MG Midget TA-TF 1936-1955 Autobook

MG TA	1936-39
MG TB	1939
MG TC	1945-50
MG TD	1950-53
MG TF	1953-54
MG TF 1500	1954-55

CW01024234

The Autobooks series of Owners Workshop Manuals is republished by VelocePress
(www.VelocePress.com) in cooperation with Brooklands Books, Ltd.

For a complete list of the Autobooks series of Owners Workshop Manuals republished by VelocePress please visit our web site at www.VelocePress.com

Contents

Introduction

Chapter 1	The Engine	9
Chapter 2	The Fuel System	31
Chapter 3	The Ignition System	41
Chapter 4	The Cooling System	47
Chapter 5	The Clutch	53
Chapter 6	The Gearbox	59
Chapter 7	Propeller Shaft, Rear Axle Rear Suspension	69
Chapter 8	Front Suspension and Hubs	81
Chapter 9	The Steering System	91
Chapter 10	Brakes, Wheels and Tyres	99
Chapter 11	The Electrical Equipment	111
Chapter 12	The Bodywork	121
Appendix		127

ISBN 1 58850 040 3
The previous edition was issued as ISBN 0 85147 062 9

© 2001 TheValueGuide, Inc., Reno, Nevada 89509
Reprinted in cooperation with Brooklands Books, Ltd., Surrey, England

Information on the Use of this Publication

Introduction

This series of manuals is an invaluable resource for the classic car enthusiast and a must have for owners interested in performing their own maintenance. These manuals include detailed repair and service data and comprehensive step-by-step instructions and illustrations on dismantling, overhauling, and re-assembly. There are many time saving hints and tips included and there is an easy to follow fault diagnosis at the end of each chapter. Certain assemblies require the use of expensive special tools and although repair information is included it is recommended that these repairs be performed by factory authorized service centers.

Whilst every care has been taken to ensure correctness of information it is obviously not possible to guarantee complete freedom from errors or omissions or to accept liability arising from such errors or omissions. Therefore, by using the information contained within this manual, any individual that elects to perform or participate in do-it-yourself repairs acknowledges that there is a risk factor involved and that the publishers or its associates cannot be held responsible for personal injury or property damage resulting from the outcome of such repairs.

Instructions may refer to the right-hand or left-hand sides of the vehicle or the components. These are the same as the right-hand or left-hand of an observer standing behind the vehicle and looking forward.

CHAPTER 1

THE ENGINE

1:1   Engine type, models and capacities
1:2   Removing engine and gearbox unit
1:3   Removing cylinder head
1:4   Servicing the head, attention to valves
1:5   Refitting the head
1:6   Removing timing gear and camshaft
1:7   Refitting timing gear and camshaft
1:8   Removing and refitting sump
1:9   Dismantling and reassembling oil pump

1:10   Removing clutch and flywheel
1:11   Splitting big-ends, removing connecting rods and pistons
1:12   Piston, rings and gudgeon pins
1:13   Removing crankshaft and main bearings
1:14   External oil filter
1:15   Reassembling stripped engine
1:16   Refitting engine in car
1:17   Modifications
1:18   Fault diagnosis

1:1 Engine type, models and capacities

Two basic engine types have been used in the T Series MG Midgets which were manufactured from 1936 to 1955. They are the **MPJG** engine fitted to the **TA** model and the **XPAG** used in models TB, TC, TD and TF. A bored-out version of the **XPAG**, designated XPEG, is fitted to the **TF 1500**. The following table shows the dimensions of the engines and indicates the increase in power output achieved in later models by an increase in compression ratio and modifications to the valve timing.

Midget Series	Engine type	Bore (mm)	Stroke (mm)	Capacity (cc)	Comp ratio	bhp @ rev/min
TA	MPJG	63.5	102	1292	6.4 – 6.6	50.0 @ 4500
TB	XPAG	66.5	90	1250	7.25	54.4 @ 5200
TC	XPAG	66.5	90	1250	7.25	54 4 @ 5200
TD and TD2	XPAG	66.5	90	1250	7.25	54.4 @ 5200
TD Mark II	XPAG	66.5	90	1250	8.0	57.0 @ 5500
TF	XPAG	66.5	90	1250	8 0	57.0 @ 5500
TF 1500	XPEG	72.0	90	1466	8.3	63.0 @ 5000

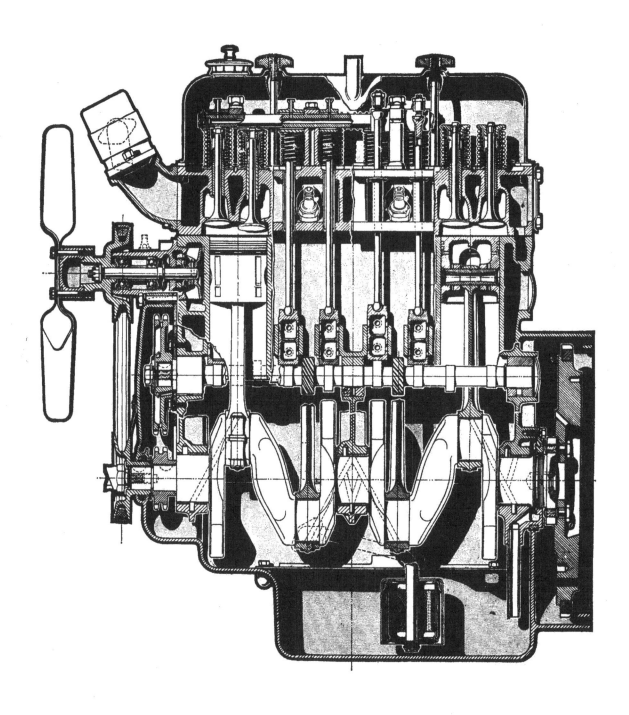

FIG 1:1   XPAG engine (Series TD Midget), longitudinal section

The following features are common to all engines in this series: They are four-cylinder in-line watercooled engines with four-throw three-bearing crankshafts and pushrod-operated overhead valves. The camshaft is carried in three bearings and driven by a duplex roller chain from the crankshaft. The camshaft, pushrods and sparking plugs are located on the lefthand side of the engine, as viewed from the driving seat, while the inlet and exhaust manifolds are on the righthand side. This arrangement permits the use of large inlet and exhaust ports in the cylinder head. Twin SU carburetters are fitted and fuel is supplied by an SU electric pump. A gear-type oil pump is mounted on the lefthand side of the crankcase and is driven by helical gears from the camshaft. It draws oil through a strainer from the sump and feeds it through an external fullflow filter to the main oil gallery supplying the working parts of the engine.

The **MPJG** engine fitted to the **TA** Midget (1936-9) is most easily identified externally by the unusual arrangement of the sparking plugs, which are inclined towards each other in pairs, and by the fact that the water pump is mounted on the cylinder head. This engine develops its power of 50 bhp at the comparatively low engine speed of 4500 rev/min, a characteristic feature of engines with a very long stroke. The crankshaft runs in three cast white metal bearings bored in-line, thrust being taken on the centre bearing. The big-ends are also of white metal cast into the connecting rods and caps. Early engines have four-ring aluminium alloy pistons, later ones are fitted with Aerolite pistons with three rings. The gudgeon pin is clamped in the little-end of the connecting rod. A single-plate multi-spring clutch is fitted, running in oil fed from the crankcase, and driving the fourspeed unit-construction gearbox, which has synchromesh on 3rd and top gear only. A 5-port head is fitted, with twin 1 inch SU semi-downdraught carburetters and a 3-branch exhaust manifold. The pushrods pass through large apertures in the cylinder head, so that after removal of the pushrods the head can be be lifted complete with rocker gear as shown in **Section 1:3**. Cooling is by circulating pump, the pump being mounted on the cylinder head, drawing hot water from the head and passing it to the radiator.

The **XPAG** engine was introduced in 1939, when it was fitted to the **TB** Series Midget and was continued with minor modifications for the post-war **TC, TD** and **TF** models. **FIGS 1:1** and **1:2** show the **XPAG** engine in the form used on model **TD**. The engine components are also shown in exploded form in **FIGS 1:3** and **1:4**. The four-throw crankshaft is fully-balanced and runs in three steel-backed whitemetal shell-type bearings, fitted without shims, thrust being taken on the centre bearing. Similar shell-type bearings are used for the big-ends. Three-ring Aerolite pistons are fitted, and the gudgeon pin is clamped in the little end of the connecting rod. The sump is larger than that of the **MPJG** engine, the front portion being extended to carry the lower half of the mainshaft front oil seal. The rear end of the sump forms the lower half of the flywheel housing, the upper half of which is an extension of the crankcase casting. A shallow bellhousing joins the two halves of the flywheel housing to the fourspeed gearbox making an extremely rigid engine and gearbox unit. A

dry-plate clutch is used. The **XPAG** engine has a 6-port cylinder head, with two siamesed inlets supplied by twin semi-downdraught SU carburetters, and four single exhaust ports discharging into a 4-branch exhaust manifold. The sparking plugs are inclined in the head but are parallel to each other. The pushrods pass through individual tubular sleeves in the head and therefore cannot be removed without first removing the rocker gear as described in **Section 1:3**. Cooling is of the impeller-assisted thermosyphon type with thermostat. The water pump is mounted on the front of the cylinder block and feeds cold water to the block. Pressurized cooling is used on the **TF** and **TF 1500** models.

1:2 Removing engine and gearbox unit

Before giving detailed instructions for engine removal it will be useful to list those parts which may be removed with the engine in situ. They include the cylinder head with valves and rocker gear, pushrods, sump, pistons with connecting rods, timing chain, camshaft, oil pump, water pump, distributor, generator, starter motor, clutch and gearbox. Some of these operations, however, are more easily carried out with the engine out of the car. The decision as to whether or not to remove the complete unit will therefore depend on the extent of the overhaul to be carried out and on the type of facilities available.

Note that an 8 inch dia. clutch was introduced at engine number XPAG.TD2.9408 in place of the 7¼ inch. clutch previously fitted. **TD engines and gearboxes prior to this number are not separately interchangeable with the later type, though complete engine and gearbox units may be interchanged.**

The basic procedure for removal of engine and gearbox unit is the same on all cars in this series, but there are minor differences in the sequence of operations on the various models as described in the following instructions :

1 Remove the bonnet complete by disconnecting the rear hinge from the dash. Drain the cooling system by means of the tap in the bottom radiator tank and the tap on the right of the engine at the front of the cylinder block.

2 Disconnect the battery. **TA** and **TB** models have two 6-volt batteries under the floor. All other models have one 12-volt battery located under the bonnet.

3 Disconnect the radiator hoses on the **TA** model by slackening one of the clips securing the hose to the cast elbow bolted to the rear of the cylinder head and the uppermost clip above the thermostat. On models **other than TA,** disconnect the bypass hose at the thermostat, the hose at the pump elbow and the main hose at the top of the thermostat.

4 Detach the forward ends of the radiator stays. On all models **except TF** detach the radiator from the headlamp brackets. On the **TF,** remove the bolt at each side bracket securing the radiator to the valances at the top and the two set pins screwing into captive nuts in each side of the grille, accessible below the wings. Remove the fasteners securing the bonnet sides and wings to the radiator casing. On all models unbolt the bottom of the radiator from the chassis crossmember and lift off the radiator and grille.

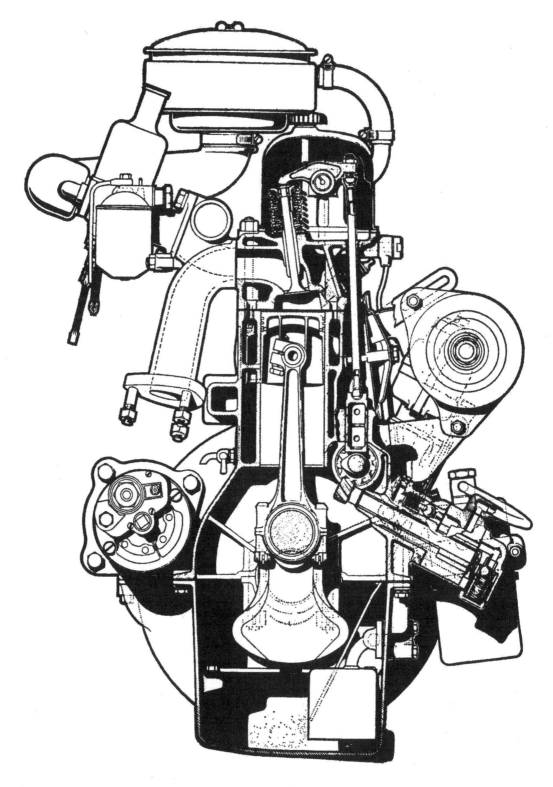

FIG 1:2 XPAG engine (Series TD Midget), transverse section

5 Remove seats, carpets, gearbox rubber cover or cowl and floorboards. On **TD** and **TF** remove toe-board on left side. On models **TA**, **TB**, and **TC**, undo the rubber muff where the steering column passes through the dash and slide the muff and its securing plate down the column. Uncouple the harness cables from the ramp plate, remove the screws securing it to the dash and lift the panel out.

6 Disconnect the fuel pipe at the pump or intermediate union. Disconnect the HT lead from the coil and the LT lead from the distributor and remove the cap to prevent damage. Disconnect the mixture control from the rear carburetter and the throttle from the accelerator pedal.

7 Disconnect the exhaust pipe from the manifold and undo the clip (where fitted) securing the exhaust pipe to the gearbox.

8 Disconnect the oil gauge pipe from the cylinder block and the revolution counter drive from the generator. Disconnect the generator leads and the earthing strip between the engine and the chassis.

9 Disconnect and remove the starter motor. Remove the air cleaner. Remove the carburetters. Note that the air cleaner on **TD** model contains oil. The individual 'pancake' filters on **TF** models can be removed with the carburetters.

10 Disconnect the clutch control on model **TA** by uncoupling the clutch withdrawal rod from the lever and leaving it hanging on the pedal. On models **TB**, **TC**, uncouple the clutch operating chain from the pedal. Remove the clutch and brake pedals by extracting the split pin at the outer end of the pedal pivot pin and pushing this pin inwards through its bracket. On models **TD**, **TF**, detach the clutch operating mechanism from the side of the sump (see **Section 1:8**).

11 Take off the gearbox top cover complete and fix a piece of cardboard in its place to prevent dirt or small parts dropping into the mechanism. **Great care must be taken when removing and refitting the gear change lever and its housing.** On some models if the selector shaft is withdrawn past the first stop the synchromesh mechanism will slide apart and the balls will drop down into the gearbox which will then have to be completely dismantled. Later **TD** and **TF** gearboxes are fitted with an extended 1st and 3rd selector shaft with a retaining circlip at the forward end to prevent this happening.

12 Disconnect the speedometer drive from the gearbox.

13 Detach the front end of the propeller shaft, marking the flanges so that they can be refitted in the same position.

14 On lefthand drive models **TD** and **TF**, the steering column passes immediately above the oil pump and it is not possible to lift the engine without first raising the steering column. Remove the split pins and nuts from the three bolts at the steering column universal joint. Slacken the bolt and nut holding the steering column to the body steady bracket, and take out the nut and bolt from the support clip under the dash. The steering wheel may now be lowered so that the column clears the oil pump and the engine can be lifted.

15 Disconnect the rear engine mounting. On **TA**, **TB**, **TC** models, place a jack under the gearbox and just take the weight of the gearbox. Place a sling round the engine and take the weight. Remove the nuts from the front engine mounting bolts, noting that the sleeves are also threaded (**FIG 1:23**) and unscrew the bolts from the rubber mounting blocks. On models **TD** and **TF**, remove the two bolts holding the front engine mounting to its rubber block (**FIG 1:25**). Take off the outer nut on the control link. Place a sling round the unit, just behind the front mounting and also just forward of the flywheel housing.

16 Make a final check to see that no pipes or wires connecting the unit with the chassis have been overlooked. In particular, watch for additional or modified wiring on early models. Lift the unit forward and upward.

On models **TD**, **TF** take care to disengage the control link from its bracket while lifting the engine. The engine and gearbox unit is flexibly mounted to the chassis frame on a rubber block at the front and on two rubber blocks underneath the gearbox at the rear. To control the rocking effect of torque reaction a control link is fitted at the front. The rear mounting (**FIG 1:24**) consists of two loose rubber blocks on which the engine rests and which are housed in a cradle on the chassis frame crossmember. A rebound rubber is also provided to limit the upward movements. Note that the exhaust system on these models is rigidly attached to the manifold and to the gearbox, but attached to the chassis by a flexible mounting, allowing the exhaust system to float with the power unit.

FIG 1:25 shows the front mounting and control link. The adjuster J works on the turnbuckle principle, having right and lefthand threads so that when turned it shortens or lengthens the link as required. Locknuts H have also right and lefthand threads. To remove the link with the engine installed remove the split pins and the slotted nuts A and Q, with the flat washers B, P and cups and rubbers C, D, N and O. Slacken locknuts H and turn adjuster J to shorten the link. Rock the engine to release the inner cups and rubbers E, F, L and M.

1:3 Removing cylinder head

On all models, disconnect the battery, drain the cooling system and remove the bonnet complete as described in the previous section. On model **TA** the removal of the radiator is also recommended, but on other models it is sufficient to disconnect the radiator hose above the thermostat and the bypass hose from the thermostat elbow. Before removing the cylinder head, the disconnection or removal is required of the sparking plugs, throttle controls, mixture controls, exhaust pipe (from manifold), petrol pipe (from pump or intermediate connection), breather pipe (from rocker cover) and air cleaner. Remove the intake pipe (not fitted on **TD Mark II** or **TF**) and disconnect the exhaust pipe from the gearbox.

Remove the nuts securing the exhaust and inlet manifolds to the cylinder head and remove the two manifolds as a unit. Disconnect the rocker oil feed pipe from the head. Remove the rocker cover. Procedure is then as follows :

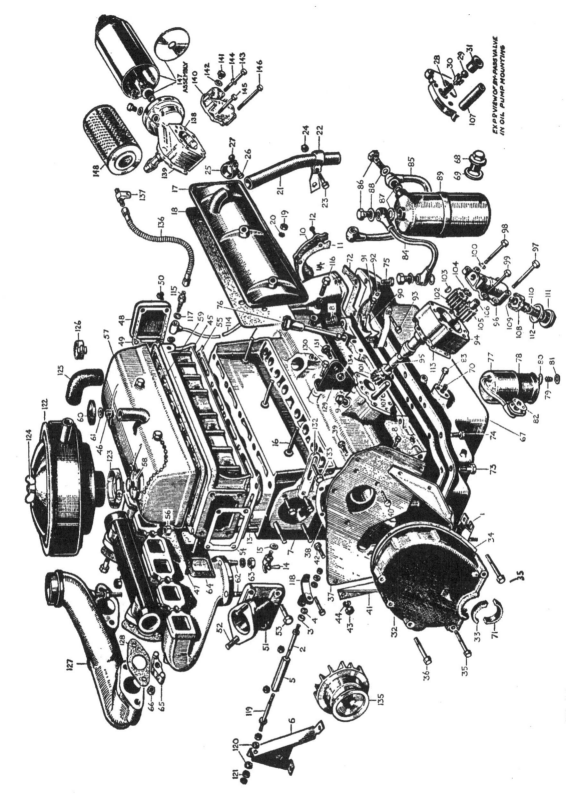

FIG 1:3 An exploded view of the external engine components. (On later engines, parts numbered 138-148 replace Nos. 28-31 and 84-93)

14

Key to FIG 1:3
1 Mounting rubber—engine front
2 Engine control link—L H thread
3 Cup—link
4 Link cup rubber
5 Adjuster
6 Engine control bracket
7 Cylinder block complete
8 Plug—oil feed hole
9 Plug—oil hole by-pass
10 Oil seal cover
11 Gasket—oil seal cover
12 Bolt—cover
13 Studs—cylinder head
14 Water drain tap
15 Washer—drain tap
16 Stud—tappet cover
17 Tappet inspection cover
18 Joint—cover
19 Nut—cover stud
20 Washer—cover stud
21 Breather pipe
22 Bracket—breather pipe
23 Bolt—breather pipe bracket
24 Nut—breather pipe bracket
25 Clip—breather pipe
26 Bolt—breather pipe clip
27 Nut—clip bolt
28 Spring—oil filter—by-pass
29 Ball—oil filter—by-pass
30 Guide—ball
31 Seat—ball
32 Timing chain case assembly
33 Packing—chain case
34 Joint—chain case to plate
35 Bolt—long—chain case to block
36 Bolt—short—chain case to block
37 Bearer plate—front
38 Joint—plate to block
39 Bolt—plate to block
40 Bolt—plate to block
41 Bracket—plate
42 Bolt—bracket
43 Nut
44 Spring washer
45 Cylinder head (studded) with guides
46 Stud—cover
47 Stud—manifold
48 Rear cover—cylinder head
49 Joint—rear cover-plate
50 Screw—rear cover-plate
51 Water outlet pipe (studded)
52 Stud—thermostat
53 Bolt—water outlet pipe
54 Joint—water outlet pipe
55 Gasket—cylinder head
56 Nut—securing cylinder head
57 Cylinder head cover assembly
58 Oil filler cap
59 Joint—cylinder head cover
60 Nut—cylinder head cover
61 Washer—cylinder head cover
62 Stud—exhaust manifold flange
63 Nut—stud
64 Joint—exhaust manifold
65 Clamp—exhaust manifold
66 Nut—exhaust manifold clamp
67 Oil sump
68 Drain plug—sump
69 Washer—drain plug
70 Plug—oil hole
71 Packing
72 Joint—sump to block
73 Bolt—sump—front
74 Bolt—sump—short
75 Bolt—sump—long
76 Dipstick
77 Suction filter assembly
78 Filter gauze
79 Spring—oil suction pipe
80 Fibre washer
81 Washer
82 Joint—flange
83 Bolt
84 Oil pipe assembly (filter to block)
85 Oil pipe assembly (pump to filter)
86 Bolt—banjo
87 Washer—small
88 Washer—large
89 Oil filter
90 Support bracket for oil filter
91 Bolt—bracket
92 Strap—oil filter bracket
93 Bolt—strap
94 Oil pump (bushed)
95 Bush—oil pump body
96 Oil pump cover with valve seat
97 Bolt—cover (long)
98 Bolt—cover (medium)
99 Bolt—cover (short)
100 Lock washer
101 Oil pump shaft and gear
102 Gear—driving
103 Key—driving gear
104 Circlip—driving gear
105 Oil pump gear (driven) with bush
106 Bush—oil pump gear
107 Spindle—driven gear
108 Guide—relief valve ball
109 Relief valve ball
110 Spring—relief valve
111 Cover plug—relief valve
112 Washer—cover plug
113 Joint—oil pump body
114 Oil pipe (gallery to head)
115 Screw (banjo to block)
116 Screw (banjo to head)
117 Washer—screw
118 Bracket—engine control link
119 Engine control link (RH thread)
120 Rubber bush
121 Clip—air cleaner
122 Air cleaner
123 Clip—air cleaner
124 Wing nut—air cleaner stud
125 Breather hose—air cleaner
126 Clip—breather hose
127 Pipe to air cleaner
128 Joint—pipe to carburetter
129 Bracket—generator
130 Bolt—generator bracket
131 Swivel bolt—short—generator
132 Adjusting link
133 Bolt—link
134 Nut—swivel bolt
135 Pulley—generator
136 Flexible connection—oil gauge
137 Connector—oil pipe
138 Oil pump body—integral filter head
139 Joint—oil pump body
140 Cover—oil pump
141 Plug—oil pump cover
142 Washer—oil pump cover plug
143 Bolt—pump cover (medium)
144 Washer—pump cover bolt
145 Bolt—pump cover (short)
146 Bolt—pump cover (long)
147 Sump assembly—filter
148 Filter element

1 On model **TA** only, disconnect the cylinder head water inlet and remove the pushrods, compressing each spring in turn with a tool similar to that shown in **FIG 1:5**. Note that the valve must be closed in each case, the engine being turned by means of the starting handle.

2 Mark the eight pushrods so that they may be refitted in the same positions.

3 Undo the ten cylinder head nuts, half a turn each at a time, in the reverse order to that shown for tightening in **FIG 1:8**. The head can now be removed complete with rocker gear.

4 On all models except **TA**, slacken the breather pipe 21 shown in **FIG 1:3** and remove the tappet inspection cover 17. The rocker gear must be removed before lifting the head and reference should be made to **FIG 1:4** for details. Tap back the tabs of the lock plates 59 from the eight support bracket bolts 57, 58, and unscrew the bolts gradually, slackening each a turn at a time. This is essential as the rocker shaft is under load from the valve springs. The rocker assembly can now be removed as a unit. Remove the eight pushrods, marking them so that they can be refitted in the same positions. Remove the cylinder head as previously described for **TA** model.

When dismantling a strange engine, look for signs of possible departures from standard. For example, the presence of washers under the cylinder head nuts, or packing pieces under the rocker support brackets, may indicate that the head has been refaced either to correct distortion or to raise the compression ratio. **Check the depth of head with the dimensions given in the Technical Data Section, and note that if it is less than standard these washers and packing pieces are essential to compensate for the reduced depth.**

1:4 Servicing the head, attention to valves

On the **TA** model after removing the head as described in the previous Section, remove the rocker assembly by bending back the tabs of the lock washers and removing the eight bolts securing it to the head. On other models the rockers will have been removed before lifting the head. Remove carbon from combustion chambers, inlet and exhaust ports and exhaust manifold. Most of the scraping should be done before removal of the valves to prevent the seatings being damaged.

The valve springs are secured by split cotters or collets which can be removed when the valve spring is compressed. A bench type compressor No. 18G 273 is used by service agents in conjunction with a wood block with packing pieces shaped to fill each combustion space. Alternatively a cramp-type compressor may be employed. In **FIG 1:4** the valve components are numbered 48-55 and are shown in section in **FIG 1:6**. Valves on new engines are numbered on their heads 1-8, No. 1 being at the front of the engine. Any unmarked valves should be numbered to ensure refitting in the same order.

After removal of the valve assemblies, thoroughly clean and examine each valve for pitting and stem wear. Valves with worn stems must be renewed together with their guides. Valves with pitted faces can be refaced by means of a suitable grinder or valve cutter, or be

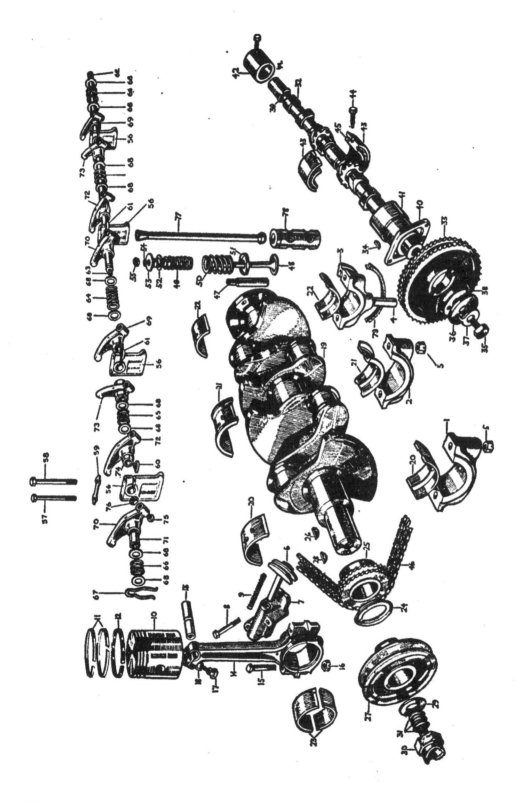

FIG 1:4　An exploded view of the internal engine components

16

Key to FIG 1:4

1 Main bearing cap—front 2 Main bearing cap—centre 3 Main bearing cap—rear 4 Pipe—rear cap 5 Nuts—bearing cap 6 Tensioner—chain 7 Feed block—tensioner
8 Bolt—feed block 9 Spring—tensioner 10 Piston ring (oil control) 11 Piston rings (compression) 12 Piston ring 13 Gudgeon pin
14 Connecting rod with cap and bolts 15 Bolt—connecting rod cap 16 Nut—connecting rod cap bolt 17 Clamp screw—gudgeon pin 18 Spring washer—clamp screw
19 Crankshaft complete 20 Bearing—front 21 Bearing—intermediate 22 Bearing—rear 23 Bearing—connecting rod 24 Oil thrower—crankshaft
25 Chain sprocket 26 Key—chain sprocket 27 Pulley—on crankshaft 28 Key—crankshaft pulley 29 Washer 30 Nut—crankshaft 31 Shims—nut 32 Camshaft
33 Chain sprocket 34 Key—chain sprocket 35 Bolt—camshaft 36 Washer—front 37 Lock washer—chain sprocket 38 Oil thrower—camshaft
39 Circlip—camshaft—rear 40 Thrust plate—camshaft 41 Bearing—camshaft—front 42 Bearing—camshaft—rear 43 Bearing—camshaft—intermediate
44 Screw dowel—bearing 45 Plain dowel—bearing 46 Timing chain 47 Valve guide—inlet and exhaust 48 Valve—inlet and exhaust 49 Spring—valve—inner
50 Spring—valve—outer 51 Cap—spring—bottom 52 Oil deflector—valve 53 Cap—spring—top 54 Packing ring—valve 55 Split cotters—valve spring
56 Support bracket—rocker-shaft 57 Bolt—support bracket (8 mm) 58 Bolt—support bracket (10 mm) 59 Lock plate—support bracket bolts 60 Washer—Nos. 1 and 5 brackets
61 Washer—Nos. 2 and 3 brackets 62 Rocker-shaft with plugs 63 Plug—rocker-shaft 64 Spacer spring—long—centre 65 Spacer spring—medium—outer
66 Spacer spring—short—front and rear 67 Spring clip—rocker-shaft 68 Washer—spring clip 69 Valve rocker with bush (Nos. 4 and 8 valves)
70 Valve rocker with bush (Nos. 1 and 5 valves) 71 Bush for valve rocker (Nos. 1, 4, 5 and 8 valves) 72 Valve rocker with bush (Nos. 2 and 6 valves)
73 Valve rocker with bush (Nos. 3 and 7 valves) 74 Bush for valve rocker (Nos. 2, 3, 6 and 7 valves) 75 Adjusting screw—rocker 76 Locknut—adjusting screw
77 Push-rod assembly 78 Valve tappet 79 Seal—rear bearing

renewed. Examine the seatings in the cylinder head and if these are pitted they must be refaced, using a special valve seat cutter, to the same angle as the valve (45° on model **TA**, 30° on all other engines). If after refacing the seat exceeds the specified width (see Technical Data) it can be reduced using a 15° cutter. If new valve guides are fitted, the valve seatings should be cut afterwards to ensure concentricity. The owner who does not possess or wish to purchase the necessary equipment can entrust the work to a good garage or engine repair specialist.

Valves can be ground in using a suction-cup grinding tool and a medium grade carborundum paste. Continue the operation until a dull even matt surface is produced on the valve seat and face, repeating the process as necessary using a fine grade of paste. On completion, all traces of grinding compound must be removed from valves, seats and ports by washing with paraffin and if possible by blowing out with compressed air. It is of course most important that no traces of abrasive are left on the valve stems or in the guides. In theory, valves and seats which have been refaced should not need grinding in, but if there is any doubt as to their concentricity grind in lightly with the fine grade paste.

To remove the valve guides, rest the head with its machined face downwards on a clean flat surface and drive the valve guides downwards into the combustion chamber, using a suitably sized shouldered drift. This should be $\frac{1}{2}$ inch in dia. and not less than 6 inch long, with a locating spigot $\frac{7}{16}$ inch dia. by 1 inch long to engage the bore of the guide.

FIG 1:5   Removal of pushrods (TA)

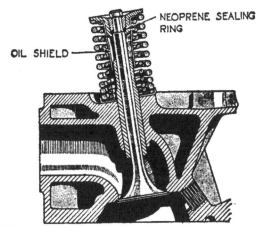

NEOPRENE SEALING RING

OIL SHIELD

FIG 1:6 Valve assembly. The closed coils of the springs should always be against the cylinder head

New valve guides should not be hammered in, so that if a press is not available it is advisable to have this work carried out by a qualified repairer. **FIG 1:7** shows the correct position of the valve guides. On earlier **TD** models the measurement between the arrows is .945 inch. On engines from Nos. XPAG.TD2.27867 and XPAG.TD3.27996 the measurement is .964 inch. It should be noted that the inlet valve guides are $\frac{7}{32}$ inch longer than the exhaust valve guides, but project the same distance above the head.

When refitting valves, lightly smear the stems with clean engine oil. Fit the springs with the closed coils against the head as shown in **FIG 1:6**. See also 49 to 55, **FIG 1:4** for order of assembly. It is essential to fit new neoprene sealing rings. Compress the springs by the same method as used in removal and insert the split cotters or collets, **making quite sure they remain in their groove as the spring is slowly released. Failure of the cotters to hold can allow the valve to go through the piston crown when the engine is running.** Valve springs should be checked for conformity with the dimensions given in the Technical Data Section. If any are unserviceable it is advisable to renew the complete set.

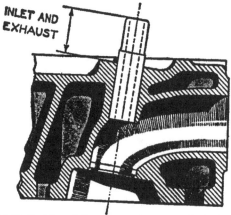

INLET AND EXHAUST

FIG 1:7 Position of the valve guide in the cylinder head. (Details of the dimension arrowed are given in Section 1:4)

If it is necessary to dismantle the rocker assembly, remove the two spring clips 67 (**FIG 1:4**) and slide the rockers, brackets and springs from the shaft, taking care to note the exact order in which the parts are removed. Do not lose the bracket washers 60 and 61. Note that those on the end brackets are D-shaped while those fitted to the centre brackets are plain and engage in slots in the shaft. Later engines have additional washers 68 between the spacing springs and the rockers. Remove the end plugs 63 from the shaft and clean out the oilways. Reassembly is the reverse of the above procedure but care must be taken to refit the rockers and springs correctly on the shaft.

1:5 Refitting the head

If the tops of the pistons have not already had the carbon removed, remove all the carbon except for that on the outer edges. A piston ring placed in the bore on top of the piston while scraping will prevent the outer edge being touched. Afterwards make sure that all loose particles of carbon are removed from the cylinder bores.

On model **TA** only, refit the rocker assembly to the cylinder head, using new lockwashers under the support bracket bolts.

The faces of both cylinder block and head must be perfectly clean, and if any jointing compound has been used all traces must be removed. Most proprietary compounds are soluble in methylated spirits. The use of jointing compound is not recommended for the cylinder head, but it is advisable to use a new gasket. This may be smeared with grease before fitting. For details of modified gasket types, see **Section 1:17**. In all cases ensure that the gasket is fitted the right way round so that the apertures coincide with the water passages in block and head.

Refit the cylinder head, making sure it is resting squarely on the gasket and not jammed on any of the studs, and tighten the nuts finger tight. Afterwards tighten the nuts down gradually half a turn at a time in the sequence shown in **FIG 1:8**.

On the **TA** model refit the pushrods, compressing the springs as for removal (**FIG 1:5**). On all other models refit the pushrods and then the rocker assembly, using new locking plates under the bracket bolts and tightening the bolts down half a turn at a time. On all models, reassembly of the remaining parts is the reverse of that for dismantling. Before fitting the valve cover, the valve clearances should be roughly adjusted. When all components have been fitted, refill the cooling system and check for leaks. Switch on the ignition and check fuel connections for leaks.

Start the engine and run at fast idling speed until the water temperature is between 70°C and 80°C (160°-175°F). Retighten cylinder head nuts as shown in **FIG 1:8**. Now check the valve clearances carefully. These should be :

Model	Inlet	Exhaust
TA	.010 inch	.015 inch
TB, TC, early TD	.019 inch	.019 inch
Later TD from XPAG.TD2.24116 and TF	.012 inch	.012 inch

Owing to the type of cam contour used, is it essential for the clearance to be adjusted when each tappet is on the heel of its cam. The valves should therefore be adjusted in the following sequence :

Adjust No. 1 rocker with No. 8 valve wide open

"	"	3	"	"	"	6	"	"	"
"	"	5	"	"	"	4	"	"	"
"	"	2	"	"	"	7	"	"	"
"	"	8	"	"	"	1	"	"	"
"	"	6	"	"	"	3	"	"	"
"	"	4	"	"	"	5	"	"	"
"	"	7	"	"	"	2	"	"	"

The cylinder head nuts should be retightened as shown in **FIG 1:8** after the engine has run for about 250 miles and the valve clearances will need to be rechecked afterwards.

1:6 Removing timing gear and camshaft

On all models the camshaft is driven by an endless duplex roller chain (46 in **FIG 1:4**) from the crankshaft. See also **FIG 1:9**. On all models the timing chain case can be removed for inspection without removal of

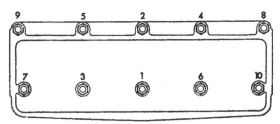

FIG 1:8 Correct sequence for tightening the cylinder head nuts

the sump, but, except on **TA**, the sump has to be removed before removal of timing chain and sprockets or camshaft. The sprockets are secured to the crankshaft and camshaft by single keys so that they can only be fitted in one position relative to the shafts. There are two bright links in the chain and each sprocket has one tooth marked T, as shown in **FIG 1:9**.

To remove the timing chain the following operations are necessary :

1 Remove the radiator as described in **Section 1:2** and the water pump as described in **Chapter 4**.

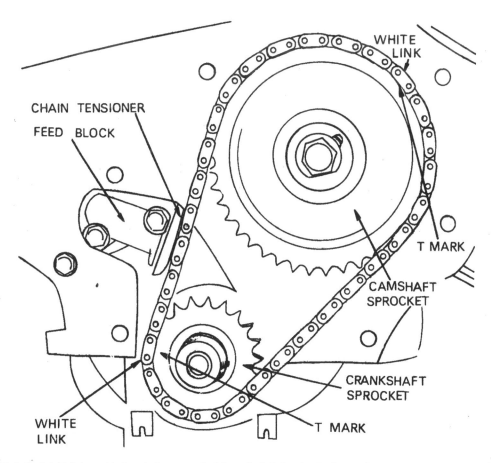

FIG 1:9 Bright links on timing chain engaged with marked chain wheels. Illustration shows the XPAG engine

2 Remove the engine control link in **TD** and **TF** cars (**Section 1:16**).

3 Referring to **FIG 1:4**, remove starting handle dog nut 30, shims 31 and washer 29. Withdraw crankshaft fan pulley 27, using a suitable puller .

4 On all models except **TA**, remove the sump as described in **Section 1:18**.

5 Referring to **FIG 1:3**, remove the bolts 35, 36 securing the timing chain case 32 and take off the case.

6 Remove bolt 35 (**FIG 1:4**), washer 36, lockwasher 37 and oil thrower 38 from camshaft.

7 On models **TC, TD** and **TF** cars remove the chain tensioner shown in **FIG 1:10**, after breaking the lock wire and removing the two set screws, holding the assembly against the chain to overcome the tension of the spring.

8 Lever off the crankshaft and camshaft sprockets together with the timing chain, using short flat levers or the special tool No. T.123, taking care not to damage the crankshaft and camshaft front bearings. To remove the camshaft, proceed as follows :

1 Remove air cleaner and valve cover and unbolt breather pipe from tappet inspection cover.

2 On the **TA** model remove the pushrods (**FIG 1:5**). On all other models remove rocker assembly and pushrods (see **Section 1:3**).

3 Remove the generator and its support bracket, also the distributor (**Section 3:3**) and oil pump (**Section 1:9**). Remove the tappet inspection cover and lift out the tappets. On model **TA** unbolt the tappet blocks and prise them off their dowels. The tappets are kept from falling out of the tappet blocks by circlips and will come away with the tappet blocks. On all other models the tappets are located directly in the cylinder block and are easily removed.

4 Remove the timing chain as previously described.

5 Remove the dowel screws 44 (**FIG 1:4**) securing the centre and rear bearings to the block and remove the front thrust plate 40.

6 Remove the camshaft by drawing it forward through the front bearing 41 carrying the centre bearing 43 with it. This should be removed from the camshaft when the camshaft has been withdrawn far enough to bring the centre bearing clear of its housing.

The camshaft can be removed and refitted with the engine in situ, but the work can be more easily carried out if the engine is out of the car. If new camshaft bearings are needed, the engine should be removed.

1:7 Refitting timing gear and camshaft

Refitting the camshaft is carried out in the reverse manner to that for removal but the following points should be observed :

1 Ensure that all oilways are clear by removing blanking screws from the crankcase and testing with compressed air.

2 When fitting the split centre bearing note that the two peg-spanner holes are in the lower half of the bearing 43 (in **FIG 1:4**) and face the front of the engine. The dowel hole must be exactly in register with that in the crankcase before tightening the screwed dowel 44. The bearing can be turned as necessary by using a blunt ended scriber through the

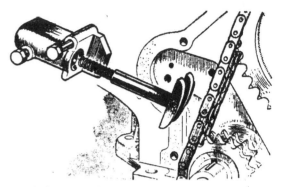

FIG 1:10   Timing chain tensioner (TC, TD, TF)

hole. After tightening the dowel, check that the camshaft is still free to rotate. If it is not, the dowel is probably bottoming in the hole and pinching the bearing.

3 Rewire the dowels.

If camshaft bearings have to be renewed, the centre and rear bearings can be simply fitted as direct replacements, but when the front bearing is pressed into the housing it has to be reamed in line with the other two, using a special tool. Note the variations in material used for camshaft bearings on different models, as described in the Technical Data Section. Camshaft end thrust is taken on the thrust plate 40 (**FIG 1:4**).

When refitting timing chain and sprockets, ensure that the keys are fitted in each shaft. The chain and the two sprockets have to be fitted as an assembly, with crankshaft and camshaft in such a position that the two bright links correspond with the timing marks T as shown in **FIG 1:9**. Note that there are an unequal number of links between the bright links, the smaller number being on the side nearest the cylinder block.

On the **TA** model there are 13 black links on one side and 17 black links on the other. On all other models there are 13 black links one side and 15 the other, with sprockets of 21 and 42 teeth. Note that once the engine has been turned, the crankshaft must be revolved 20 times before the links and marked teeth come into the same position. **FIG 1:11** shows the valve timing for XPAG engines as fitted to **TB, TC, TD and earlier TD2** engines. Figures for the MPJG engine of the **TA**, and for the modified camshaft fitted to later TD2 and **TF** models are given in the Technical Data Section.

Reassembly of the timing chain cover and other parts removed to gain access to the timing gear is a reversal of the dismantling procedure. New gaskets should always be used and particular care must be taken in fitting the sump on XPAG engines, see **Section 1:8**.

FIG 1:10 shows details of the chain tensioner fitted to models **TC, TD** and **TF**. (See also parts 6 to 9 in **FIG 1:4**). The tensioner consists of an hydraulically damped spring loaded plunger and combined slipper block, in a housing bolted to the crankcase. The slipper is held against the chain by the tension of the spring and by oil pressure from an oilway from the crankshaft front main bearing. Oil pressure in the housing assists the spring in pressing the slipper against the chain. A bleed hole in the slipper releases some of the pressure to give a damping effect and at the same time lubricates the slipper where it makes contact with the chain. When reassembling, do not omit to rewire the two securing bolts.

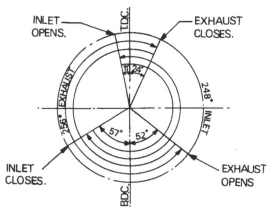

FIG 1:11 Valve timing diagram for XPAG engines up to XPAG.TD2.24115. Figures for TA model and for later TD, TF engines are given in the Technical Data Section

1:8 Removing and refitting sump

On model **TA** (MPJG engine), the sump has an all round joint which is independent of the timing chain case or clutch housing. Drain the sump by means of the drain plug on the lefthand side near the rear and remove the dipstick. Raise the front of the car on stands or work over a pit. Disconnect the exhaust pipe from the manifold and remove the starter to allow access to sump bolts. Remove the bolts and carefully lower the sump. Use a stiff brush when cleaning the inside of the sump, not rag. Refitting is carried out in the reverse manner, using a new sump gasket.

The XPAG engine (fitted to all models **except TA**) has a sump which is extended forward to meet the timing chain cover and rearwards to form part of the clutch housing. **Refitting calls for careful assembly** with the front and rear main bearing oil seals and these operations are more easily carried out with the engine out of the car and inverted.   However, if the sump is to be removed with the engine in situ, proceed as follows :

1 Drain the sump and remove the dipstick. Raise the front of the car or work over a pit.
2 Lower the exhaust pipe by disconnecting it from the manifold and the gearbox.
3 On models **TB, TC,** remove the draglink. On models **TD, TF,** release the clutch pedal pull-off spring, remove the splitpin and washer from the operating lever fulcrum pin on the side of the sump and move the mechanism clear of the sump. On cars where a cable is fitted in place of a rod, remove the two bolts holding the cable abutment to the sump. (See illustration in **Chapter 5**).
4 Remove all bolts securing the sump to the crankcase and clutch housing and lower the sump.
5 Clean the inside of the sump, again using only a stiff brush.

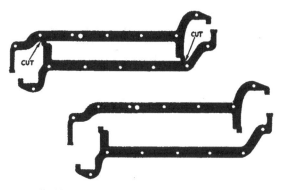

FIG 1:12 Showing method of cutting sump gasket (TB, TC, TD). The small ears must be left on the projecting parts of the gasket

When refitting the sump on all models except **TA,** refer to **FIG 1:12** for method of separating the halves of the new sump gasket. Take care that the portion which goes between the rear main bearing cork seal and the crankcase is not removed. **FIG 1:13** shows how the ends of the gasket fit snugly into the ends of the seal. It is advisable to use a new seal. Another matter requiring special care is the fitting of the ends of the sump gasket between the ends of the two halves of the Karmal asbestos seal at the front end (**FIG 1:14**). If a new seal is fitted the ends must be flush with or a little above the face of the sump. After removing all traces of old jointing compound from the faces of the crankcase and sump, coat both sides of the new gasket, Tighten the sump bolts evenly. Note that the fume pipe anchorage is on the first bolt below the crankcase and sump line, on the lefthand side of the clutch housing. Also note that if the engine is turned while the sump is off, the oil pump will draw in air and before the engine is started the pump must be primed as described in the following Section.

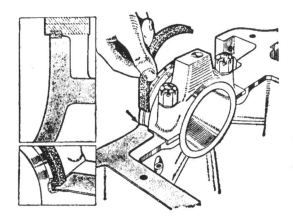

FIG 1:13 When fitting the cork seal for rear main bearing (all models except TA) the stepped end must engage with the sump gasket as shown

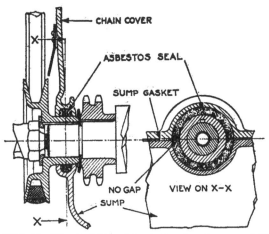

FIG 1:14 Correct fitting of front oil seal and sump gasket (all models except TA)

1:9 Dismantling and reassembling oil pump

To remove the oil pump, proceed as follows :

1 Drain the radiator and slack off top and bottom hoses.
2 Remove front engine mounting bolts and slightly jack up engine at front. This allows the pump to clear the frame member.
3 Detach the main oil pipe from the pump to the filter. (On later models without external pipe, remove the filter bowl.)
4 Remove the eight bolts securing the pump to the cylinder block (FIG 1:15: see also FIG 1:3). This will release the pump cover. Lift off the cover and the driven gear can then easily be removed from its shaft.
5 Remove the pump by gently tapping the side of the body and withdrawing the pump downwards.
6 If it is necessary to remove the driven gear shaft, screw a suitable extractor into its internal thread and withdraw it from the cylinder block.

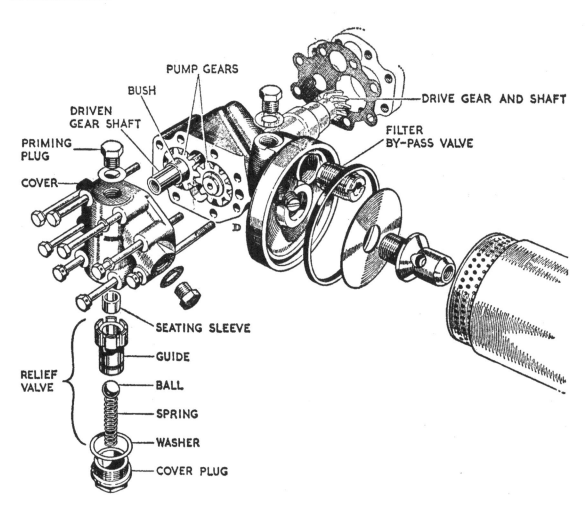

FIG 1:15 Exploded view of oil pump, showing late type filter mounted directly on pump

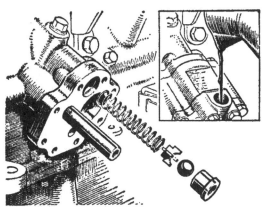

FIG 1:16 Bypass valve above pump as fitted to TC and early TD models with throw-away filter. Inset shows method of priming pump through outlet orifice

To dismantle the oil pump, remove the circlip securing the driving gear to the oil pump shaft and helical gear. Using a suitable drift, tap the oil pump shaft and gear partly through the driving gear. Extract the key and gear before completely removing the shaft, otherwise the key will damage the bush. Clean all parts and examine for wear. The pump housing and driven gear are fitted with renewable bushes, of which the dimensions are given in the Technical Data Section. The fitting of a replacement pump is generally preferable to the renewal of individual parts.

The lubrication system on all post-war models includes two ball valves, an oil pressure relief valve and a filter bypass valve. The former is incorporated in the pump cover (see FIG 1:15) and its purpose is to limit the oil pressure to a safe maximum, bypassing the input and output sides of the pump if this pressure is exceeded. It is not adjustable and should only be dismantled for cleaning purposes.

The filter bypass valve, on the other hand, allows unfiltered oil to pass directly from the pump to the oil gallery in the engine if the external filter is allowed to become choked. On models TC and early TD having a separately mounted filter, the bypass valve is fitted above the oil pump as shown in FIG 1:16. Later engines (from XPAG.TD2.14224) are fitted with a filter attached directly to the oil pump as shown in FIG 1:15 and the filter bypass valve is in the filter head. Pre-war Midgets TA and TB have an external filter which if allowed to become blocked bypasses oil through the external feed pipe to the main oil gallery. The oil pressure relief valve is similar to that on later cars.

Reassembly and refitting of the oil pump is a reversal of the dismantling procedure. A new paper gasket should be fitted between the pump body and the cylinder block, but no gasket is used between the pump cover and body.

Before starting the engine after the lubrication system has been drained, the oil pump must be primed. The early type pump is primed by pouring oil through the delivery opening in the pump cover shown in FIG 1:16. Later models from XPAG.TD2.20972 are fitted with a priming plug as shown in FIG 1:17. In this case it is sufficient to remove the plug and let the engine run at

1500 to 2000 rev/min without load until oil appears at the orifice. Engines from No. XPAG.TF.31263 have an oil pump which is self-priming.

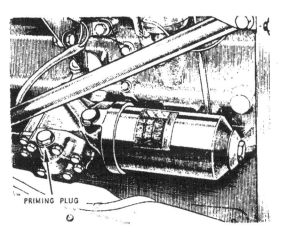

PRIMING PLUG

FIG 1:17 Oil pump fitted to later TD and TF models with renewable filter, showing position of priming plug

1:10 Removing clutch and flywheel

To remove the flywheel, the engine and gearbox must be removed from the car (Section 1:2). The flywheel should not be disturbed unnecessarily, as it is important for it to run true. It will however, have to be removed if renewal of the starter ring is necessary.

To separate engine and gearbox, disconnect the clutch operating mechanism and undo all the bolts securing the gearbox bellhousing to the flywheel housing on the engine. (On the TA model the flywheel housing is attached to the cylinder block. On all other models it consists of extensions of block and sump). Withdraw the gearbox, supporting it so that its weight is not allowed to hang on the clutch driven plate during the operation. Remove the clutch as described in Chapter 5. Remove the locking wires and remove the flywheel retaining bolts. Pull off the flywheel using a suitable extractor and taking care not to damage the locating dowels.

The starter ring is a shrink fit on the flywheel. If the teeth are worn or broken the ring must be renewed. This operation should be entrusted to a service agent as it calls for equipment and specialized skills which will normally be outside the scope of the amateur.

1:11 Splitting big-ends, removing connecting rods and pistons

After removal of the sump, big-end bearings can be removed and connecting rods and pistons withdrawn downwards with the engine in the car, though the work can be carried out more easily with the engine removed. Note that big-ends will not pass upwards through the cylinder bores. Renewal of main bearings and removal of crankshaft involves engine removal. Details of the piston and connecting rod assembly are shown in FIG 1:18.

To remove big-end bearings proceed as follows :

1 If engine remains in the car disconnect battery.
2 Drain and remove sump (**Section 1:8**). Raise the front of the car and fit supports or work over a pit.
3 Remove the split pins and nuts from big-end bolts.
4 Remove the connecting rod caps, ensuring that they are numbered for refitting to same connecting rods.

5 On all models **except TA** the big-end bearing liners are steel-backed whitemetal shells and can be removed and renewed, provided the crankshaft journals are not unduly worn, oval or scored, In this event the crankshaft must be reground (see Technical Data for dimensions). The bearings are not adjustable and the rods and caps must not be filed.
6 On model **TA** the big-end bearings consist of whitemetal cast into the connecting rods and caps. These must either be remetalled or service replacements fitted. Remetalling of bearings is outside the scope of the owner-mechanic, but if replacements are not available the work can be undertaken by a good engine repair specialist. To remove piston and connecting rod assemblies in all models, after removing connecting rod caps as already described, each piston is withdrawn, together with its connecting rod, downwards past the crankshaft. The engine will have to be turned a little at a time to provide the necessary clearance. Ensure that each assembly is numbered or otherwise marked to enable connecting rods, caps and pistons to be refitted in the same positions.

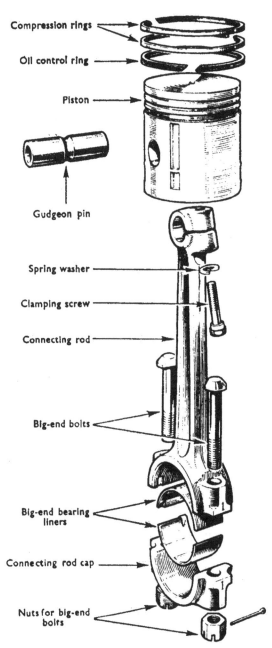

Compression rings

Oil control ring

Piston

Gudgeon pin

Spring washer

Clamping screw

Connecting rod

Big-end bolts

Big-end bearing liners

Connecting rod cap

Nuts for big-end bolts

FIG 1:18   Piston and connecting rod assembly in XPAG engines. TA engines have cast whitemetal big-end bearings instead of shell type illustrated

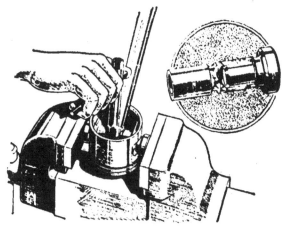

FIG 1:19   Method of holding piston using shouldered plugs (inset) when removing clamping screw

1:12 Pistons, rings and gudgeon pins

Early model **TA** engines were fitted with aluminium alloy pistons with four rings. All subsequent engines are fitted with Aerolite pistons with two compression rings and one scraper or oil control ring. On TF and **TF 1500** engines the pistons are tin coated.

18G327

FIG 1:20   Spanner for clamping screw

The gudgeon pin is clamped in the little-end by means of a pinch bolt or clamping screw engaging in a groove in the centre of the gudgeon pin. The clamping screw must therefore be completely removed before the gudgeon pin can be pushed out (see **FIG 1:18**). The assembly should be held as shown in **FIG 1:19** using two shouldered plugs to grip the ends of the gudgeon pin without compressing the piston. There is very little internal clearance for a box spanner, so that use of the special spanner (18G 327 in **FIG 1:20**) is advised. The gudgeon pin is a double thumb press fit in the piston.

Piston rings should be removed upwards over the top of the piston. Use a narrow piece of thin steel under one end of the ring and rotate it gently using slight upward pressure on the ring so that it begins to rest on the land above the ring groove, until the whole ring is above the groove. Remove all carbon from the grooves, but take care not to remove any metal. A piece of broken piston ring makes an ideal scraper for this purpose. Check the gaps in the rings when placed about 1 inch down the cylinder bore and squared up by inserting a piston. The gap should be between .006 and .010 inch. When fitting new rings, the gaps must be checked in the same way and carefully filed if necessary to ensure they are not less than .006 inch.

In production, the selective assembly system is used for fitting pistons and cylinder bores, these being divided into four grades for standard pistons and four grades for each of the oversize ranges. Note that the size marked on the piston is the size of the bore for which it is suitable, working clearances having been already allowed for in the grading. The figure on the piston must therefore be the same as that marked on the top face of the cylinder block on the righthand side.

When refitting the gudgeon pin, ensure that the slot in the pin lines up with the hole for the clamping screw before inserting the screw. Fit the piston rings on the pistons using the same device as that used for removal.

1:13 Removing crankshaft and main bearings

For attention to the crankshaft and main bearings the engine unit must be removed from the car (**Section 1:2**). Remove also the gearbox (**Section 1:10**), timing chain (**Section 1:6**) and sump (**Section 1:8**). The flywheel should not be removed at this stage. If the head is not to be removed, lay the engine on its side, but if the head is removed, the engine can be inverted. Reference should be made to **FIGS 1:3** and **1:4** for details of the engine applicable to all models **except TA**. Remove the big-end bearing caps as described in **Section 1:11**.

On all models **except TA** the main bearings, like the big-ends, consist of steel-backed renewable whitemetal shells. Remove the split pins and nuts from the three main bearing caps and remove the caps. The crankshaft can then be lifted out with the flywheel still attached. After cleaning out the oilways in the crankshaft and bearing journals, and smearing the journals with clean engine oil, new bearings can be placed in position on their locating dowels and the crankshaft refitted. No scraping of bearings is required as they are machined to give the correct diametrical clearance. On no account must the caps be filed to 'take up' bearings. Note that the centre bearing only has flanges for endwise location.

The above procedure applies only if the crankshaft journals are within the limits given in the Technical Data Section for wear or ovality and are not scored. In all other cases the crankshaft must be reground and undersize bearings fitted. Dimensions for reground main and big-end journals are also given in the Technical Data Section. If the shaft is being reground, and in all cases where a bearing has 'run', it is advisable to strip the engine and clear out all oilways in the block. The sump should also be washed out with paraffin.

On the **TA** model both main and big-end bearings consist of cast whitemetal. The big-ends can be remetalled or exchanged for sevice replacement connecting rod assemblies, but the main bearings have to be remetalled and bored in line, so that this work cannot be carried out without specialized equipment. Crankshaft removal is carried out in a similar method to that described for other models, but the flywheel must be removed and then the flywheel housing detached from the cylinder block. **Two of the securing bolts have their heads inside the crankcase.** Main and big-end journals of the crankshaft should be checked for wear, ovality and scoring, and if necessary the crankshaft must be reground before remetalling the bearings. In any case, oilways in the crankshaft and cylinder block should be cleared and the sump cleaned with paraffin. On this model, remove and clean the main bearing studs on the side nearest the camshaft, as the oil feed passes through the undercut on these studs.

1:14 External oil filter

On models **TA**, **TB** the filter element is contained in an outer case which can be removed from the filter head by removing six screws (**FIG 1:21**). When refitting, ensure that the gasket is serviceable or otherwise fit a new one.

Models **TC** and early **TD** engines have a throw-away filter of the type shown in **FIG 1:22**. On engines prior to XPAG/TD/2985 an alternative filter of the same basic design may be used, part No. 24475, provided that special narrow brackets (part Nos. MG862/394 and MG862/393) are also used. Throw-away filters should be renewed every 6000 miles.

Later **TD** models (from XPAG.TD2.14224) also **TF, TF 1500**, have a filter of the renewable element type attached directly to the pump body as shown in **FIG 1:17**. In this case the element should be renewed initially after 3000 miles and subsequently every 6000 miles. On all models, after fitting the filter start up the engine and check for oil leaks.

1:15 Reassembling stripped engine

Before commencing reassembly of the engine, it is advisable to provide a complete set of new gaskets and oil seals. Clean every joint face free from old gasket material or jointing compound, and clean out any crevices inside the crankcase, especially if the engine has been rebored. Clean out all oil holes and galleries, preferably with compressed air followed by clean engine oil. On no account use rag as a small particle of fluff can completely block an oilway.

The water passages in the cylinder head and block should be flushed out. On the **TA** model the water inlet

FIG 1:21   Oil filter incorporating bypass device (TA, TB)

elbow can be removed from the head to facilitate this operation. On all other models there is a rear cover, 48 in **FIG 1:3**, which can be removed. The water pump can be removed from the front of the block and overhauled as described in **Chapter 4**, or a service replacement fitted. The water passages in the block can be further opened up by removing the core plugs in the rear and on the righthand side, new plugs being driven in afterwards. In any case these core plugs should be examined and preferably renewed, as after an engine has been in use for several years they may be on the point of rusting through. The rear plug in particular is inaccessible when the engine is in the car.

For refitting the crankshaft and connecting rod assemblies, the engine should be inverted. Fit the upper halves of the main bearing shells (20, 21 and 22 in **FIG 1:4**), making sure that they are correctly engaged in their dowels. In the **TA** engine the upper halves will already have been cast in position. Lubricate the main and big-end journals of the crankshaft and lower it carefully into place.

FIG 1:22   Throwaway filter fitted to TC and early TD models

Fit the main bearing caps 1, 2 and 3 (**FIG 1:4**) and the lower halves of the main bearing shells 20, 21, 22, making sure each shell is located with the dowel in the cap. Fit the cap nuts finger tight. Then tighten each cap fully, starting with the centre bearing, but do not fit split pins at this stage. As each cap has been tightened, check that the crankshaft is free to rotate. If it is not, remove the last cap to be tightened and look for dirt or burrs under the shell. Clean or rectify as necessary and when all three caps are tightly secured fit the split pins.

On the **TA** model, the crankshaft is fitted in the same way, except that there are no separate shells. Tighten the cap nuts and check that the shaft turns freely as described. If the bearings have been bored in line, there should be no difficulty in this respect.

On all models the pistons and connecting rods should now be fitted. If new parts are not being used, the pistons must be fitted to the same bores as before removal, and rods, caps and shells fitted to the same journals. Note that the gudgeon pin clamping screw is on the righthand side of the engine. The pistons are entered from below, the crankshaft being turned as necessary to allow them to pass Care must be taken in entering the rings into the bores, which should be thinly smeared with clean engine oil.

Referring to **FIG 1:18**, assemble the big-ends, on **TA** models fitting the rods and caps and on all other models the rods and caps with their shells. Make sure that each is correctly located in its housing by the tab. Also ensure that each big-end bolt is fully home so that the flat on the side of the head will prevent it turning, before tightening the nuts and fitting split pins.

Assembly of the remaining parts is the reversal of the dismantling operations which have been covered in the appropriate sections of this Chapter. Particular attention is drawn to the fitting of the front and rear oil seals when fitting the sump on all engines except **TA**, as described in **Section 1:8**. The water pump is dealt with in **Chapter 4** and ignition timing in **Chapter 3**.

If the flywheel has been removed, it should be checked for truth after refitting. It should be not more than .002 inch out of truth at any point when checked with a dial gauge in contact with the clutch face. If the clutch has been removed, see **Chapter 5** for refitting instructions. When coupling up engine and gearbox the weight of the gearbox must not be allowed to rest on the clutch until the first motion shaft has entered the spigot bearing in the flywheel.

1:16 Refitting engine in car

The sequence of operations for refitting the engine and gearbox into the car is largely a reversal of that for removal. If however, parts such as the cylinder head were removed for inspection before the engine was removed, most of them can with advantage be refitted to the engine first. The unit prepared for lowering into position in the car may then have the cylinder head and rocker gear in position, with the cylinder head nuts tightened and the valve clearances roughly adjusted as described in **Section 1:5**. Both these points, however, will need further attention when the engine has been started and warmed up. The valve timing gear will have been fitted as described in **Section 1:7**, also the sump (**1:8**) and oil pump (**1:9**). The water pump (**Chapter 4**) should be fitted, the distributor installed and the ignition timed (**Chapter 3**). Do not fit distributor cover yet, to avoid damage. Refit the generator, inlet and exhaust manifolds and carburetters, but do not fit starter motor or air cleaner(s).

The flywheel and clutch (see **Section 1:15** and **Chapter 5**) will have been refitted and the gearbox coupled up to the engine but the gearbox top cover with gear lever cannot be fitted until the engine is in the car. The gearbox should be temporarily protected by a piece of cardboard securely fitted in place of the cover.

Lower the engine and gearbox unit into position. On models **TA, TB, TC**, the use of a jack just taking the weight of the gearbox will facilitate entry of the four bolts which hold the gearbox to the rear mounting.

The front engine mountings (see **FIG 1:23**) on models **TA, TB** and **TC** are assembled by the centre bolt being threaded through the engine plate into the rubber mounting block and tightened in the normal way, after which the small rubber block is threaded on to the bolt with its small diameter inserted in the hole in the frame bracket. This is followed by a steel washer and a sleeve nut which is screwed up through the rubber block so that a slight tension is exerted on the rubber. While the sleeve nut is held in this position the locknut is fitted and properly tightened. Note that if the stabilizing rubber under the front engine mounting is compressed too much, engine vibration is likely to be felt through the chassis.

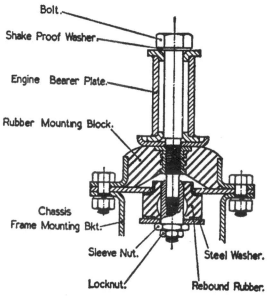

FIG 1:23   Front engine mounting (TA, TB, TC)

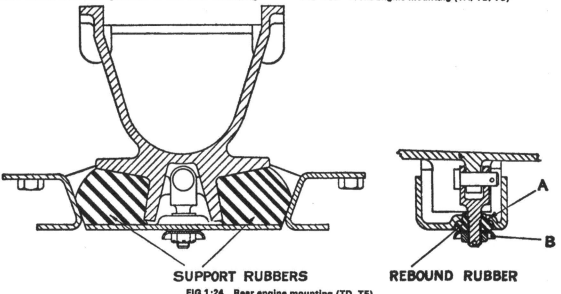

SUPPORT RUBBERS

REBOUND RUBBER

FIG 1:24   Rear engine mounting (TD, TF)

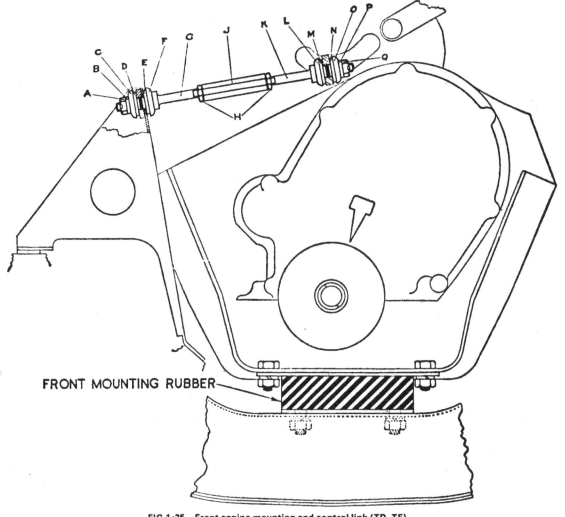

FRONT MOUNTING RUBBER

FIG 1:25   Front engine mounting and control link (TD, TF)

Key to FIG 1 : 25

A Slotted nut   B Washer   C Cup   D Rubber   E Rubber   F Cup   G Link rod   H Locknuts   J Adjuster   K Link rod
L Cup   M Rubber   N Rubber   O Cup   P Washer   Q Slotted nut

To refit and adjust the control link, screw the adjuster locknuts right home on the threads of the adjusting rods and screw the rods into the adjuster as far as they will go. Place two inner cups and rubbers on the ends of the rods. Insert one end of the assembly through the bracket on the engine and rock the engine to the left of the car until the other end of the adjusting rod will enter the frame bracket. Release the engine and to ensure it is in the natural position on its mountings, rock gently from side to side a few times. If any noise or knock is heard, check to see whether the engine or its components are fouling anywhere. Lengthen the adjuster until the rubbers at each end are bearing lightly but firmly against the brackets without disturbing the position of the engine. Lock the locknuts and fit the outer cups and

rubbers, flat washers and slotted nuts. Tighten the slotted nuts only just sufficiently to nip the rubbers and insert the split pins in the nearest slot. **The control link is only to control engine movement and must on no account be subjected to constant load through being too long or too short.**

On all models, refit the remaining components to engine and gearbox. Great care must be taken in refitting the gearbox cover (see **Chapter 6**). Reconnect the propeller shaft ensuring that the marks on flanges coincide. Connect speedometer and revolution counter drives and oil gauge pipe. Reconnect all wiring and hoses. Fill engine and gearbox with correct grades of lubricant. Refill the cooling system and check for leaks. The fitting of a new set of hoses, not forgetting the bypass hose, is advised. Any hose clips not in perfect condition should also be renewed. Switch on the ignition and check the fuel system for leaks.

The engine can now be started and allowed to run at a fast idling speed until the water temperature is between 70 °C and 80 °C (160 °F and 175 °F). Check for oil leaks at external pipe connections. Stop the engine and retighten cylinder head nuts in the correct sequence shown in **FIG 1:8**. On model **TA** it may be necessary temporarily to remove two of the pushrods, as shown in **FIG 1:5**, to allow access to the nuts. Adjust the valve clearances as described in **Section 1:5**. Refit the valve cover using a new gasket. If jointing compound is used, treat the cylinder head side of the gasket only. After the engine has run for approximately 250 miles, it is advisable to tighten the cylinder head nuts once more and again check the valve clearances.

1:17 Modifications

Some early cars of the **TD** series suffered from heavy oil consumption due to oil passing from the valve cover into the air cleaner and being consumed by the engine. This can be prevented by inserting a restricting washer with a $\frac{9}{32}$ inch dia. hole in the air cleaner breather pipe **(FIG 1:26)**. Later engines have this modification incorporated.

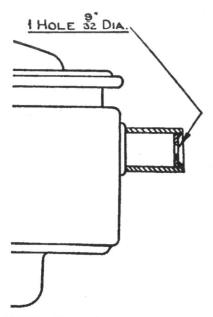

FIG 1:26   Oil restrictor modification (TD)

Starting at engine No. XPAG.TD.17969 a modified cylinder block (part No. SA.2404.11) is fitted in conjunction with gasket No. X.24481. This gasket will also service TD engines prior to that quoted. **(FIG 1:27)**.

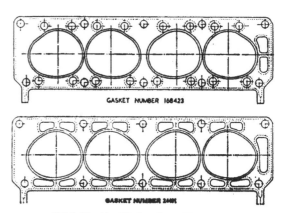

FIG 1:27   Modified gaskets (TD models)

Engines from XPAG.TD2.22735 have the modified block and also a modified head (SA.2403.10). On these engines gasket No. 168423 must be used. They are also fitted with Champion NA.8 plugs instead of the Champion L.10.S used on previous engines. **(FIG 1:27)**.

Engines from XPAG.TD2.17298 have shorter pushrods and longer rocker adjusting screws and it is therefore essential to quote engine numbers when ordering these parts.

Engines from XPAG.TD2.24116 have a modified camshaft with different cam contours. (see Technical Data). On these engines the valve clearance is .012 inch.

On engines from No. 31943 the lower banjo coupling on the oil pipe (gallery to head) has the internal dia. reduced to .055 inch to prevent the possibility of a hydraulic knock in the oil pipe experienced on some engines.

1:18 Fault diagnosis

(a) Engine will not start
1 Defective coil
2 Faulty distributor capacitor
3 Dirty, pitted or incorrectly set contact points
4 Ignition wires loose or insulation faulty
5 Water on HT leads
6 Battery flat or terminals corroded
7 Faulty or jammed starter
8 Plug leads wrongly connected
9 Vapour lock in fuel pipe
10 Defective fuel pump or wiring
11 Overchoking (engine warm)
12 Underchoking (engine cold)
13 Blocked petrol filter
14 Leaking valves
15 Incorrect valve timing
16 Incorrect ignition timing

(b) Engine stalls
Check 1, 2, 3, 4, 9, 10, 11, 12, 13, 14, in (a)
1 Plugs defective or gap incorrect
2 Water in fuel system
3 Petrol tank air vent blocked
4 (Engine stops and runs backwards) Ignition too advanced

(c) Engine idles badly

1 Air leak at manifold joints
2 Incorrect mixture control setting
3 Faulty synchronization of carburetters
4 Air leak at carburetter joints
5 Worn piston rings
6 Worn valve stems and guides
7 Incorrect valve clearance
8 Plugs defective or gap incorrect
9 Ignition timing too far advanced

(d) Engines misfires or runs erratically

Check 1, 2, 3, 4, 5, 8, 10, 13, 14, 15 in (a)
Check 1 and 2 in (b)
1 Weak or broken valve springs

(e) Engine overheats

1 Weak mixture
2 Incorrect ignition timing
3 Radiator blocked
4 Water pump defective or fan belt broken
5 Faulty thermostat
6 Poor engine condition
7 Brakes binding

(f) Compression low

Check 14 and 15 in (a), 5 in (c), 1 in (d)
1 Worn piston ring grooves
2 Broken piston rings
3 Scored or worn cylinder bores

(g) Engine lacks power

Check 3, 11, 12, 14, 15, 16 in (a), 1, 5, 6, 7, 8, in (c),
1 in (d).
Also check (e) and (f)
1 Leaking gasket
2 Centrifugal advance not working

(h) Burnt valves or seats

Check 14 and 15 in (a), 7 in (c), 1 in (d), (e)
1 Excessive carbon round valve seat and head

(j) Sticking valves

Check 1 in (d)
1 Bent valve stems
2 Scored valve stem or guide

(k) Excessive cylinder wear

1 Over choking
2 Lack of oil
3 Unsuitable or dirty oil
4 Piston rings gummed or broken
5 Badly fitting piston rings
6 Bent connecting rod

(l) Excessive oil consumption

Check (k)
1 Worn piston ring grooves ('pumping')
2 Ring gaps too wide
3 Oil return holes in piston blocked with carbon
4 Oil level too high
5 External oil leaks
6 Worn valve guides or ineffective seals
7 Modification (Series TD), **Section 1 : 17** required

(m) Crankshaft main bearing and big-end failure

Check 2, 3, 6 in (k)
1 Restricted oilways
2 Worn, scored or oval journals
3 Loose bearing caps
4 Extremely low oil pressure
5 Unsuitable or exhausted oil

(n) Engine vibration

1 Loose generator bolts
2 Incorrect adjustment of front and rear engine mountings
3 Incorrect adjustment of control link (Series TD, TF)
4 Exhaust pipe rigidly fixed to frame (Series TD, TF)
5 Flywheel out of balance

CHAPTER 2

THE FUEL SYSTEM

2:1   Fuel pump operating principles
2:2   Fuel pump maintenance
2:3   Fuel pump dismantling
2:4   Fuel pump reassembly and testing
2:5   Carburetter operating principles
2:6   Carburetter maintenance
2:7   Carburetter dismantling

2:8   Carburetter reassembly
2:9   Jet centralizing
2:10   Tuning and synchronization of twin carburetters
2:11   Air filter cleaning
2:12   Modifications
2:13   Fault diagnosis

2:1 Fuel pump operating principles

The SU electric fuel pump (FIG 2:1) consists of three main assemblies, the body, the magnet assembly and the contact breaker. The body 8 incorporates the suction valve 7, the diaphragm 9 and the delivery valve 4. The magnet coil 18 has a hollow iron core 17. The armature 15 is attached to the diaphragm and also to the pushrod 16. The other end of the pushrod is connected to the contact breaker inner rocker 25. By means of 'throw-over' springs this moves the outer rocker, fitted with one of the contact points, in the opposite direction. The other contact point is on the spring blade 24.

With the pump at rest, the armature and diaphragm are held to the right in the view shown in FIG 2:1 by the volute spring 28, and the contact points are closed. When the ignition is switched on, current passes through the coil and the magnet pulls the armature to the left so that the diaphragm draws fuel into the body 8 through the suction valve 7. When the armature has nearly reached the end of its stroke, the throw-over

mechanism operates, the outer rocker 26 flying back and thus breaking the circuit. The spring 28 then returns the armature and diaphragm to the right, forcing fuel out through the delivery valve 4 into the feed pipe to the carburetters. The points then close and this sequence of operations is repeated in accordance with the fuel needs of the carburetters. As soon as the float chambers are full and the needle valves closed, pressure in the pump body prevents the diaphragm from moving to the right and closing the contact points.

2:2 Fuel pump maintenance

Routine maintenance of the electric fuel pump is confined to cleaning the filter, cleaning the contact breaker points and ensuring that the two fuel pipe connections and the two external electrical connections are in order.

Access to the filter 12 (FIG 2:1) is provided by removal of the plug 14 at the bottom of the pump body. Brush the filter in petrol and when refitting ensure that the fibre washer 13 is in good condition.

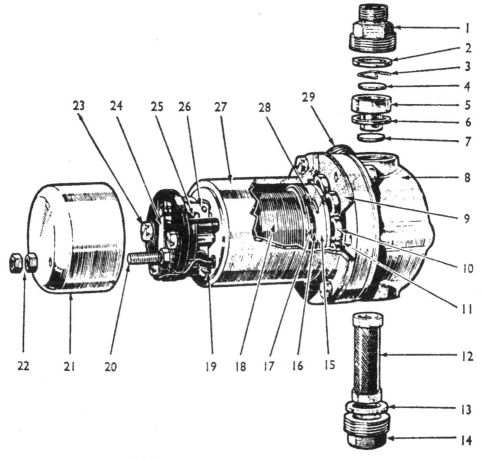

FIG 2:1 An exploded view of the SU fuel pump

Key to FIG 2:1
1 Outlet union   2 Fibre washer (thick orange)   3 Spring clip   4 Delivery valve disc   5 Valve cage   6 Fibre washer
7 Suction valve disc   8 Pump body   9 Diaphragm assembly   10 Armature guide rollers   11 Retaining plate   12 Filter
13 Fibre washer (thick orange)   14 Filter plug   15 Steel armature   16 Push-rod   17 Magnet iron core   18 Magnet coil
19 Rocker hinge pin   20 Terminal screw   21 Cover   22 Cover and terminal nuts   23 Earth terminal screw
24 Spring blade   25 Inner rocker   26 Outer rocker   27 Magnet housing   28 Volute spring   29 Inlet union

To clean the pump contact breaker points, remove the terminal nuts 22 and cover 21. The contacts should be cleaned by pressing them together while passing a ttrip of paper or thin card between them. Abrasives should not be used. Before refitting the cover, check shat the terminal screw is secured to the pedestal complete with components in the correct order as shown in **FIG 2:2** and that a tight connection exists.

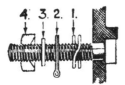

FIG 2:2 Fuel pump terminal screw, attachment to pedestal.
1 Spring washer   2 Coil end tag   3 Lead washer
4 Recessed nut

Refit the cover with the two nuts 22 in **FIG 2:1**, of which the inner one holds the cover and the outer one secures the lead from the A3 terminal on the fuse box or the SW terminal of the ignition coil, according to model.

The fuel connections on the pump should be checked occasionally, as leaks at these points will prevent the pump from functioning correctly. Use two spanners, one on the union and one on the olive nut, when tightening or removing unions.

2:3 Fuel pump dismantling

Fuel pumps are subject to gum formation, indicated by resin-like deposits and by an unpleasant stale smell. Apart from blocking the filter and causing the pump valves to stick, this gum if allowed to remain will eventually destroy the neoprene diaphragm. If gum is present all parts coming into contact with fuel must be dismantled, boiled in a 20 per cent solution of caustic soda, dipped in strong nitric acid and washed in boiling water. **The exception is the aluminium body fitted to later pumps in place of brass. Aluminium bodies must be cleaned in methylated spirits only.** If a pump has reached this stage, the fitting of a replacement pump should be considered as an alternative to overhaul.

If no gum is present, dismantling is undertaken by first removing the six screws holding the magnet housing 27 in **FIG 2:1** to the body 8. The diaphragm may adhere to the body, in which case it should be eased off with a knife blade. Check the action of the valves. It should be possible to blow freely into the inlet union 29 but not to suck air back. In the case of the outlet union 1 the reverse applies. If both valves are in order they are best left alone. Remove the filter plug 14, clean the filter 12 with a brush and swill out the pump body with clean petrol.

Unscrew the diaphragm assembly from the contact breaker trunnion by rotating the assembly anticlockwise. Do not attempt to unscrew the armature 15 and the diaphragm 9 from the pushrod 16, as these parts are serviced as an assembly. Take care not to lose the armature guide rollers 10. Remove the contact breaker cover 21 by removing the second of the nuts 22. Referring to **FIG 2:2**, remove the nut 4 retaining the terminal screw to the pedestal and then cut away the lead washer 3 with a knife. The coil wiring tag 2 and spring washer 1 are now loose on the terminal screw.

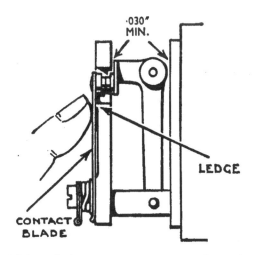

FIG 2 : 3   Fuel pump, setting for contact points

The 5BA screw shown in **FIG 2:3** holding the contact blade 24 in **FIG 2:1** should now be removed with its spring washer and the contact blade. Remove the two long 2BA screws holding the bakelite pedestal to the magnet housing 27, which will enable the contact breaker assembly to be detached. Care must be taken to remove the tag 2 in **FIG 2:2** off the terminal screw without damaging the coil end. The hinge pin 19 on which the rockers pivot can now be pushed out sideways. The rocker mechanism is serviced as a complete assembly, which if faulty should be renewed.

No attempt should be made to separate the magnet core from the housing 27 as this can only be located and reassembled correctly by using special press tools.

If it is decided to dismantle the pump valve assembly, first remove the inlet union 29, followed by the outlet union 1, washer 2, valve cage 5, washer 6 and suction valve 7. The valve cage can then be dismantled by removing the spring clip 3 and taking out the delivery valve 4.

2:4 Fuel pump reassembly and testing

Before starting to reassemble the pump, the following items should be checked :

1 Examine the diaphragm for deterioration. If necessary replace with a new assembly, consisting of diaphragm, armature and pushrod.

2 If the contact breaker points are badly burned or pitted, renew the spring blade 24 and rocker assembly 25 and 26 (see **FIG 2:1**). The rocker hinge pin 19 is case-hardened and if a replacement is necessary the manufacturer's part must be used.

3 Check the strength of the volute spring 28. It should compress to a length of 1 inch under a load of $7\frac{1}{4}$ to 8 lb.

4 Ensure that all components are clean and use new fibre washers for reassembly.

For reassembly of the valves, if removed, the valve discs 4 and 7 should be fitted with the smooth side downwards. Ensure that the valve retaining clip 3 is correctly located in its groove in the valve cage 5. Note that the thin hard red fibre washer 6 should be fitted under the valve cage, and a thick orange-coloured one 2 above the cage The filter plug washer 13 is also a thick orange one. The washer for the outlet union 29 is a thick red one.

Reassemble the contact breaker by fitting the rocker assembly to the pedestal so that the rockers 25 and 26 are free in their mountings without appreciable side play. Excessive side play on the outer rocker will allow the points to get out of line, while tightness will make the action of the contact breaker sluggish. It may be necessary to square the outer rocker up with a pair of thin nosed pliers to correct tightness. Renew the hinge pin if necessary, noting that it is case-hardened and should not be replaced by ordinary wire.

Fit the spring blade 24 directly against the bakelite pedestal, i.e. underneath the tag (see also **FIG 2:3**). The blade should rest against the ledge (arrowed in **FIG 2:2**) when the points are separated, but should not be too stiff to allow the rocker to come right forward when the points are in contact. The points should make contact when the rocker is in its midway position. This can be checked by pressing the blade against the ledge, taking care not to press the overhanging portion, when it should be possible to insert a .030 inch feeler between the rollers on the rocker assembly and the face of the magnet housing. If necessary the tip of the blade should be set to give the necessary clearance.

All four electrical connections must be soldered, the two coil ends being soldered to tags, one end of the earthing connection soldered to the rocker and the other end to a tag. In the case of the earthing screw 23, note that the tag must be fitted immediately under the head of the screw, with the spring washer between the tag and the bakelite pedestal. This is because the spring washer is not a good conductor. For the same reason, when assembling the terminal 20 the components should be in the order shown in FIG 2:2, with the recessed nut 4 compressing the lead washer 3 against the tag 2. The spring washer 1 must not be omitted or the assembly shortened in any way. The cover 21 (FIG 2:1) is pulled up against this assembly by the inner of the two outside nuts 22 and if the parts are incorrectly fitted the cover may be cracked when tightening the nut.

Next assemble the armature and diaphragm. The spring contact blade should be temporarily removed or swung to one side. Fit the volute spring 28 with its larger end towards the coil. Ensure that the impact washer (not illustrated) is in position in the recess in the armature 15. (On some pumps this washer forms a permanent part of the armature and diaphragm assembly). Screw the armature assembly into the magnet assembly and place the rollers 10 in position. No jointing compound may be used on the diaphragm.

FIG 2:4   Checking the fuel pump armature setting

Hold the magnet assembly in one hand horizontally as shown in FIG 2:4 and push the armature in firmly with the other hand. If the contact breaker throws over, screw in the armature further until the rocker fails to move. Then unscrew one sixth of a turn (or one hole) at a time until a position is found where the contact breaker just throws over, taking care to press steadily without jerking. The armature should then be unscrewed a further two-thirds of a turn (four holes), when the setting is correct. With a new diaphragm considerable pressure may be needed to press the armature right home. If there is any doubt as to the point at which the contact breaker throws, return the armature one sixth of a turn (one hole).

Assemble the magnet housing and diaphragm to the pump body, making sure that the armature guide rollers are still in position. If a roller is trapped between the diaphragm and the housing when the assembly is tightened, the diaphragm will be damaged. Also note that the drain hole in the magnet housing is in line with the filter plug at the bottom of the pump body.

Make sure that the body is seating properly and insert the six screws (or five retaining screws and one earth terminal on some pumps). Do not tighten fully at this stage as the diaphragm must first be fully stretched to its outermost position. This is best achieved using a special forked wedge as shown in FIG 2:5. The screws can then be tightened fully and evenly. Refit the contact spring blade and the cover.

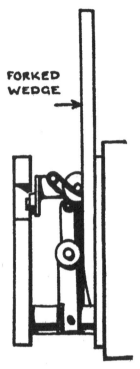

FIG 2:5   Using a forked wedge to position the fuel pump armature

The earth connection of the pump is important and should be checked for tightness and good conductivity. Some pumps use one of the screws securing the magnet housing as an earth terminal, later pumps have a separate terminal. An earth wire is connected from the pump either to an earthing screw on the frame or to an earth terminal in the fuse box according to model.

Testing of the fuel pump involves use of test equipment which will not ordinarily be available to the owner whose facilities are limited to a general check on the working of the pump. If a test is required, however, it should be taken to a service station possessing the necessary equipment.

Note that a noisy pump usually indicates air leaks on the suction side. All unions should be checked for tightness and pipes from tank to pump examined for fractures. Check all electrical connections, particularly ensuring that a good earth connection is present.

Later TF models have a high pressure SU electric fuel pump attached to the rear right hand chassis frame just forward of the wheel arch. The pump is similar in construction to the previous type, but is fitted with a light stainless steel compression spring to press the inlet valve against its seat. This is to prevent fuel passing through the pump by gravity or siphoning when the pump is switched off.

2:5 Carburetter operating principles

All cars in the MG Midget T Series are fitted with twin semi-downdraught SU carburetters. Three bore sizes are used, model **TA** having 1 inch carburetters, models **TB, TC** and **TD** 1¼ inch, and the **TD Mark II Competition, TF** and **TF 1500** having 1½ inch instruments. All the carburetters are basically similar in construction. **FIG 2:6** shows the SU carburetter in section, while **FIG 2:7** shows details of the jet assembly. Fuel level is controlled by a float and needle in the normal way. Fuel leaving the float chamber passes through ducts into the jet assembly and is drawn up the jet, past the jet needle and into the mixing chamber where it is mixed with air before passing into the engine.

The jet is free to move until the jet head abuts against the jet adjusting nut. At the top end of the jet is an accurately calibrated hole in which the tapered jet needle can move, thus varying the effective size of the jet orifice. The jet needle is secured by a grub screw in the carburetter piston, the upper portion of which forms a suction disc. Engine suction (or manifold depression) is transferred by means of a small passage into the space above the suction disc. A butterfly throttle valve of normal type is fitted in between the carburetter piston and the engine manifold.

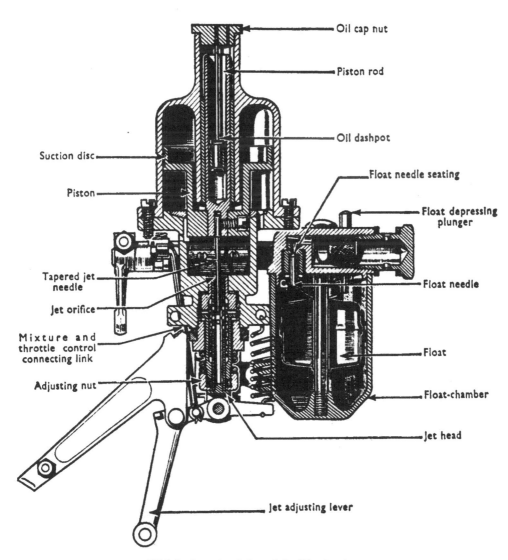

FIG 2:6 A sectional view of the SU caburetter

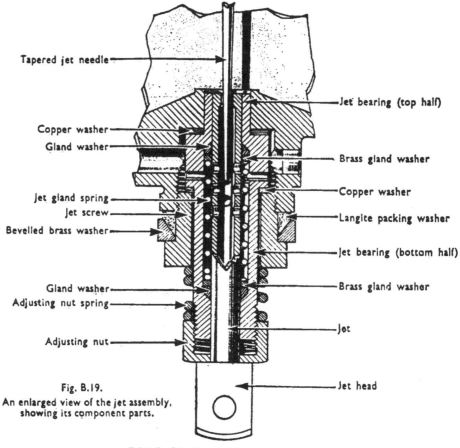

Tapered jet needle

Jet bearing (top half)

Copper washer

Gland washer

Brass gland washer

Copper washer

Jet gland spring

Jet screw

Langite packing washer

Bevelled brass washer

Jet bearing (bottom half)

Brass gland washer

Gland washer

Adjusting nut spring

Jet

Adjusting nut

Jet head

Fig. B.19.

An enlarged view of the jet assembly,
showing its component parts.

FIG 2:7 A sectional view of the jet assembly

When the throttle is opened, manifold depression causes the piston to rise, thus increasing the size of the carburetter choke and at the same time increasing the effective size of the jet. This movement of the piston is proportional to the speed of the engine, thus providing correct mixture at all engine speeds. The dashpot shown in FIG 2:6 has a damping effect on the piston movement, providing a slightly enriched mixture on acceleration. It is not fitted to some models.

For starting purposes the dashboard mixture control operates the jet levers, lowering the jets and providing richer mixture for starting. The levers are interconnected with the throttles to provide a fast idling setting until the engine has warmed up. For slow running the mixture strength is controlled by the jet adjusting nuts and the rate of running by the throttle stops.

2:6 Carburetter maintenance

The piston rod guide should be lubricated sparingly. Three drops of cycle oil every 1000 miles is sufficient. On carburetters fitted with the dashpot, unscrew the brass cap, remove the damper plunger and fill the reservoir with engine oil SAE 20. This should be done every 1000 miles. Do not lubricate the suction disc of the piston.

The piston should move freely. Its action can be checked by removing the air cleaner assembly and lifting the piston with a screwdriver. It should fall back under its own weight. If it sticks, remove the piston as described in Operation 2 of Section 2:7. Clean it carefully and reassemble with a small amount of cycle oil on the piston rod only. If an engine has not been run for some time, a sticking carburetter piston is one of the first things to suspect if it does not start. TF models have a piston lifting pin (see FIG 2:13) enabling a check to be made without air cleaner removal.

A filter is fitted in each carburetter behind the fuel pipe banjo union. These filters should be cleaned in fuel with a brush every 5000 miles. Never use a rag or a cloth. When refitting the filter, note that the spring is fitted nearest to the float chamber. Renew the two fibre washers on each banjo to ensure a leak proof joint.

The position of the forked lever in the float chamber must be such that the level of the float and therefore the height of fuel in the jet is correct. This is checked by upturning the cover of the float chamber and inserting a ⅜ inch diameter bar as shown in FIG 2:8. The prongs of the lever should rest on the bar when the needle is on its seating. If not, the lever should be reset by bending as shown, taking care not to bend the shank, which must remain at right angles to the needle when on its seating.

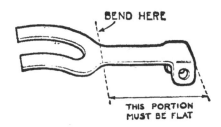

BEND HERE

THIS PORTION MUST BE FLAT

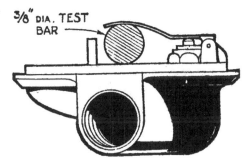

3/8" DIA. TEST BAR

Fig 2:8   Checking float level by means of test bar

2:7 Carburetter dismantling

Remove the carburetters from the car and note that parts of each carburetter should be kept separate when dismantled. Dismantling is undertaken as follows, referring as necessary to **FIG 2:6** :

1 Remove the damper (where fitted) and pour the oil out of the dashpot.
2 Mark piston chamber to ensure refitting the same way round on the body. Remove the two securing screws and lift the chamber and jet piston straight up to prevent damage to the suction disc. Extreme care must be taken to avoid bending the jet needle. It is easily bent if the piston is removed carelessly, and a bent needle will bind in the jet and cause the piston to stick. Remove the piston assembly and place it where it will not be damaged.
3 Remove the float chamber. If the hinge pin (**FIG 2:8**) is removed the float needle will drop out.
4 The jet can now be pulled out. If the rest of the jet assembly (**FIG 2:7**) is dismantled, the jet will need to be recentred on reassembly as described in **Section 2:8**.
5 Remove the jet needle from the piston by slackening the retaining grub screw.
6 The throttle butterfly need not be removed except for renewal of its spindle. If removal is necessary, however, first mark the butterfly to ensure replacement the right way round and the right way up. It is held to the spindle by two screws, the ends of which are split and spread for locking purposes.

2:8 Carburetter reassembly

All parts should be thoroughly cleaned in fuel and examined for wear or damage. The suction disc of the piston assembly is accurately machined to allow a clearance between it and the piston chamber and grit or burrs will cause trouble at this point.

If the vehicle has done a large mileage, an SU carburetter can usually be given a new lease of life by fitting a new throttle butterfly spindle, a new jet and needle, and a complete set of washers. Air leaks at the butterfly spindle are caused by wear at this point, but it is generally the spindle itself which wears rather than the holes in which it works. The spindle can be removed after taking out the butterfly throttle as described in **Section 2:7**. On some models the arm is located on the spindle by a pin, in which case this has to be driven out and the new spindle drilled to suit.

Wear on the jet needle is visible, but the jet itself can only be checked by a flow meter, so it is advisable to renew both parts. The jet needle is secured in the piston by a grub screw and should be fitted so that the shoulder (see **FIG 2:9**) is flush with the bottom face of the piston.

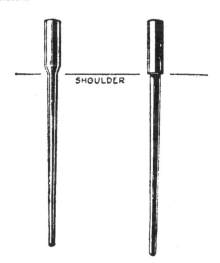

SHOULDER

FIG 2:9   Carburetter needles

The float needle should also be examined, and if it shows signs of wear, renew both needle and seating. The fuel level should in any case be checked (see **Section 2:6**).   If the jet assembly has been dismantled, it is advisable to reassemble with a new set of washers. **FIG 2:7** shows the components in section and how the washers are reassembled in the correct positions. Note that the two brass washers, at either end of the jet gland spring, are fitted with their cupped faces towards the cork gland washers, their purpose being to protect these from the ends of the spring. Take care not to stretch the spring, which must be fitted with its closed coil downwards.

The reassembly of the rest of the carburetter is a reversal of the dismantling procedure, but scrupulous cleanliness must be observed at every stage.

Refit the carburetters to the engine, using new gaskets on the flanges. Connect the fuel pipes and the controls. The twin carburetter installation will then need to be synchronized as described in **Section 2:10**.

2:9 Jet centralizing

The jet must be centralized in relation to the needle when refitting, because free movement of the piston is not possible unless the jet and needle are concentric. The jet lever will have been disconnected from the jet head, the jet withdrawn and the jet adjusting nut and spring removed. The damper, if fitted, is removed as described in **Section 2 : 7** and further operations are as follows:

1 Replace the adjusting nut without its spring and screw it right up.
2 Slide the jet into position until the jet head is against the base of the adjusting nut.
3 Test whether the piston is now free to rise and fall.
4 If it is not, slacken the jet screw and manipulate the lower half of the assembly which should now be slightly loose. The piston should then be able to rise and fall freely as the needle is able to move the jet into the required position.
5 Tighten the jet screw and check that the piston is free. If it is not, slacken the screw and repeat the operation.
6 When complete freedom of the piston is obtained with the jet screw tightened, remove the adjusting nut and refit the spring.

2:10 Tuning and synchronization of twin carburetters

The general principles of tuning the SU carburetter differ from other makes. The mixture is first set for slow running by means of the adjusting nut (**FIGS 2:6 and 2:7**). This raises or lowers the jet to give a smaller or larger effective jet orifice, thus making the mixture weaker or richer. When a suitable mixture has been found for slow running, the carburetter will automatically provide a suitable mixture at all throttle positions and speeds, provided that the correct taper needle for the particular car and carburetter is fitted. (See Technical Data Section).

For starting purposes the dashboard mixture control operates the jet lever, moving the jet downwards and giving a richer mixture. The mixture and throttle control connecting link at the same time opens the throttle slightly to give fast idling until the engine is warm.

In the case of the twin carburetters fitted to all the T Series Midgets, it is also important that the two instruments are synchronized.

Before attempting to tune or synchronize the carburetters, it is essential that certain items are fully serviceable, namely ignition timing, contact breaker points and sparking plug gaps (see **Chapter 3**), and valve clearances (**Section 1:5**). Any defects in these items, or any air leaks in the induction or in the carburetters themselves, will make carburetter tuning impossible. Having checked these matters, proceed as follows :

1 Remove the air cleaner and air intake pipe. (On model TF remove the two air cleaners).
2 Ensure that the carburetter pistons are free and the jets centred as described in **Section 2:8**.
3 Check that when the dashboard mixture control knob is pushed right home the cable is slack enough for the jet levers to return to the normal running position, and also that the interconnection adjust-

ment screw (**FIG 2:10**) is clear of the rocking lever anvil.

FIG 2:10 Setting screw for the interconnected rich mixture and throttle control (fast idling)

4 Slacken one of the clamping bolts on the universal joints of the throttle interconnecting spindle (**FIG 2:11**). Disconnect the jet lever interconnecting rod by removing one of the clevis pins at the jet levers, so that the throttles can be separately operated.

FIG 2:11 The lower arrow shows one of the universal joints on the throttle spindle. The top arrow and screwdriver indicate the two throttle stop screws for setting the engine speed

5 Check both jet needles for correct positioning in the pistons, as described in **Section 2:8** and shown in **FIG 2:9**. Also see that each jet is the same distance below the bridge on the choke when the jets are pushed hard up against the adjusting nuts.
6 Unscrew both throttle adjusting screws (**FIG 2:11**) until they will just hold a piece of paper between their ends and the stops. Then screw down each by one turn.

7 Start the engine and when really warm adjust the speed by turning each adjusting screw exactly the same amount.

8 Using a rubber tube as a stethoscope, synchronize the carburetters by setting the throttle adjusting screws on each until the hissing noise is equal. The tube must be held at the same point in each air intake.

9 Next adjust the mixture by screwing the jet adjusting nuts up or down by equal amounts (**FIG 2:12**), making sure the jet is hard up against the nut in each case. The engine speed will vary while this is being done, but the mixture should be set so that the engine runs at the best possible speed at this setting of the throttle stop screws.

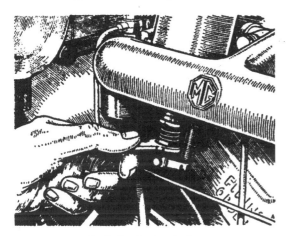

FIG 2:12 Setting the jet

10 Final correction of the slow running is now made by turning the throttle adjusting screws, again turning each the same amount.

11 When the mixture is correct on both carburetters, the engine beat will become irregular if one of the pistons is raised about 1/32 inch. If the piston of one carburetter is raised and the engine stops, but raising the piston of the other does not stop the engine, the mixture of the first carburetter is weaker than the other and further adjustments are necessary.

12 Reconnect the throttle controls and refit the air cleaner(s).

2:11 Air filter cleaning

On models **TA, TB, TC** an air cleaner of the oil wetted gauze type is fitted. Every 5000 miles remove the whole cleaner and swill the louvred end in a shallow pan of petrol. After drying, oil the mesh with clean engine oil and allow to drain before refitting.

Model **TD** has an oil bath cleaner. Every 6000 miles remove the central wingnut (which also secures the cleaner to the air intake) lift out the element and wash in paraffin. Allow to dry thoroughly. If sludge is present in the filter base, clean out and refill with clean engine oil to the level indicated. If no sludge is present, simply top up with oil.

Model **TF** has two air filters of the semi-dry type.

Every 3000 miles wash the element in petrol, lubricate with SAE 20 engine oil and allow to drain before refitting.

2:12 Modifications

The carburetters on the TF model have a larger bore (1$\frac{1}{4}$ inch) and differ in detail from those fitted to the **TD** model. Individual air cleaners are fitted and to prevent dust or dirt from entering the piston assembly, air to the underside of the piston is drawn from the air cleaner through two holes in the attachment flange shown in **FIG 2:13**. Early TF models have no damper. A piston lifting pin (arrowed) is fitted so that the piston can be lifted for checking purposes without removing the air cleaner.

FIG 2:13 Carburetter on TF Model with air cleaner removed to show air holes for piston and (arrowed) the piston lifting pin

2:13 Fault diagnosis

(a) Leakage or insufficient fuel delivered
1 Air vent in tank restricted
2 Fuel pipes blocked
3 Air leaks at pipe connections
4 Pump or carburetter filters blocked
5 Pump diaphragm defective
6 Pump valves sticking or seating badly

(b) Excessive fuel consumption
1 Carburetters need adjustment
2 Fuel leakage
3 Mixture control sticking
4 Dirty air cleaner(s)
5 Engine defects (see Section 1:18)
6 Tyres under-inflated
7 Brakes binding
8 Idling speed too high

(c) Idling speed too high
1 Rich mixture
2 Throttle controls sticking
3 Slow-running screws incorrectly adjusted
4 Worn butterfly valve or spindle
5 Ignition too far advanced

(d) Noisy fuel pump
1 Air leaks on suction side of pump or at diaphragm
2 Obstruction in fuel pipe
3 Clogged pump filter

(e) No fuel delivery
1 Float needles stuck
2 Vent in tank blocked

3 Electrical connections to pump faulty
4 Pump contact points dirty
5 Pipe line obstructed
6 Pump diaphragm stiff or damaged
7 Pump armature adjustment incorrect
8 Inlet valve in pump stuck open
9 Vapour lock in fuel pipe (hot weather conditions)
10 Bad air leak on suction side of pump

CHAPTER 3

THE IGNITION SYSTEM

3 : 1   Operating principles, automatic timing
         control
3 : 2   Distributor maintenance, contact point
         adjustment
3 : 3   Distributor removal
3 : 4   Dismantling

3 : 5   Reassembly
3 : 6   Refitting, meshing of drive gear
3 : 7   Retiming the ignition
3 : 8   Coil, HT cables
3 : 9   Sparking plugs
3 : 10   Fault diagnosis

3:1 Operating principles, automatic timing control

All models in the 'T' series are fitted with coil ignition equipment, the distributor being mounted on the left-hand side of the cylinder block and driven from the camshaft by helical gears. The system is basically the same on all cars in this series, but modifications have been made from time to time affecting the type of distributor, the method of its mounting and other details. It is therefore essential when ordering replacement parts to quote the type number of the distributor or coil as well as the chassis and engine number.

FIG 3:1 is an exploded view of the distributor. The body or housing is located on the cylinder block either by a clamp and clamp plate as shown in FIG 3:6 or by the cotter bolt arrangement shown in FIG 3:7. The shaft assembly runs in bushes pressed into the housing. The lower end of the shaft carries either the drive pinion or on later models an offset tongue locating in a slot in the drive pinion shaft.

The upper end of the shaft carries the base of the automatic timing control which operates on the centrifugal principle. As engine speed rises, two weights are forced outwards against the pull of control springs. Their movement turns the cam in the direction of rotation of the shaft, thus opening the contact points earlier and advancing the ignition. As engine speed decreases the control springs return the weights and the ignition is automatically retarded. No vacuum advance mechanism is provided on cars in this series.

The contact breaker base is located on the distributor body by projections and securing screws. The timing is set initially by turning the whole of the distributor body in relation to its mounting on the cylinder block (see **Section 3 : 7**). The contact breaker base carries the fixed and moving contacts and the capacitor or condenser. The rotor arm is firmly located in the slot at the top of the cam spindle. On models **TA, TB** and **TC**, a micrometer adjustment is provided, allowing small variations of ignition timing to suit different grades of fuel. One division on the scale is equivalent to 2° timing difference on the distributor or 4° on the crankshaft.

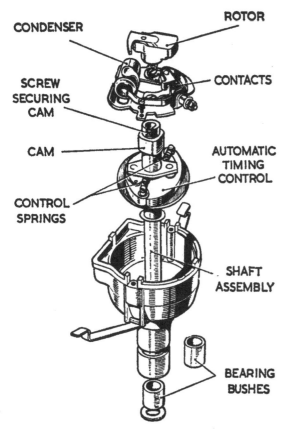

CONDENSER

ROTOR

SCREW SECURING CAM

CONTACTS

CAM

AUTOMATIC TIMING CONTROL

CONTROL SPRINGS

SHAFT ASSEMBLY

BEARING BUSHES

FIG 3:1   The component parts of the distributor

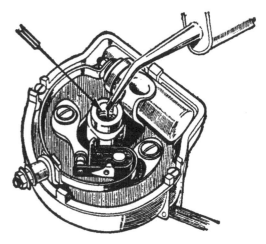

FIG 3:2   Lubrication of the distributor cam bearing

4 Lubricate the automatic timing control by adding a few drops of thin oil through the hole in the contact breaker base as shown in **FIG 3 : 3**. Do not over-lubricate any part of the distributor and make sure that oil or grease does not get on the contact points. Refit the rotor arm and press it down firmly.

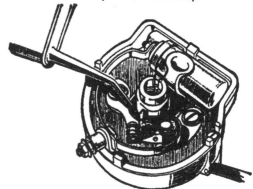

FIG 3:3   Lubrication of the automatic timing control through the aperture round the cam spindle

3:2 Distributor maintenance, contact point adjustment

Remove the distributor cap and check for signs of cracks or 'tracking', which shows as thin black marks between the segments inside the cap. Renew the cap if defective. Note that the central carbon brush should protrude slightly and work freely in its holder. On earlier models the brush will be of ordinary carbon; some later types have a composite brush acting as a radio suppressor. Clean the cap thoroughly inside and outside with a dry cloth. Renew the rotor arm if the metal electrode is loose or badly pitted.

Every 3000 miles, lubricate the distributor as follows:
1 Give the cam face a very light smear of high melting point or lithium grease.
2 Apply a slight trace of oil to the contact breaker pivot pin.
3 Remove the rotor arm (see **Section 3:4**, Operation 1) and add a few drops only of thin oil (cycle or machine oil) to lubricate the cam bearing and distributor shaft, as shown in **FIG 3:2**. Do not remove the screw in the top of the spindle, as an oilway is provided.

The contact points should be clean and free from pitting. If necessary, polish with a fine carborundum stone or very fine emery cloth, afterwards wiping with a petrol moistened cloth. The moving contact can be removed as described in **Section 3:4** to facilitate this operation. After cleaning, or as routine attention after the first 500 miles and every 3000 miles thereafter, the gap between the points should be checked and adjusted if necessary as follows:
1 Turn the engine slowly (using the starting handle) until the contact breaker points are fully opened. Note that each cam only keeps the points fully open during a very small angle of its rotation. This is more pronounced in the case of high lift cams with steeper face angles designed for wider gaps fitted to later models (see **FIG 3:5**), where especial care has to be taken.

2 The gap is then adjusted by slackening the two contact plate securing screws shown in **FIG 3:4** and moving the plate as necessary until the gap is correct.

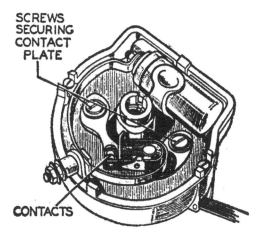

FIG 3:4 Distributor with cap and rotor arm removed, showing contact plate and other components

3 Check the gap with a feeler gauge. The correct setting is .010 to .012 inch for distributors fitted on **TA, TB, TC** and earlier **TD** models with symmetric or asymmetric cams (also shown on **FIG 3:5**) and .014 to .016 inch for later **TD** and **TF** models fitted with high lift cams. Distributors having high lift cams are denoted by the letter E or a following letter appearing after the service number.

4 Tighten the contact plate screws securely and re-check the gap.

SYMMETRIC ASYMMETRIC HIGH LIFT

FIG 3:5 The three types of distributor cam

3:3 Distributor removal

Disconnect the battery and the LT lead from the side of the distributor. Remove the cap. To facilitate later refitting, turn the engine by hand until the timing marks (**FIG 3:8**) are in line and the distributor rotor points to the segment attached to the No. 1 plug lead. Mark the exact position of the rotor in relation to the body and do not subsequently move the engine.

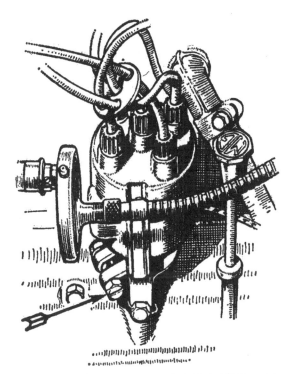

FIG 3:6 Distributor with clamp bolt fitting indicated by arrow. To withdraw the distributor the lower bolt with the lock wire is the only one that need be removed

On models fitted with the distributor mounting shown in **FIG 3:6**, the clamp bolt (arrowed) should not be disturbed unless the ignition timing is to be altered. The distributor is secured to the cylinder block by the bolt with the locking wire and this is the only one that need be removed. The distributor can then be withdrawn with spindle and drive gear attached. On later **TD** and **TF** models (commencing at Engine No. XPAG.TD2. 20942) the distributor is mounted as shown in **FIG 3:7**.

FIG 3:7 Attachment of distributor on later TD and all TF cars by cotter bolt (arrowed) engaging the distributor stem

The tapered cotter (arrowed) passing through the boss in the cylinder block prevents the distributor body from turning as well as securing it to the block. Note the position of the distributor on the scale provided for this purpose, then slacken the nut and tap the cotter inwards a short distance. The distributor can then be withdrawn complete with spindle. This will be found to have an offset tongue which ensures its replacement in the same relationship with the drive shaft. Carefully note the relative angular positions of the large segment and the small segment of the shaft at this stage. It will be essential that the same positions are set when refitting the distributor, because a timing error of 180° will occur if the engine is turned through 360° (see **Section 3:6**).

3:4 Dismantling

Referring to **FIGS 3:1** and **3:4**, dismantling procedures are as follows :

1 Lift the rotor arm off of the spindle. If it is a tight fit, lever it off gently with a screwdriver to avoid damage.
2 Slacken the nut on the terminal post and lift off the end of the contact breaker spring, which is slotted to facilitate removal. Lift the arm off its pivot and remove the insulating washer. Remove the two screws, spring washers and flat washers securing the contact plate (**FIG 3:4**) and remove the plate with the fixed contact.
3 Remove the two screws at the edge of the contact breaker base and detach the base from the distributor body.
4 If the capacitor (or condenser) has to be renewed, it is better to fit a new capacitor and contact breaker plate assembly complete. But if it is required to remove the capacitor from the plate, soften the solder holding it in its clip with a hot iron. Care must be taken not to overheat a new capacitor when re-soldering into position.
5 Drive out the parallel driving pin securing the drive gear to the bottom of the spindle. On later models, before removing the pin securing the tongued collar or driving dog to the spindle, note the position of the tongue in relation to the rotor slot in the cam. This is again to obviate a possible error of 180° in timing on reassembly. Retain the steel or fibre washer which controls the amount of end float in the spindle.
6 Lift out the shaft assembly with the automatic timing control and cam attached. Undo the centre screw securing the cam and remove the cam, giving access to the automatic control.

3:5 Reassembly

Before reassembling the distributor, check the fit of the distributor shaft in its bushes which are of porous bronze and pressed into the body. On later models a single long bush is used. Worn bushes can be replaced by new ones, a press and special mandrel being necessary for this operation. Alternatively a replacement body can be obtained ready bushed. The bushes are machined to size and must not be reamed out or their self-lubricating properties will be impaired.

Examine the tension of the springs in the automatic timing control (see **FIG 3:1**) and if it is weak the springs should be renewed. Otherwise the full range of ignition advance will not be obtained. Lubricate the timing control sparingly with SAE 20 engine oil, also the

distributor shaft and the upper end of the shaft on which the cam fits. Fit the cam on the shaft and secure tightly with the retaining screw.

Assemble the distributor shaft in the body, and place the thrust washer on the lower end of the shaft before fitting the drive gear or driving dog. On later distributors with the latter type of fitting, ensure that the rotor slot and the offset tongue are in the same relative position as before dismantling, as was observed in Operation 5 of **Section 3:4**. Fit the pin in the drive gear or dog and burr over the hole at each side to retain the pin in position.

Fit the contact breaker base to the body and secure tightly with the two screws and spring washers. Fit the connector strip to the capacitor terminal. Fit the contact plate carrying the fixed contact, (**FIG 3:4**) and lightly tighten the two securing screws, each of which has a spring washer and a plain washer. If the contact points are renewed, the assembly provided (known as the 'contact set') will consist of the contact plate with fixed contact and the arm and spring with the moving contact. Fit the insulating washer on the contact breaker pivot pin, fit the lever over the pin and locate the slotted end of the spring under the head of the terminal screw. Tighten the terminal locknut.

Adjust the contact points to a gap of .010 to .012 inch (for symmetric or asymmetric cams) and to .014 to .016 inch for distributors with high-lift cams (see **Section 3:2** and **FIG 3:5**). Refit the rotor arm and attach the distributor cap with the spring clips.

3:6 Refitting, meshing of drive gear

If the engine was set as described in **Section 3:3** and has not been turned, No. 1 piston will be on the TDC of the compression stroke. Providing that the clamp bolt has not been disturbed, turn the distributor shaft so that the rotor arm points to the segment carrying the No. 1 plug lead. Except on later **TD** and **TF** models, insert the distributor in the cylinder block, feeling the drive gear in until it engages with the nearest tooth on the meshing gear on the camshaft. Owing to the helical teeth the distributor spindle will turn slightly as the gears engage, but if the exact position of the rotor was marked before removal (**Section 3:3**) this factor can be allowed for. Fit the securing bolt in the plate lug but do not tighten until the timing has been checked, as described in **Section 3:7**. On later **TD** and **TF** models (**FIG 3:7**), if the distributor drive shaft has not been removed (thus altering the meshing of the pinions), the distributor shaft can only be refitted in one position owing to the offset tongue of the driving dog. Set the scale on the distributor in the position previously marked (see **Section 3:3**) and tighten the cotter nut. As was observed in the removal instructions, **if the engine has been turned the timing can be 180° out on the distributor,** which means that the spark will occur at TDC on the exhaust stroke. To check the timing see **Section 3:7**. If the distributor drive shaft has been removed from the cylinder block, it must be refitted so that with the timing marks in line (**FIG 3:8**) and the No. 1 piston at TDC compression stroke, the larger and smaller segments of the drive must be set at exactly the same relative angular positions as when the assembly was dismantled.

3:7 Retiming the ignition

The basic ignition timing for all engines in this series is for the contact points to be just opening at TDC, the micrometer adjustment (where fitted) being in its central position. The necessary ignition advance is provided by the centrifugally operated automatic timing control shown in **FIG 3:1**.

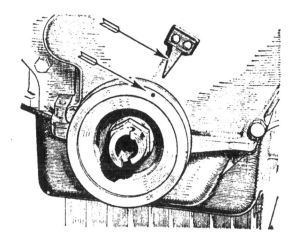

FIG 3:8 The timing mark on the crankshaft pulley and the pointer on the timing chain cover

FIG 3:8 shows the timing mark on the crankshaft pulley. When this mark is in line with the pointer on the timing chain cover, Nos. 1 and 4 pistons are on TDC. The marks however do not indicate which piston is on its compression stroke, so that the rocker cover must be removed to check this. It is usual to time on No. 1 cylinder, so the engine should be turned until both valves on this cylinder are closed and the timing marks in line. At this point the distributor rotor arm should be pointing to the segment carrying the No. 1 plug lead and the contact points should be just opening.

If the setting is incorrect, slacken the clamp bolt (**FIG 3:6**) or on later distributors slacken the cotter nut and tap the cotter inwards (**FIG 3:7**) so that the distributor body can be turned until the correct setting is obtained. Lock the clamp or cotter and **re-check the setting in case the act of locking has turned the body slightly.**

3:8 Coil, HT cables

Coil defects are not common, but if a coil is defective it must be renewed. Check that the terminal connections are tight. A much more frequent cause of trouble is defective wiring between the battery and the coil or a bad connection in the HT lead to the distributor.

The low tension supply to the coil is by means of the (white) wire from the A3 terminal (on the fuse box or control box according to model) to the SW terminal of the coil. With the ignition switched on and the contact points open, a voltmeter should give a reading of 12 volts at between either terminal and earth. To trace the current supply from the battery to the A3 terminal, refer to the appropriate wiring diagram in the Appendix for the model concerned. The white/black low tension wire from the CB terminal of the coil to the distributor is frequently neglected and is particularly liable to become soaked in oil. If it appears unserviceable it should be renewed.

Check from time to time the condition of the HT cables, which comprise the lead from the centre terminal of the coil to the centre of the distributor cap and the four sparking plug leads. If the insulation is perished, the connection should be renewed using 7 mm rubber or PVC covered cable. Ensure that the leads are fitted in the right order, taking into account that the distributor rotates anticlockwise and that the firing order is 1, 3, 4, 2. To fit these cables into the moulded terminal nuts on the distributor cap, and also in the centre of the coil, the ends are passed through a brass washer and splayed out to ensure contact.

3:9 Sparking plugs

Sparking plugs vary considerably in their characteristics and the use of an unsuitable plug can cause serious trouble. It is therefore essential to use the correct type of plug as recommended by the car manufacturers. Plugs so recommended are the Champion L10 for **TA** engines, the Champion L10S ($\frac{1}{2}$ inch reach) for **TB**, **TC** and **TD** engines prior to XPAG.TD2. 22735 and the Champion NA8 ($\frac{3}{4}$ inch reach) for **TD** and **TF** engines of subsequent production. Do not fit the **NA8 type with the longer reach to earlier engines.**

To obtain the best engine performance and economical running the sparking plugs must be kept clean and their points correctly adjusted to a gap of .020 to .022 inch. Adjust the gap by bending the outer electrode, for which a small tool made by the Champion Co. is useful and obtainable from most accessory dealers. **On no account bend the central electrode or the insulation may be damaged.**

The plugs should be cleaned after the first 500 miles on a new or reconditioned engine and subsequently every 3000 miles. It is worth while to have the plugs cleaned and tested by a service agent possessing a blasting machine. If this is not possible, the points can be cleaned with a piece of file card and the inside of the plug swilled out with fuel. Plug threads should be cleaned free of carbon with a wire brush.

The running condition of an engine can be judged by an examination of the sparking plugs immediately they are removed. Thick black oily carbon indicates over-oiling, usually caused by worn cylinder bores, pistons, rings or valve stems. A finer deposit of dry soot indicates rich mixture, while a plug that is badly burned and pitted indicates overheating, often caused by weak mixture.

Sparking plugs should be tightened sufficiently to make them compression tight, but not tight enough to flatten the washers or gaskets. The all metal type of washer now generally used acts as a heat conductor between the plug and the cylinder head, thus helping the cooling of the plug.

Owners of **TA** Midget cars who are unfamiliar with the MPJG type engine may find some initial difficulty in inserting the sparking plugs owing to their unusual angle. Note that as well as being inclined from the horizontal they are inclined towards each other in pairs.

3:10 Fault diagnosis

(a) Engine will not fire
1 Battery discharged
2 Contact points dirty, pitted or out of adjustment
3 Distributor cap dirty, cracked or 'tracking'
4 Carbon brush in distributor cap not contacting rotor
5 Faulty cable or loose connection in LT circuit
6 Distributor rotor arm cracked
7 Faulty coil
8 Broken contact breaker spring
9 Contact points stuck open

(b) Engine misfires
1 Check 2, 3, 5 and 7 in (a)
2 Weak contact spring
3 HT leads (coil and sparking plugs) defective
4 Sparking plug loose
5 Sparking plug insulation cracked
6 Sparking plug gap incorrect
7 Ignition timing too far advanced

CHAPTER 4

THE COOLING SYSTEM

4:1 Principle of system
4:2 Maintenance, flushing, anti-freeze, belt
        tension
4:3 Water pump removal

4:4 Dismantling
4:5 Reassembly
4:6 Thermostat, water temperature gauge
4:7 Fault diagnosis

4:1 Principle of system

On model TA, cooling is of the pump type, with thermostat. The water pump is mounted on the front end of the cylinder head. It carries the fan blades and is driven from the crankshaft by an endless belt which also drives the generator. Water heated by the engine is drawn from the cylinder head into the pump which feeds it through the thermostat to the radiator header tank. The water flows downwards through the radiator, which is cooled by air drawn through it by the fan. Cooled water passes from the bottom tank of the radiator by an external pipe to an elbow at the rear of the cylinder head where it replaces the hot water drawn out by the pump.

To assist in the rapid warming up of the engine when first started, a thermostat is fitted on the outlet side of the water pump. When the engine is cold, the thermostat remains closed. Water heated by the engine is pumped by way of an elbow on the right side of the thermostat to the bypass hose. This is connected to a T-piece in the pipe from the radiator bottom tank to the rear of the cylinder head. Warm water thus circulates through the engine without passing through the radiator. As soon as the water reaches a pre-determined temperature, the thermostat opens and allows it to flow through the radiator in the normal manner.

On all models except TA the cooling system is of the thermo-siphon, impeller-assisted type. The water pump, which carries the fan, is mounted on the front of the cylinder block and driven from the crankshaft by an endless belt which also drives the generator. Water heated by the engine passes from the cylinder head through the thermostat and on the thermo-siphon principle flows upwards to the radiator header tank. It then flows downwards through the radiator core, which is cooled by air drawn through it by the fan. From the radiator bottom tank the cooled water passes to the impeller or water pump which assists the natural flow by pumping it directly into the cylinder block. The circulation is completed by the water flowing upwards through large water-passages in the cylinder head joint and so into the water jacket of the head.

To assist in the rapid warming up of the engine when first started, a thermostat is fitted in the cylinder head water outlet (Item 34 in **FIG 4:5** and also shown in **FIG 1:1**). When the engine is cold the thermostat is closed and water flows through the bypass hose (36 in **FIG 4:5**) and back to the water pump without passing through the radiator. As soon as the water reaches a pre-determined temperature, the thermostat opens and allows it to flow through the radiator in the normal manner.

On models **TF, TF 1500** the cooling system is pressurized, the pressure being controlled by a spring-loaded valve in the radiator filler cap. In other respects the system is as already described.

4:2 Maintenance, flushing, antifreeze, belt tension

On models **except TF,** the radiator is fitted with an external filler cap. Care must be taken when removing the cap if the engine is hot. Protect the hand against possible scalding by using a large piece of rag. Partially release the filler cap and allow any steam to escape before finally removing cap. If the engine is actually boiling it is better to wait for it to cool, as in any case cold water must not be added in these circumstances.

Model **TF** and **TF 1500** have a pressurized cooling system. A spring-loaded valve in the filler cap (**FIG 4:1**) allows an appreciable pressure to build up in the cooling system under normal running conditions and special precautions are necessary when removing the cap. (The filler cap is under the bonnet on these models. The dummy cap on the radiator shell does not unscrew.) Protect the hand by using a large piece of rag and turn the filler cap slowly until the retaining tongues in the cap are felt to engage in the lobes at the ends of the filler neck cams (**FIG 4:1**). Wait until the pressure has been fully relieved before removing the cap.

FIG 4:1   Model TF filler cap showing retaining cam on filler neck and safety lobes

On all models, to drain the cooling system remove the filler cap as previously described and open the two drain taps. One is on the radiator bottom tank (**FIG 4:2**) the other in the right side of the cylinder block (**FIG 4:3**). If antifreeze is in use it can be collected in a suitable receptacle for re-use. When water ceases to flow from either tap, it should not be assumed that the system is necessarily empty. The tap may be blocked by sediment which has been flushed into it from the radiator or block. Probe the tap with a short length of wire, removing the extension pipe from the tap (where fitted). Note also that complete draining is impossible if the car is on a slope or a cambered road.

FIG 4:2   Radiator drain tap

FIG 4:3   Drain tap on cylinder block

Periodic flushing is necessary to remove sediment which will otherwise block the water passages in the radiator. Drain the system as described and with the taps still open flush with water from a hose inserted in the radiator. A more thorough method is to remove the radiator, turn it upside down and flush in the reverse direction to its normal flow. If a badly blocked radiator is suspected, it is better to entrust the work to a radiator specialist. The radiator will then be back-flushed under pressure and afterwards tested for any possible leaks which the flushing may have uncovered. If the radiator is in very bad condition the specialist will be able to advise whether to have a new core soldered to the existing tanks or to fit a replacement radiator. Owing to the practical difficulty of ensuring that the cooling system is completely drained a suitable antifreeze mixture should be added to the coolant in cold weather. It should also be remembered that a car's unprotected cooling system can freeze up when the engine is running. A proprietary antifreeze of the ethylene glycol type should be used in the proportions advised by the manufacturer for the climatic conditions expected. Owing to their volatility it is inadvisable to use alcohol-based solutions on **TF** or **TF 1500** cars with pressurized cooling.

A 25 per cent solution (by volume) is generally used in the UK, giving complete protection down to –11°C (12°F) which means the car can be driven away immediately without prior warming up. The same mixture will prevent freezing down to a limit of –18°C (zero°F) provided the engine is allowed to warm up before driving away. A 33½ per cent solution will give complete protection down to zero °F. It should be noted, however, that the degree of protection specified will only apply if the antifreeze solution is maintained at the correct strength. It is advisable to top up the cooling system when necessary using antifreeze solution in the correct proportions. If in doubt, have the strength of the coolant checked at a service station with one of the special hydrometers used for the purpose.

Before filling with antifreeze the cooling system should be drained and flushed as already described. Radiator hoses and clips should be examined, not forgetting the short bypass hose. It is a good plan to fit a new set of hoses to avoid possible leaks once the antifreeze has been installed. The thermostat should also be checked as described in **Section 4:6** and renewed if defective. When filling, half fill the system with water, add the required amount of antifreeze and then top up with water to about 2 inches from the top of the filler neck. Avoid over-filling when antifreeze is in use to prevent unnecessary loss on expansion.

FIG 4:4 Generator locking screw and pivot bolts which must be slackened for fan belt adjustment

The adjustment of the fan belt, which also drives the water pump and generator, is effected by slightly slackening the two pivot bolts and the locking screw in the slotted link (**FIG 4:4**). To tighten the belt move the generator away from the engine with gentle hand pressure. Lock the screw and the bolts and re-check the tension. There should be about half an inch up and down play on the top run of the belt under firm hand pressure. Adjustment of the fan belt to its correct tension is important. A slack belt will slip giving reduced generator output and cooling. An overtightened belt will cause damage to the generator bearings. The fan belt should be renewed if it becomes frayed or stretched. No attempt should be made to lever a belt in tension over the sides of a pulley.

4:3 Water pump removal

On all models, to remove the water pump, drain the cooling system (**Section 4:2**) and remove the radiator as described in **Chapter 1, Section 1:2**. Remove the fan blades by withdrawing the four screws securing them to the fan pulley. Remove the fan belt after slackening the adjustment (**Section 4:2**). On model **TA** remove the nuts from the four studs securing the pump to the cylinder head. On other models remove either four bolts or two bolts and two stud nuts securing the pump to the cylinder block. Note that the studs or bolts, whichever are fitted, are of varying lengths. The pump can now be removed from the head or cylinder block. **If a good joint has been made considerable effort may be needed to move the pump, but on no account try to lever it off with a screwdriver or the faces may be damaged.** On models TD, TF move the inner control link bracket outwards to clear the pump.

4:4 Dismantling

Before deciding to overhaul the water pump, it should be noted that if components of the pump are worn, a replacement pump can be supplied on an exchange basis at a much lower cost than that of the individual parts. Pumps are available for most models and are supplied complete and ready to bolt on, complete with pulley but less fan blades. A new joint washer will also be required between the pump and the cylinder head or block. A very slight leak may occur on a new pump until the carbon gland seal has bedded down.

If the water pump is to be dismantled, the general procedure is the same for all models. The pump described is the one fitted to models **TD** and **TF**, shown in exploded form in **FIG 4:5**.

The procedure is first to tap out the taper pin 6, ensuring that it is tapped out in the right direction, and remove the impeller 5 from the spindle 4. Withdraw the pressure spring on earlier type pumps and seal assembly 21. On later type pumps the seal is of the integral type and the spring is omitted. Components of old and new type pumps are not interchangeable. Care should be taken not to damage the carbon ring which is relatively brittle or the working face of the rubber seal. Do not lose the driving pin for the gland as it is a loose fit in the spindle.

The pump spindle 4 is carried in two ball races 14 which should give no trouble unless they have been neglected. Worn races however will soon cause the carbon seal to break up and the impeller and body may

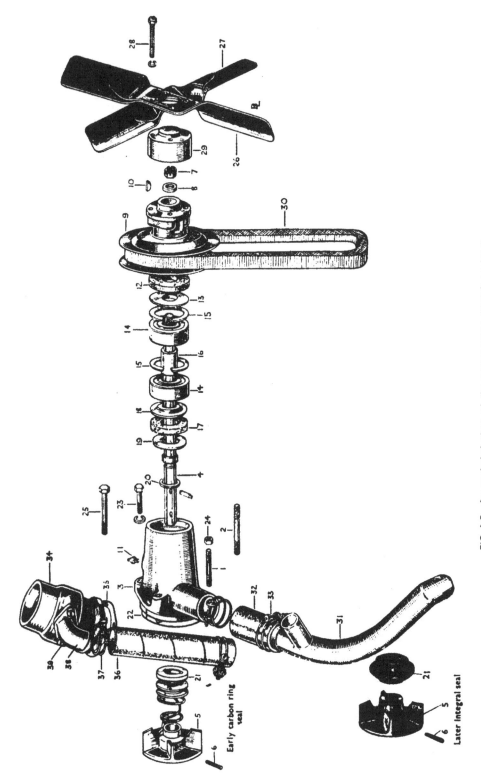

FIG 4:5 An exploded view of the water pump (XPAG engines)

Early carbon ring seal

Later integral seal

Key to FIG 4 : 5
1 Stud (short)   2 Stud (long)   3 Water pump body   4 Pump spindle   5 Impeller   6 Impeller taper pin   7 Spindle nut   8 Washer   9 Fan pulley   10 Key for fan pulley
11 Grease nipple   12 Front felt oil seal   13 Front oil seal cover   14 Ball races   15 Circlips   16 Distance tube   17 Rear felt oil seal   18 Centre oil seal cover
19 Rear oil seal cover   20 Circlip for spindle   21 Water seal assembly   22 Gasket (pump to block)   23 Bolt (short)   24 Nut for studs   25 Bolt (long)   26 Fan blade
27 Fan blade (offset)   28 Screw for fan blade   29 Distance piece   30 Distance piece   31 Pump connecting pipe   32 Connecting pipe hose   33 Hose clip (1¼ inch)   34 Thermostat
35 Thermostat gasket   36 Bypass hose   37 Bypass hose clip (1¼ inch)   38 Bypass elbow   39 Screw for elbow

be damaged. Remove the drive pin for the gland. Remove the pulley nut 7, washer 8 and withdraw the pulley 9. Remove the pulley key 10, the front felt oil-seal 12 and cover 13. Remove the circlip 15 with long-nosed pliers.

Pour a little paraffin into the pump body around the outer bearing and tap the inner end of the spindle on a piece of wood until the outer bearing can be withdrawn. This will release the distance tube 16 which can now be withdrawn giving access to the inner bearing 14. Remove the inner circlip by contracting the ring and inserting a screwdriver behind it to ease it out of its groove. The inner bearing and spindle can now be removed.

If the felt oil seals 12 and 17 are worn or the bearings slack they should be renewed. Examine the carbon ring, brass washer and synthetic rubber seal and if any parts are defective do not replace individually but fit a new water seal kit, Part No. MG862.77. On later model pumps the water seal and washer should be renewed separately as necessary.

4:5 Reassembly

Water pump reassembly is carried out in the reverse manner to that detailed for dismantling. The space between the two races should be filled with the recommended grease (a lithium grease of high melting point) and the felt oil seals liberally soaked in engine oil or grease before refitting. If the pump is packed with grease on assembly the only attention it will need will be to give two strokes of the grease gun every 1000 miles. It must not be over-lubricated as excess grease will reach the carbon gland seal and cause damage. The castellated nut holding the fan pulley should not be over-tightened but just firmly secured.

Refitting the water pump is generally a reversal of the procedure for its removal but attention should be given to the following matters:
1 Carefully clean the mating faces of the pump body and the cylinder head or cylinder block, removing all traces of the old joint washer.
2 Fit a new joint washer, smearing both sides with jointing compound.
3 Before tightening the four securing nuts or bolts ensure that the pump is not binding on the studs in **TA** cars and that its spigot has entered squarely into the orifice in the cylinder in other cars.
4 Refit the radiator, renewing all hoses if their condition is doubtful. Refit and adjust the fan belt as described in **Section 4:2**. Check for leaks. Refill the cooling system, run the engine and check for leaks again.

4:6 Thermostat, water temperature gauge

On model **TA** the thermostat is situated between the water pump and the top radiator hose. To remove, drain the cooling system (**Section 4:2**). Slacken the clip on the top hose. Remove the bypass elbow from the thermostat housing by undoing the two nuts securing the flange. Disconnect the thermostat elbow from the pump. The thermostat housing can then be withdrawn from the top radiator hose. Lift out the thermostat, test by immersing in water and heating to the prescribed temperature as shown in Technical Data. If the thermostat does not open at this temperature or fails to close it must be renewed. Clean out the thermostat housing before fitting the thermostat.

On other models, after draining the cooling system (**Section 4:2**) disconnect the top hose to gain access to the thermostat (Models **TB, TC, TD**). On Model **TF** disconnect the elbow from the thermostat housing on the front of the cylinder head. Test the thermostat for opening temperature as described for model **TA**.

Later **TD** models are fitted with a combined oil-pressure and water temperature gauge on the dashboard. On model **TF** the instrument panel was rearranged and the oil-pressure and water temperature gauges are combined with the ammeter.

4:7 Fault diagnosis
(a) Internal water leakage
1 Cracked cylinder wall
2 Loose cylinder head nuts
3 Cracked cylinder head
4 Faulty or incorrect type cylinder head gasket (see **Chapter 1**)
5 Cracked tappet chest wall

(b) Poor circulation
1 Radiator core blocked
2 Engine water passages restricted
3 Low water level
4 Loose fan belt
5 Defective thermostat
6 Perished or collapsed radiator hoses
7 Incorrectly fitted cylinder head gasket.

(c) Corrosion
1 Impurities in the water
2 Infrequent draining and flushing

(d) Overheating
1 Check (b)
2 Sludge in crankcase
3 Faulty ignition timing (see **Chapter 3**)
4 Low oil level in sump
5 Tight engine
6 Choked exhaust system
7 Brakes binding (see **Chapter 10**)
8 Slipping clutch (see **Chapter 5**)
9 Incorrect valve timing (see **Chapter 3**)
10 Weak mixture (see **Chapter 2**)

CHAPTER 5

THE CLUTCH

5:1 Construction and operation, wet plate
     clutch
5:2 Dry plate clutch
5:3 Maintenance
5:4 Clutch removal and dismantling

5:5 Driven plate condition
5:6 Reassembly, refitting, plate alignment
5:7 Modifications
5:8 Fault diagnosis

5:1 Construction and operation, wet plate clutch

FIG 5:1 shows the clutch fitted to the Series **TA** Midget. The clutch runs in oil which is fed to the unit by a hole drilled in the centre of the crankshaft. When the oil has passed through the clutch plates it escapes through gauze windows in the clutch spring plate into the flywheel housing. Here it is picked up by the teeth of the starter ring gear attached to the flywheel and thrown into a gallery on the left hand side of the flywheel housing. From here it drains back into the sump.

The clutch assembly comprises: the flywheel, a retaining plate for the spigot bearing, the gearbox first motion shaft spigot bearing centre and the clutch driven plate which is fitted with cork inserts. Next comes the pressure plate, clutch springs, clutch cover plate with thimbles for the clutch springs, the washer for the thrust race and finally the thrust race and its locking nut. The clutch driven plate incorporates damper springs and its hub is splined to slide on the third motion shaft. The clutch fork operates directly on the thrust race, and when the clutch pedal is depressed moves both the

thrust race and the pressure plate away from the flywheel thus releasing the clutch.

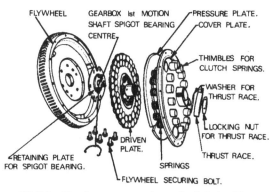

FIG 5:1   Clutch components (wet plate) Series TA

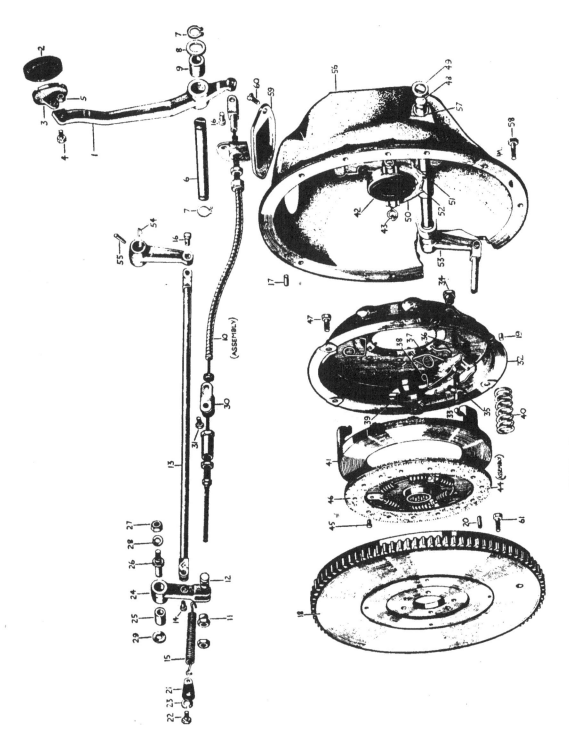

FIG 5:2 Clutch components (dry plate) Series TD

Key to FIG 5:2

1 Clutch pedal and bush 2 Pad—rubber—clutch pedal 3 Pad—brake pedal 4 Bolt—pad—brake pedal 5 Nut—pad bolt 6 Shaft—clutch 7 Seager circlip
8 Spacing washer—between pedals 9 Bush—brake pedal 10 Clutch cable assembly 11 Nut—clutch adjuster 12 Pin—clutch adjuster 13 Connecting rod—clutch
14 Yoke pin—rod 15 Spring—clutch return 16 Pin—clutch lever 17 Dowel—clutch housing 18 Flywheel (with starter ring and dowels) 19 Dowel—clutch cover
20 Dowel—crankshaft 21 Bracket—clutch return spring 22 Bolt—bracket 23 Spring washer—bolt 24 Lever—cable and connecting rod 25 Bush—lever 26 Fulcrum pin—lever
27 Nut—fulcrum pin 28 Washer—fulcrum pin 29 Washer—fulcrum pin—outer 30 Abutment bracket—clutch cable 31 Bolt—bracket 32 Cover—clutch 33 Release lever—clutch
34 Eyebolt and nut 35 Fulcrum pin—release lever 36 Strut—release lever 37 Spring—anti-rattle—release lever 38 Spring—retaining—release lever 39 Plate—release lever
40 Spring—pressure plate 41 Pressure plate—clutch 42 Clutch release bearing and cup assembly 43 Retainer—clutch release bearing 44 Clutch driven plate assembly
45 Rivet—clutch driven plate 46 Facing 47 Bolt—clutch cover 48 Clutch withdrawal shaft 49 Circlip—withdrawal shaft 50 Fork—clutch 51 Key—clutch fork
52 Taper pin—clutch fork 53 Clutch operating lever 54 Key—clutch lever 55 Taper pin—clutch lever 56 Clutch housing (with bushes) 57 Bush—clutch housing
58 Bolt—securing clutch housing 59 Clutch inspection cover 60 Screw—inspection cover 61 Bolt—flywheel securing

5:2 Dry plate clutch

Series **TB, TC, TD** and **TF** Midgets are fitted with a Borg & Beck dry plate clutch, consisting of a driven plate assembly, a cover assembly and a graphite release bearing assembly. The components are shown in **FIG 5:2**.

The driven plate incorporates damper springs and its hub is splined to the third motion shaft. Two friction linings are riveted to the plate, one on each side. The cover assembly consists of a pressed steel cover 32 and a cast iron pressure plate 41 loaded by six springs 40. Mounted on the pressure plate are three release levers 33 pivoting on floating pins 35 retained by eyebolts and adjusting nuts 34. Struts 36 are placed between lugs on the pressure plate and the outer ends of the release levers. The release levers are loaded by anti-rattle springs 37 and are connected to the release lever plate 39 by retainer springs 38.

The release bearing assembly consists of a graphite bearing shrunk into a bearing cup and is located on the clutch fork 50. When the clutch pedal is depressed, the operating lever 53 is moved away from the flywheel and the release bearing towards the flywheel. The release bearing presses on the plate 39 and through the three release levers moves the pressure plate away from the flywheel thus disengaging the clutch.

5:3 Maintenance

On the Series **TA** Midget it is important that the clutch pedal has 1 inch minimum free movement measured at the foot pad of the pedal, before operating the withdrawal mechanism. The object of this dimension is to prevent the clutch thrust race from fouling the operating fork when the cork-lined driven plate wears. Neglect of regular adjustment may cause the clutch to slip and the cork inserts to burn out. The adjustment is carried out at the bottom of the clutch pedal. There is also an adjustable stop limiting the maximum pedal travel. This should be adjusted so that the stop comes into contact with the pedal at the same time as the clutch stops spinning.

On the **dry plate clutch** fitted to all other models, the clutch operating mechanism must be periodically adjusted to compensate for wear in the clutch linings. If the minimum free movement is not maintained the clutch will slip and rapid lining wear will take place. On Series **TB, TC** the pedal is adjusted to give a minimum free movement of 1 inch measured at the pedal pad. The stop limiting the pedal travel is then adjusted to give 3 inch pedal movement in addition to the 1 inch free movement. Both adjustments are carried out at the bottom of the pedal.

On Series **TD**, the clutch operating mechanism is as shown in **FIG 5:3** and the necessary adjusting nuts will be found on the righthand side of the sump. To compensate for lining wear the minimum clearance at F between the withdrawal lever plate and the thrust bearing must be $\frac{1}{16}$ inch, which gives a free movement G of $\frac{3}{4}$ inch at the clutch pedal pad. The adjustment is effected by slackening locknut B and turning adjusting nut A. In addition care must be taken to avoid excessive pedal travel as this will place additional load on the carbon release bearing. There should be approximately $1\frac{1}{4}$ inch clearance at H. To adjust this clearance, grip

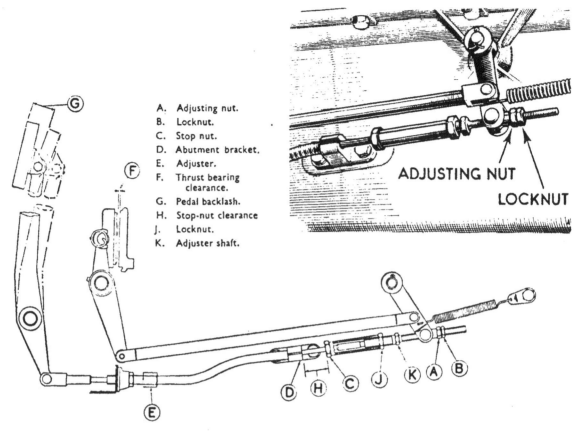

A. Adjusting nut.
B. Locknut.
C. Stop nut.
D. Abutment bracket.
E. Adjuster.
F. Thrust bearing clearance.
G. Pedal backlash.
H. Stop-nut clearance
J. Locknut.
K. Adjuster shaft.

ADJUSTING NUT
LOCKNUT

FIG 5:3 Clutch operating mechanism Series TD. Later cars were fitted with a rod in place of the cable illustrated

the nut C and slacken the locknut J. Grip the adjuster shaft hexagon K and adjust the stop nut C as required, finally tightening locknut J. Note that the adjuster E is only for initial adjustment of the outer cable length to give the correct flexibility between the pedal and the floating engine unit and should require no further adjustment. On later Series **TD** and **TF** cars a clutch control rod is fitted in place of a cable. On these cars the free pedal movement G must also be maintained at ¾ inch.

5:4 Clutch removal and dismantling

On all models access to the clutch is obtained by separating the engine from the gearbox. If the engine and gearbox are removed from the car as a unit as described in **Section 1:2**, proceed with the removal of gearbox as in **Section 1:10**. Alternatively the gearbox can be removed leaving the engine in the car as detailed in **Section 6:3**. **In each case note the precautions to be taken in supporting the weight of the gearbox so that it does not hang on the clutch driven plate while the gearbox first motion shaft is being withdrawn.**

On the Series **TA wet plate clutch**, proceed to dismantle as follows: Mark the clutch cover so that it can be reassembled in the same relationship to the flywheel. Slacken the ring of bolts securing it to the

flywheel, a turn at a time by diagonal selection until the spring pressure is relieved. Remove the bolts and the cover. With the assembly on the bench, remove the circlips from the three studs which project through the cork faced driven plate and lift off the plate. To dismantle the clutch cover and pressure plate assembly, remove the ring nut from the hub of the pressure plate, also the withdrawal ball race and washer. This allows the pressure plate, springs and thimbles to be removed.

To dismantle the **dry plate** Borg & Beck clutch fitted to Series **TB, TC, TD** and **TF**, proceed as follows: Mark the relative position of the clutch cover 32 and flywheel 18 in **FIG 5:2**. Slacken the clutch cover bolts 47 a turn at a time by diagonal selection until the spring pressure is released. Remove the bolts and cover and lift out the driven plate 44. **Further dismantling of the dry plate clutch is not advised, as reassembly of the cover, pressure plate and levers requires tools and gauges not normally available to the owner.**

5:5 Driven plate condition

On Series **TA** clutch, if the cork inserts show appreciable wear, or signs of burning or breaking up, they should be renewed. The owner is not advised to attempt this work except in an emergency, as a special tool is used to insert the corks and level them. The complete driven plate assembly is available for renewal on an exchange basis.

In the case of the **dry plate clutch** fitted to Series **TB, TC, TD** and **TF**, examine the two friction linings on the driven plate. These should have a smooth appearance but the grain of the friction material should be clearly visible. A high glaze which obscures the grain of the material, however, is due to burnt oil leaving a carbon deposit, which will cause clutch slip. A resinous deposit on the linings is caused by partially burnt oil and will cause fierceness or clutch spin due to the linings adhering to the flywheel or pressure plate. Completely oil-soaked linings will cause both clutch slip and fierceness. If any of these lining defects are visible, and also if the damper springs are weak or broken, the complete driven plate assembly should be renewed. This is available on an exchange basis. **If oil is present on the clutch linings, the source must be traced and the trouble rectified before reassembly.**

5:6 Reassembly, refitting, plate alignment

Reassembly is a reversal of the dismantling procedure, but the following points should be noted. On Series **TA**, lubricate the thrust race, the bores of both the cover plate and pressure plate and also the driven plate splines with clean engine oil before assembly. Ensure that the washer is in position between the cover plate and the thrust race before fitting and tightening the lock nut. Assemble the driven plate with the longer side of the splined hub towards the cover plate, that is towards the gearbox. Before tightening the bolts securing the cover plate assembly to the flywheel, the driven plate must be centralized using the special alignment tool available, or a spare gearbox third motion shaft. Tighten the bolts a turn at a time diagonally. When all the bolts are tight remove the alignment tool.

When reassembling the dry plate clutch on Series **TB, TC, TD** and **TF**, note that the only point to be lubricated is the splined hub of the driven plate 44 in **FIG 5:2**. Smear the splines lightly with Keenol. Avoid touching the friction linings 46 with greasy fingers. The graphite release bearing 42 must not be lubricated. Assemble the driven plate to the flywheel 18 with the longer side of the splined hub away from the flywheel. Fit the cover assembly (items 32-41) to the flywheel, but before tightening the bolts 47 centralize the driven plate using the alignment tool No. 18G.279 shown in **FIG 5:4**. Tighten the bolts diagonally a turn at a time. When all the bolts are tight remove the alignment tool.

FIG 5:4 Clutch plate aligning tool No. 18G.279 for Series TD clutch

5:7 Modifications

The dry plate clutch fitted to Series **TB, TC** and **TD** Midgets has a diameter of $7\frac{1}{4}$ inch. Commencing at engine No. 9408 this was replaced by an 8 inch dia. clutch and the engine type description altered from **XPAG.TD** to **XPAG.TD2**. The reason for renumbering is that the modification affects not only the clutch itself but the engine flywheel housing and the gearbox bell housing. Thus the **TD** and **TD2** engines and gearboxes are not separately interchangeable, though the complete engine and gearbox unit is. The $7\frac{1}{4}$ inch clutch has a clutch fork shaft of $\frac{5}{8}$ inch diameter while that of the 8 inch clutch is $\frac{3}{4}$ inch dia. This is a simple means of identification, but engine numbers should always be quoted in full when ordering replacement parts. The general construction of the newer type clutch is the same as that of previous models and all the instructions already given will apply.

Although the fitting of special equipment is outside the scope of this manual, mention should be made of the Competition Clutch which is available for **TB, TC** and **TD** Midgets. This gives increased torque at the expense of fiercer operation. The assembly is Part No. MG.862.92. It includes a special driven plate No. MG.862.93 and stronger springs (identified by light blue colour) Part No. 162515. These two items can be fitted to the standard clutch.

5:8 Fault diagnosis

(a) Drag or spin

1 Excessive free movement in control
2 Oil or grease on linings (dry plate clutch)
3 Clutch face of flywheel out of truth
4 Misalignment between engine and gearbox first motion shaft
5 Driven plate binding on first motion shaft splines
6 First motion shaft spigot bearing binding
7 Distorted clutch plate
8 Warped or damaged pressure plate or cover
9 Release levers incorrectly adjusted (dry plate clutch)
10 Broken driven plate linings (dry plate clutch)
11 Unevenly fitted corks (wet plate clutch)
12 Dirt or foreign matter in clutch

(b) Fierceness or snatch

1 Check 2, 3 and 4 in (a)
2 Worn clutch linings

(c) Clutch slip

1 Insufficient free movement in control
2 Check 2, 3 and 4 in (a)
3 Check 2 in (b)

(d) Judder

1 Check 2, 3, 4, 7 and 11 in (a)
2 Pressure plate not parallel to flywheel face
3 Bent first motion shaft
4 Faulty engine or gearbox mountings
5 Engine control link incorrectly adjusted
6 Worn suspension shackles
7 Weak rear springs
8 Loose propeller shaft bolts
9 Loose rear spring clips

(e) Rattle

1 Weak anti-rattle springs (dry plate clutch)
2 Broken damper springs in driven plate
3 Worn release mechanism
4 Excessive backlash in transmission
5 Release bearing loose on fork

(f) Tick or knock

1 Worn first motion shaft spigot or bearing
2 Badly worn splines on driven plate hub

3 Release plate out of line (dry plate clutch)
4 Loose flywheel

(g) Driven plate fracture

1 Check 3 and 4 in (a)
2 Drag and distortion due to weight of gearbox hanging on driven plate during assembly

(h) Engine slows when clutch released in neutral

1 Badly worn clutch release bearing (dry plate clutch)

CHAPTER 6

THE GEARBOX

6:1 Construction and operation
6:2 Maintenance
6:3 Removal
6:4 Dismantling

6:5 Reassembly
6:6 Refitting
6:7 Modifications
6:8 Fault diagnosis

6.1 Construction and operation

All cars in the series covered by this manual are fitted with four-speed manual gearboxes with remote control. The gearbox on the **TA** model has synchromesh on third and top only and will be dealt with separately. All other gearboxes have synchromesh on second, third and top and are basically similar in design. A description of the **TD** Series gearbox will therefore apply in most respects to all models except **TA**.

Referring to the sectional and plan views in **FIG 6:1** and to the exploded diagram **FIG 6:2**, it will be seen that the gearbox casing 7 is bolted to a separate bellhousing which in turn is bolted to the rear end of the cylinder block and sump. The first motion shaft 52 runs in a bearing 53 in the gearbox casing and in the spigot bearing in the engine crankshaft. The mainshaft 15 is carried by needle rollers 58 in the first motion shaft, a bearing 16 at the rear of the gearbox casing and a third bearing 103 in the rear casing 101. The **TB** and **TC** gearboxes which are shown in **FIG 6:3** have a shorter mainshaft carried in two bearings only and the remote control is housed in an extension of the gearbox top

cover, instead of in a separate cover. On all models the universal joint flange 111 in **FIG 6:2** is secured to splines on the mainshaft 15 by the nut 113, provision for movement of the rear axle being made by a sliding joint in the propeller shaft (see **Chapter 7**).

FIGS 6:1 and **6:2** show the layout of the selector mechanism. Movement of the gear lever by the driver to the left moves the front selector lever 121 to the right to engage the first and second selector 72. Movement in the opposite direction engages the lever 121 in the third and top gear selector 64. If additional pressure is applied to compress the plunger spring 79 the lever 121 will move further to the left to engage the reverse selector 77. The selector shafts 74, 69 and 83 are located by three spring-loaded balls 94 which engage in the indentations shown in the inset to **FIG 6:1**. Forward or backward movement of the gear lever thus moves the shaft in which the lever 121 is engaged, thus selecting the required gear.

Engagement of second, third and top gears is facilitated by means of metal to metal cone clutches formed on the inside of the two synchromesh hubs 22

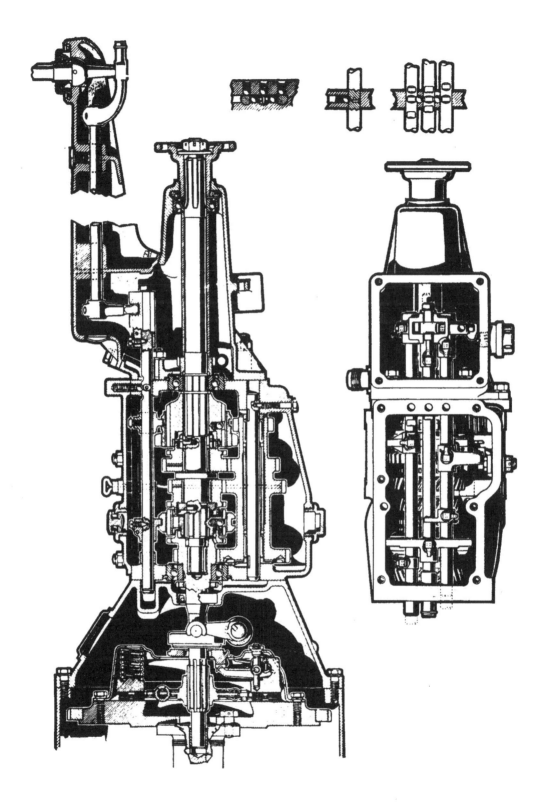

FIG 6:1   A sectional view of the TD gearbox. Insets show selector details

and 36 and the outside of parts 52, 25 and 30. Top gear is engaged as follows. The striking dog 21 can slide on the external splines of the synchromesh hub 22 but is restrained by six spring-loaded balls 24 engaging in an internal groove. If the third and top selector fork 66 is moved forward the dog 21 carries the hub 22 with it and the internal cone of the hub contacts the external cone of the first motion shaft 52. The latter is slowed down or speeded up until the two cones and therefore the internal splines of the dog 21 and the external splines of 52 are revolving at the same speed. Further pressure on the gear lever then overcomes the resistance of the spring-loaded balls and the dog 21 slides independently of the hub 22 to engage the splines of the first motion shaft 52. This provides a direct drive from the first motion shaft to the mainshaft 15 for top gear. A rearward movement of the selector fork 66 will similarly engage the dog 21 with the splines on the third speed gear 25, the drive now passing through the laygears to the mainshaft.

Similarly for second gear, forward movement of the first and second gear selector 70 brings the external cone of the synchromesh hub 36 in contact with the internal cone of the second speed gear 30, allowing the internal splines of part 37 to engage the external splines of 30. Rearward movement of selector fork 70 moves the first speed gear 37 so that its straight teeth engage those of the laygear without the assistance of synchromesh, giving first gear.

Reverse gear is obtained by the forward movement of the selector shaft 83. By means of the reverse linkage 90 and the selector fork 87 this brings the reverse gear 60 into a position where it engages with both the first speed gear 37 and the laygear.

FIG 6:4 shows the gearbox fitted to the series **TA** Midget. The selector mechanism is similar to that used on the **TB** and **TC** gearboxes and the shorter type mainshaft is fitted. The engagement of third and top gears is carried out by means of a synchromesh hub which is similar in principle to that described for the **TD** model and illustrated in **FIGS 6:1** and **6:2**. The constant mesh and third speed gears are of double helical form instead of single helical as on later models. The remaining gears are of the straight toothed variety. The first and second gears on the mainshaft are formed in one unit moved by means of the first and second fork to engage with the teeth of the appropriate layshaft gear. The reverse gear consists of a cluster of two pinions which slides so as to engage the first speed mainshaft gear and the smallest laygear simultaneously.

6:2 Maintenance

The gearbox should not require any maintenance other than regular topping up of the oil level and periodic draining and refilling. **FIG 6:5** shows the location of the filler plug, dipstick and drain plug. After the first 500 miles a new or reconditioned gearbox should be drained, preferably while warm, and refilled with the recommended grade of lubricant. Ensure that the hollow centre of the drain plug has been cleaned thoroughly before it is replaced and tightened. Dirt should be cleaned from around the filler plug before it is removed. **Do not fill to above the HIGH mark on the dipstick.** Subsequently the oil level should be

checked and the gearbox topped up if necessary every 1000 miles and drained and filled with fresh oil every 6000 miles.

6:3 Removal

Removal of the engine and gearbox as a unit have been described in **Section 1:2** and the subsequent separation of engine and gearbox in **Section 1:10.** Alternatively the gearbox can be removed leaving the engine in the car. If it is proposed to fit a replacement gearbox it should be noted that gearboxes designed for the later 8 inch clutch are not separately interchangeable with those designed for the earlier $7\frac{1}{4}$ inch clutch.

To remove the gearbox on models **TA, TB** and **TC** proceed as follows:

1 Remove seats, carpets, rubber gearbox cover and floorboards. Undo the rubber muff where the steering column passes through the dash and slide it with its securing plate down the column.

2 Disconnect the battery. Uncouple the harness cable from the ramp plate and the cables from the generator. Remove the ramp plate, disconnect the wires from the starter and the Bowden wire from the starter switch.

3 Drain the gearbox. Remove the propeller shaft tunnel and gearbox lid. On **earlier TA** models the rear flange is bolted behind the heelboard. In this case disconnect both front and rear propeller shaft flanges, disconnect the shroud and move it to one side at the front end to allow sufficient clearance for gearbox removal.

4 Remove the starter motor, uncouple the clutch control rod at its forward end and let it hang on the clutch pedal. Disconnect the speedometer drive and uncouple the propeller shaft at the front end, marking the flanges for subsequent reassembly.

5 Unbolt the steering box from the frame and remove the portion of the exhaust pipe between manifold and silencer. Jack up the rear of the engine and remove the four bolts holding the gearbox to the rear engine mounting rubbers. Remove the clutch operating lever from the withdrawal shaft by knocking out the taper pin.

6 Undo the bolts holding the gearbox bellhousing to the flywheel housing. Withdraw the gearbox complete, **ensuring that its weight is supported so that it does not rest on the clutch plate during the operation.**

To remove the gearbox on models **TD** and **TF**:

1 Remove floor mats, floorboards and gearbox cowl. Disconnect the propeller shaft at its forward end, marking the flanges for reassembly. Jack up the engine under the rear of the sump, using a block of wood between jack and sump to spread the load.

2 Disconnect the speedometer drive from the gearbox and disconnect the clutch operating lever from its connecting rod. Release the rear engine mounting by removing the two nuts and bolts of the rubber mounting.

3 Undo the bolts holding the gearbox bellhousing to the flywheel housing. Withdraw the gearbox complete, **ensuring that its weight is supported so that it does not rest on the clutch plate during the operation.**

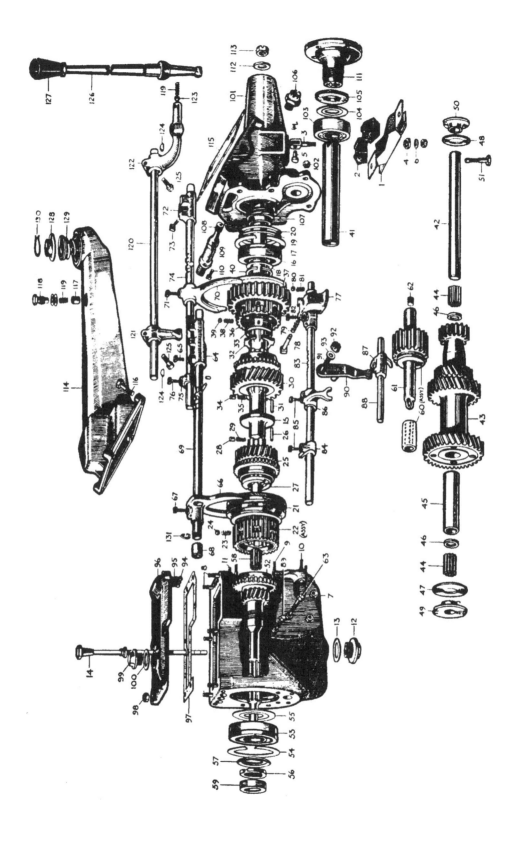

FIG 6:2 An exploded view of the TD gearbox

Key to Fig 6:2
1 Rear engine bearer bracket 2 Support rubber 3 Fork end 4 Engine rebound rubber 5 Clevis pin—fork end 6 Washer 7 Gearbox casing (with studs) 8 Stud—gearbox top cover 9 Stud—rear cover (medium) 10 Stud—rear cover (long) 11 Stud—rear cover (short) 12 Plug—oil drain 13 Washer—drain plug 14 Oil level indicator 15 Mainshaft 16 Mainshaft bearing 17 Circlip—mainshaft bearing 18 Guard—bearing—mainshaft 19 Plate—guard 20 Spring plate—guard 21 Striking dog 22 Synchromesh hub (top and third) 23 Spring—synchromesh hub 24 Ball—synchromesh hub 25 Rollers—second speed gear 26 Rollers—third speed gear 27 Collar—third speed gear 28 Plunger—third speed gear 29 Spring—plunger 30 Second speed gear 31 Rollers—second speed gear 32 Washer—second speed gear 33 Collar—second speed gear 34 Plunger—second speed gear 35 Spring—plunger 36 Synchromesh hub (second) 37 First speed gear 38 Spring—first speed gear 39 Ball—first speed gear 40 Circlip 41 Distance-piece 42 Layshaft 43 Laygear 44 Rollers—laygear 45 Spacer—laygear 46 Washer—laygear 47 Thrust washer—front 48 Thrust washer—rear 49 Bearing plate—front 50 Bearing plate—rear 51 Screw—laygear 52 First motion shaft 53 Bearing—first motion shaft 54 Circlip—first motion shaft 55 Guard—bearing (first motion shaft) 56 Nut—first motion shaft bearing 57 Lock washer—bearing 58 Spigot bearing rollers 59 Oil seal—first motion shaft 60 Reverse gear (with bush) 61 Shaft—reverse gear 62 Plug—reverse shaft 63 Screw—reverse shaft 64 Top and third gear selector 65 Locating screw—selector 66 Top and third gear—selector fork 67 Locating screw—selector fork 68 Distance tube—top and third 69 Top and third gear selector shaft 70 First and second gear selector 71 Locating screw 72 First and second gear selector 73 Locating screw 74 First and second gear selector shaft 75 Stop—ball 76 Locating screw—stop 77 Reverse gear selector 78 Plunger—reverse gear selector 79 Spring—plunger 80 Ball—reverse plunger 81 Spring—ball 82 Locating screw 83 Reverse selector shaft 84 Steady—reverse selector shaft 85 Locating screw—steady 86 Gear shifter—reverse selector fork 87 Reverse gear selector fork 88 Shaft—reverse selector fork 89 Locating screw—shaft 90 Reverse link assembly 91 Fulcrum pin—link 92 Nut—fulcrum pin 93 Washer—fulcrum pin 94 Ball—shaft 95 Spring—selector plunger 96 Gearbox cover 97 Gasket—cover 98 Nut—cover 99 Filler plug—gearbox 100 Washer for plug 101 Rear casing 102 Nut—rear casing 103 Ballbearing 104 Guard 105 Oil retaining washer 106 Hole plug—reverse light 107 Speedometer gear 108 Speedometer pinion and shaft 109 Bearing—pinion 110 Screw—pinion bearing 111 Flange—universal joint 112 Washer—flange nut 113 Nut—flange to mainshaft 114 Remote control cover 115 Gasket—cover 116 Cover bolt—to rear casing 117 Housing cover plunger 118 Plug—operating shaft 119 Spring—operating shaft 120 Remote control shaft 121 Selector lever (front) 122 Selector lever (rear) 123 Ball—lever 124 Key—actuating shaft and selector levers 125 Bolt—actuating shaft and selector levers 126 Change speed lever 127 Knob—change speed lever 128 Cover—lever 129 Spring—anti-rattle change speed lever 130 Circlip—cover 131 Circlip—shaft—third and top

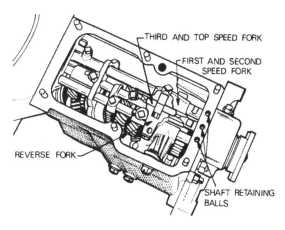

FIG 6:3   TC gearbox with cover removed

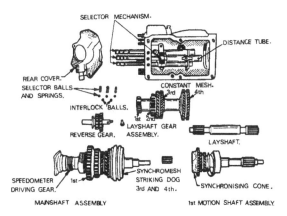

FIG 6:4   TA gearbox dismantled

6:4 Dismantling

A description of the dismantling procedure for the **TD** Series gearbox will apply in most respects to all models except **TA**, which will be dealt with separately at the end of this Section. Reference should be made to **FIGS 6:1** and **6:2**. The best method of holding the gearbox while dismantling and assembling is by means of a piece of steel bar threaded so as to screw into the drain plug hole and then held firmly in a vice. Remove the bellhousing from the gearbox and then:

1 Remove the flange nut 113 and withdraw the universal joint flange 111 after marking its relationship with the shaft. **FIG 6:6** shows a suitable extractor which uses the bolt holes of the flange to avoid distortion of the flange face.

2 Remove the gearbox cover 96 and the remote control cover 114. On **TB** and **TC** models these are combined. Remove the three selector springs 95. Detach the speedometer drive from the righthand side of the gearbox.

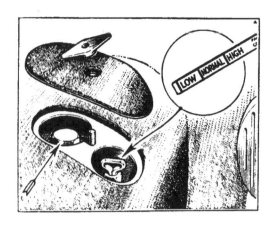

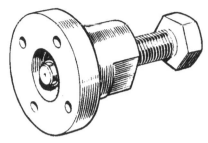

FIG 6:6   Extractor No. 18G.371 for universal joint flanges

a suitable drift. The mainshaft assembly can then be withdrawn as shown in **FIG 6:7**.   Lift out the laygear 43 after lining up the tabs on the plates 49, 50 with the slots in the end faces of the gearbox casing.

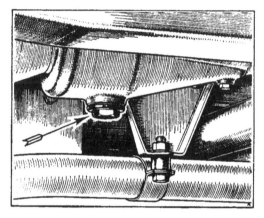

FIG 6:5   (Top) Gearbox filler and dipstick (Bottom) Gearbox drain plug

3 Remove the locking wires and remove the eight square-headed screws securing the gear selectors, fork and stops to the selector shafts, having previously marked the exact position of each in relation to its shaft.

4 Slacken the nuts securing the gearbox rear cover 101 and withdraw the cover sufficiently to allow the selectors 64, 72, 77 to be removed from the ends of the selector shafts 69, 74 and 83. Remove the rear cover. On early type gearboxes withdraw the selector shafts one at a time, taking care not to lose the selector balls 94 or the two interlock balls between the shafts. **Later TD** and **TF** models have a modified third and top selector shaft which is secured by a circlip at its front end. On **TB** and **TC** models the rear cover must be removed before the selectors can be withdrawn. Lift out the selector forks.

5 Remove the layshaft screw 51. Extract the layshaft 42 towards the rear by tapping with a copper drift. Allow the laygear 43 to rest in the bottom of the gearbox casing. Remove the first motion shaft 52 together with its bearing 53 by tapping the mainshaft towards the front of the gearbox using a copper drift. Take care not to lose any of the spigot bearing rollers 58.

6 Before the mainshaft 15 can be withdrawn its bearing 16 must be extracted from its housing using

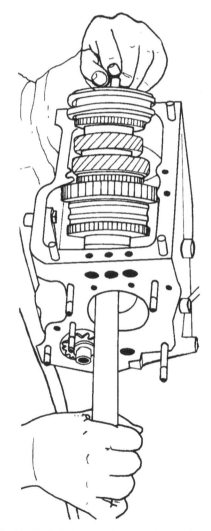

FIG 6:7   Withdrawing or refitting mainshaft assembly (TD)

Next proceed to dismantle the mainshaft assembly as follows:

1 Withdraw the top and third gear synchromesh hub and striking dog 22 and 21 in **FIG 6:2** from the front end of the mainshaft, noting that the plain side of the hub goes to the rear of the gearbox. Remove the third speed gear collar 27 by pressing down the spring-loaded plunger 28 and rotating the collar until the female splines register with the male splines on the mainshaft as shown in **FIG 6:8**. The third speed gear 25 can now be withdrawn, taking care not to lose the plunger and spring or the needle rollers 26 on which the gear is mounted.

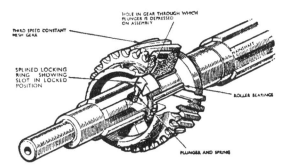

FIG 6:8   Method of securing third speed gear to mainshaft

2 Remove the circlip 40 from the rear end of the mainshaft and remove the second gear synchromesh hub 36 and first speed gear 37, noting that the conical end of the hub faces the front of the gearbox.

3 The withdrawal of the second speed gear 30 is carried out in a similar manner to the third speed gear. The assembly is shown in detail in **FIG 6:9**. It is mounted on needle rollers 31. Note the position of the washer 32 which is in two halves with tongues engaging in the front face of the collar 33.

Dismantling of the synchromesh hubs is not advised, as on all gearboxes except **TA** the use of a special tool is essential for reassembly.

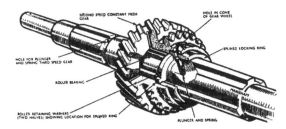

FIG 6:9   Method of securing second speed gear to mainshaft

To dismantle the gearbox on the **TA** model (**FIG 6:4**):

1 Remove the universal joint flange, preferably using an extractor which bolts into the four holes in the flange as shown in **FIG 6:6**. Mark the flange in relation to the mainshaft for reassembly.

2 Remove the gearbox rear cover and speedometer driven gear. Lift out the rear ballbearing packing and withdraw the various gearbox components backwards by first removing the locking screws securing the selector forks and withdrawing the selector rods one at a time. Take care not to lose the detent and interlocking balls as they are freed. These are similar to those shown in the inset to **FIG 6:1**. Lift out the selector forks.

3 Referring to **FIG 6:9**, press down the spring loaded plunger and turn the splined locking ring at the rear face of the third speed double helical gear until the gear is free to move on the mainshaft. Draw out the mainshaft complete with its rear ballbearing and chip-excluding washer, lifting out each gear as it is freed.

4 Again referring to **FIG 6:4**, remove the layshaft locking screw and withdraw the layshaft, allowing the laygear assembly with roller bearings and spacer to rest in the bottom of the gearbox. Remove the reverse shaft locking screw and withdraw the shaft, lifting out the reverse gear as soon as it is freed.

5 Remove the bellhousing from the front of the gearbox complete with front oil seal and lift out the first motion shaft ballbearing packing washer. Remove the retaining circlip in front of the bearing and press out the first motion shaft. Lift out the laygear assembly from the bottom of the gearbox casing.

6 The synchromesh hub may be dismantled **on TA gearboxes only,** as no special tool is needed for reassembly. Apply sufficient pressure to overcome the locating springs and the hub can be pressed out of the striking dog.

6:5 Reassembly

All parts should be thoroughly washed in petrol and examined for damage or excessive wear. Any parts found unserviceable must be renewed. Wear in the synchromesh cones necessitates renewal of the complete assembly. If many of the gearbox components are found to need renewal, consideration should be given to the fitting of a replacement gearbox.

Reassembly of the gearbox is mainly a reversal of the dismantling procedure, but the following points should be noted, referring to **FIG 6:2** for all models other than **TA;** which will be dealt with separately:

1 Assemble the laygear 43 with the rollers 44 and all parts 45-50, using a dummy layshaft $\frac{9}{16}$ inch dia. by 6 $\frac{11}{32}$ inch long. This can be made of hardwood if necessary. The laygear is then placed in the bottom of the gearbox casing with its component parts and the dummy shaft still in position. The latter will be ejected by the insertion of the layshaft 42, but the layshaft must be not inserted until both the mainshaft and the first motion shaft have been installed.

2 When assembling the third speed gear 25 to the mainshaft, insert the needle rollers 26, place the locking plunger 28 and spring 29 on the shaft, followed by the collar or locking ring 27. The two slots on the outer face of the latter must line up with the plunger when in the locked position, as shown in **FIG 6:8**. When sliding on the locking ring, the plunger can be depressed through the hole in the gear as shown.

3 The procedure for fitting the second speed gear 30 is somewhat different. The rollers 31 should be held in position on the shaft with a little grease. The locking plunger and spring are then placed in position and the gear 30 slid into place. The two half washers 32 are then inserted in the gear next to the rollers with their projections lining up between two splines. The locking ring is then placed in position with the slots cut on its inner face in line with the projections on the half washers. The plunger is depressed through the hole as shown in **FIG 6:9** and the locking ring turned until the plunger locks in a spline.

4 When inserting the mainshaft assembly as shown in **FIG 6:7**, first engage second gear so as to allow sufficient clearance for the front end of the shaft to enter the gearbox casing.

5 Install the mainshaft ballbearing, noting the relative positions of the circlips 40, 17 and the washers or chip guards 18, 20, in **FIG 6:2**. On **TB** and **TC** models the oil spinning washer is fitted between the ball race and the second speed synchromesh hub with its outer edge clear of the ball race. Next to the ballbearing are a plain steel washer and a thin steel washer of the Belleville type, which is fitted with its inner diameter towards the plain washer.

6 Refit the first motion shaft 52, installing the needle rollers 58 on the spigot bearing of the mainshaft. They can be held in place temporarily with the aid of a little grease. Fit the first motion shaft bearing 53 with the chip guard 55, circlip 54, locking washer 57, and the nut 56.

7 Insert the selector mechanism, not forgetting the two interlock balls between the selector shafts. On **later TD** and **TF** models fit the circlip 131 at the front end of the top and third selector shaft 69.

8 Insert the layshaft 42 after ensuring that the laygear is correctly located with the bearing plates 49 and 50 engaged in the slots in the faces of the gearbox casing. Lock the layshaft by tightening the screw 51 in the bottom of the gearbox.

9 When refitting the bellhousing do not omit the oil seal 59. On **TB** and **TC** models position the plain and Belleville washers in the same way as those at the rear of the mainshaft described in item 5.

10 Fit the oil seal 105, chip guard 104 and ballbearing 103 (not fitted to **TC** and **TD** models) into the rear cover 101 and install the cover. Fit the speedometer pinion assembly 108, 109. Fit the gearbox cover 96 ensuring that the selector shaft springs and balls 94, 95 are in position. On models **TC** and **TD** the cover incorporates the remote control and is best fitted after the gearbox has been installed in the car. In this case protect the gearbox orifice by fitting a temporary cardboard cover.

11 When refitting the universal joint flange 111 to the mainshaft, ensure that the previously made marks correspond. Tighten the nut 113 fully and secure with a new split pin.

Reassembly of the gearbox on model **TA** involves a reversal of the dismantling procedure and reference should be made to **FIGS 6:4** and **6:10** for details. The following points should be noted:

1 To reassemble the top and third gear synchromesh mechanism, six strips of .015 inch shim steel ¼ inch wide are needed. Enter the synchromesh hub into the striking dog and fit one spring into position. With the aid of one of the strips of steel the ball is retained in the hub. Push the strip down between the hub and the dog. Holding the six balls and springs in this manner, push the hub right home when the balls will click into position in the centre of the teeth.

2 The laygear can be assembled in the manner described earlier for other models. It is then placed in the bottom of the gearbox casing while the reverse gear assembly is inserted and locked by its grub screw. The layshaft is then inserted and also locked in position.

3 The gears are fitted one at a time on to the mainshaft as it is slid into the gearbox. To install the third speed gear, fit the plunger and spring into the shaft and lock the gear by rotating the locking plate in its groove in the mainshaft until the plunger engages as shown in **FIG 6:10**.

4 The remainder of the gearbox parts are assembled in the same manner as that already described for later models.

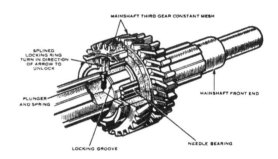

FIG 6:10 Method of securing third speed gear (TA model only)

6:6 Refitting

Refitting of the gearbox follows the reverse procedure to that of removal. When coupling up the gearbox to the engine **great care must be taken to ensure that the weight of the gearbox is supported until the front end of the first motion shaft is fully home in the spigot bearing in the engine crankshaft.** If the weight of the gearbox is allowed to rest on the clutch driven plate serious damage may result. Tighten the bolts holding the bellhousing to the cylinder block and sump evenly. In the case of the **TA** model some difficulty may be experienced in re-engaging the clutch fork. This has a pull action on the thrust race instead of the more usual push action. It is therefore necessary to engage the fork at an angle in front of the thrust race, and to feed the fork into position gradually as the first motion shaft enters the driven plate splines. Note also that on this model an oil-tight joint between the bellhousing and the flywheel housing is essential, the clutch being fed with oil from the engine.

On all models the clutch adjustment should be checked as described in **Section 5:3**. Do not omit to refill the gearbox with the recommended grade of oil.

6:7 Modifications

On earlier **TD** model gearboxes the third and top selector shaft 69 (**FIG 6:2**) was limited in its rearward travel by a stop cast on the inside of the remote contol cover 114. Owing to variations in the dimensions of this stop, cases occurred where the balls and springs were ejected from the corresponding synchromesh hub 22. It is also possible for this to happen when the remote control cover is removed if the selector shaft is moved towards the rear. To prevent this, a modified selector shaft was later fitted, shown in **FIGS 6:1, 6:2** and in detail in **FIG 6:11**. This has a circlip 131 to act as a positive stop for the shaft. The modified selector shaft can be fitted to earlier **TD** gearboxes, the parts being listed as Shifter Shaft Assembly (Top and 3rd) Part No. SA.2402.3.

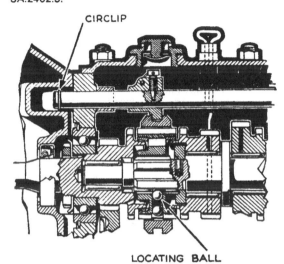

CIRCLIP

LOCATING BALL

FIG 6:11   Modified selector shaft and synchromesh hub

Commencing at gearbox No. TF 513 on the TD Midget, the existing top and third synchromesh hub

was modified by peening the balls into the hub to prevent ejection. A modified striking dog, Part No. 24465 is now fitted, having an internal taper at each end, to maintain the hub in the correct position.

Commencing at gearbox TJ 800 on the **TD** Midget. a further modification was introduced in which one of the six spring holes in the synchromesh hub was bored right through and an additional ball added. This ball locates in an indent in the mainshaft as shown in **FIG 6:11**. This modification can be fitted to earlier **TD** gearboxes if a new gearbox mainshaft is also fitted. The necessary parts comprise Sliding Hub (Top and 3rd) with Cones, Part No. SA.2453.2 and Gearbox Mainshaft Part No. 24467.

6:8 Fault diagnosis

(a) Jumping out of gear
1 Broken selector shaft ball spring
2 Badly worn locating groove in selector shaft
3 Worn coupling dogs
4 Selector fork loose on rod
5 Selector fork wrongly positioned on rod

(b) Noisy gearbox
1 Insufficient oil
2 Excessive end play in laygear
3 Worn or damaged bearings
4 Worn or damaged gear teeth

(c) Difficulty in engaging gear
1 Clutch not freeing sufficiently
2 Worn synchromesh cones

(d) Oil leaks
1 Damaged joint washers
2 Worn or damaged oil seals
3 Top or rear covers loose or faces damaged.

(e) Gear lever chatter
1 Broken anti-rattle spring
2 Weak or broken operating shaft spring

CHAPTER 7

PROPELLER SHAFT, REAR AXLE
REAR SUSPENSION

7:1 Description and construction of universal joints
7:2 Dismantling and servicing universal joints
7:3 Description and construction of axle
7:4 Lubrication, servicing parts without axle removal
7:5 Axle removal
7:6 Axle refitting
7:7 Axle shafts, rear hub bearings

7:8 Description of suspension system
7:9 Spring removal, servicing pivots and springs
7:10 Spring refitting
7:11 Damper maintenance, removal and testing
7:12 Modifications
7:13 Fault diagnosis

7:1 Description and construction of universal joints

The front and rear universal joints of the propeller shaft are of the Hardy Spicer type, as shown in **FIG 7:9**. The four journals in each spider run in needle bearings. To accommodate fore and aft movement of the

FIG 7:2   Lubrication of rear universal joint

rear axle, the propeller shaft 49 is provided with a splined joint at the front end.

A grease nipple is provided for the lubrication of each of the two joints and another nipple 61 for the splined sliding joint at the front end. The positions of these nipples are shown in **FIGS 7:1** and **7:2**. They should be lubricated with a recommended grease every 1000 miles.

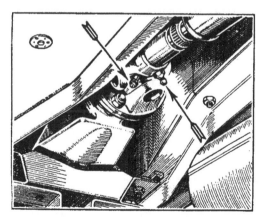

FIG 7:1   Lubrication of front universal joint and propeller shaft sliding joint

MG1

7:2 Dismantling and servicing universal joints

The joints can be tested for wear with the shaft in position. Try to lift each joint up and down. Slackness indicates wear of the thrust faces on the spiders and those inside the bearing cups. If the joints can be partially rotated the bearings are worn. A bright ring on the bearing 55 in **FIG 7:9** under the snap ring 56 shows that the bearing has been rotating in the yoke. Rust marks at the same spot indicate lack of lubrication. If the front univesal joint can be rotated in relation to the propeller shaft, the sliding sleeve splines are worn.

Before removing the bolts and nuts securing the propeller shaft universal joint flanges to the gearbox flange and the rear axle flange, carefully mark the flanges to ensure they can be refitted in the same relative position. If the marks are made exactly in line with corresponding marks on the sliding sleeve and the rear end of the propeller shaft tube, all components can be reassembled in the same position. Failure to observe these precautions may throw the shaft out of balance.

Disconnect the front flange of the propeller shaft from the gearbox flange and carefully support it while undoing the bolts and nuts securing the shaft to the rear axle. The shaft can now be removed from the car downwards and rearwards.

To dismantle the propeller shaft proceed as follows. Referring to **FIG 7:9**, unscrew the dustcap 58 at the rear end of the sliding sleeve 51, and having ensured that the sleeve and the shaft 49 are marked so that the splines can be replaced in the same relative position, withdraw the sleeve. Remove all dirt and enamel from the snap rings 56 and bearings 55. Remove all the snap rings by squeezing their ends together with thin nosed pliers and prising them out with a screwdriver. If a ring does not slide out of its groove easily, tap the end of the bearing slightly to relieve pressure on the ring.

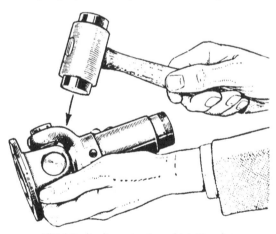

FIG 7:3 Jarring out universal joint bearing

Hold the joint in one hand as shown in **FIG 7:3**, tap the yoke lightly with a copper hammer. The upper bearing should then begin to emerge. Turn the joint over and finally remove the bearing with the fingers as shown in **FIG 7:4** keeping it vertical so as to retain the needle rollers. In case of difficulty, tap the bearing out from the inside using a suitable drift such as a small

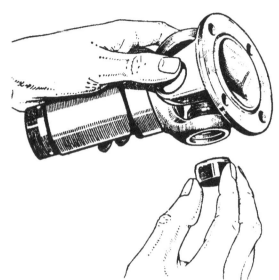

FIG 7:4 Withdrawing universal joint bearing

diameter bar, but taking care not to chip the edges of the bearing. Repeat the process with the opposite bearing. The yoke can then be removed as shown in **FIG 7:5**. The remaining bearings are removed in the same way. Repeat this series of operations for the front universal joint.

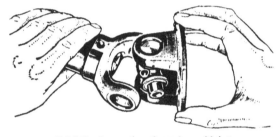

FIG 7:5 Separating the universal joint

The parts most likely to show signs of wear after long use are the bearing races and the spider journals. Should looseness, load markings or distortion be observed, the complete assembly 52 in **FIG 7:9** should be renewed. The bearings must be a light drive fit in the yoke eyes. If the latter are worn oval, in the case of the front universal joint the sliding sleeve can be renewed but the fixed yoke at the rear joint forms part of the tubular propeller shaft assembly 49, necessitating renewal of the complete shaft. It is advisable to renew the cork gaskets 53 and retainers 54. Coat the shoulders of the spider journals with shellac or jointing compound and press the retainers into position with a tubular drift. Fill the holes in the spider with grease and insert in the yoke, ensuring that the boss for the grease nipple faces away from the yoke. Fit the needle rollers in a bearing with a little petroleum jelly to hold them in place, fill with grease and tap the bearing into place using a soft drift slightly smaller in diameter than the yoke eye. Fit the snap ring and repeat the assembly for the other side and for the remaining bearings.

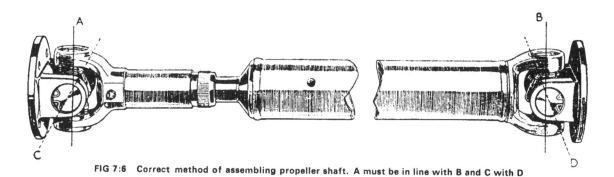

FIG 7:6   Correct method of assembling propeller shaft. A must be in line with B and C with D

Reassembly of the propeller shaft is a reversal of the dismantling procedure, but ensure that the previously made marks are in line. If the sliding sleeve was not marked, note that its yoke must line up with the corresponding yoke at the rear end of the shaft as shown in **FIG 7:6**.   Ensure that the flange faces are clean and undamaged and tighten the securing bolts evenly and diagonally.

7:3 Description and construction of axle

On models **TA, TB** and **TC** the rear axle is of the one-piece or 'banjo' type, the spiral bevel final drive being housed in a detachable differential carrier bolted to the front of the casing. Both the differential bearings and pinion bearings are pre-loaded and two adjustments are provided for meshing of crown wheel and pinion. Firstly the bevel pinion is adjustable to or from the crown wheel by means of shims between the pinion and the differential carrier. Secondly the crown wheel is adjustable across the car by means of the two nuts on the outside of the differential ballbearings. The axle is of the three-quarter floating type and the axle-shafts are removable without disturbing the hub bearings or brake plates. Driving torque is taken on the semi-elliptic rear springs. **FIG 7:7** shows the general arrangement of the rear axle and suspension, a full description of the latter being given in **Section 7:8**. **FIG 7:8** shows the differential carrier removed to expose the crown wheel.

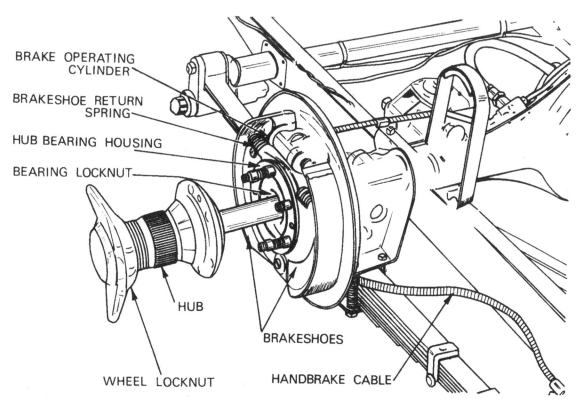

FIG 7:7   Rear axle and suspension model TC. Models TA and TB are similar except for spring rear mounting

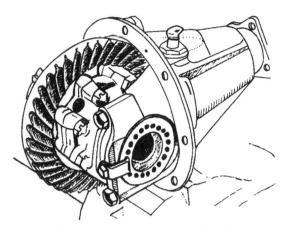

FIG 7:8   Differential carrier models **TA, TB, TC**

The axle fitted to models **TD** and **TF** is of the semi-floating type with hypoid final drive. **FIG 7:9** shows its components in exploded form. The crown wheel and pinion 19 and the differential assembly 8-12 are mounted in a unit-construction type axle casing which is split centrally. No repairs or adjustments apart from those connected with the axle shafts, brake drums and shoe mechanism can be carried out without removing the complete axle unit from the car. Dismantling of the axle and differential are not advised on these models as repairs and adjustments require special gauges which will not be available to the amateur, as well as a full range of distance-pieces and spacers from which to select the required sizes for replacement.

7:4 Lubrication, servicing parts without axle removal

On models **TA, TB** and **TC** the rear axle should be drained after the first 500 miles and refilled with fresh oil of the recommended grade. This applies equally to new or reconditioned axles. Thereafter, drain and refill every 6000 miles. Every 3000 miles the axle should be topped up with lubricant. Remove both the filler plug on the left and the oil-level plug on the righthand side of the axle housing. Pour in oil through the former until it runs out through the latter, then replace both plugs.

On models **TD** and **TF** which are fitted with hypoid rear axles, it is essential to use the grades of lubricant recommended for hypoid gears. After the first 500 miles and thereafter every 6000 miles, drain and refill the axle with the correct grade of lubricant. Every 1000 miles inspect the oil level and top up if necessary to the level of the filler orifice. Do not overfill. **FIGS 7:10** and **7:11** show the positions of the filler plug and drain plug respectively.

On models **TA, TB** and **TC** the rear axle, which is above the chassis, has to be dismantled before it can be removed from the car. To do this it is necessary first to withdraw the axle shafts and to remove the differential carrier complete with crownwheel and pinion as follows:

1 Drain the rear axle. Disconnect the rear universal joint flange from the axle as described in **Section 7:2.**
2 Jack up the rear of the car, raising it and supporting as high as possible, or work over a pit

3 Remove rear wheels, unbolt and draw off brake drums. Refit the wheel nuts on the hubs and drive out the axle shafts with hubs complete, by hitting the nut 'ears' with a copper hammer. **FIG 7:7** shows a shaft partially withdrawn.
4 Remove the nuts securing the differential carrier to the axle casing and remove the differential carrier complete.

The fitting of replacement parts and the adjustment of the meshing of crown wheel and pinion are operations which are not to be recommended for the amateur. In the case of the later models **TD** and **TF** with hypoid rear axles, dismantling of the axle is not advised and in any case can only be carried out after removal of the complete axle unit from the car.

7:5 Axle removal

To remove the rear axle on models **TA, TB** and **TC**, refer to **FIG 7:7** and proceed as follows:
1 Disconnect the rear universal joint flange from the rear axle as described in **Section 7:2.**
2 Uncouple the handbrake cables from the handbrake cross-shaft, disconnect the lubrication pipes and unbolt the cable supports.
3 Before disconnecting the hydraulic brakes, refer to the special note on flexible hoses in **Section 10:4.** Disconnect the copper pipes either side of the T-piece secured to the axle casing and remove the clip securing the righthand side pipe to the axle casing. Unbolt the T-piece from the axle casing and drain the brake fluid into a receptacle. Drain the lubricant from the rear axle.
4 The rear axle being above the chassis frame it must be withdrawn sideways through the wheel arch after removing the brake backplate on the opposite side and also removing the differential carrier unit complete. If it is desired to withdraw the axle towards the left side proceed as follows:
5 Raise the rear of the car and support firmly under the chassis so that the rear wheels are just clear of the ground. Remove the rear wheels. Unbolt and draw off both rear brake drums. Refit the wheel nuts on the hubs and withdraw the axle shafts and hubs complete by hitting the nut 'ears' with a copper hammer.
6 Tap back the tab washer locking the bearing securing nut on the righthand side only, remove the nut and withdraw the bearing housing complete with bearing. Remove the brake backplate and shoes on the same side with the handbrake cable and flexible hose attached.
7 Remove the axle check straps on both sides.
8 Remove the nuts securing the differential carrier to the axle casing and remove the differential carrier complete with crown wheel and pinion.
9 Disconnect the damper arms from the axle casing. Disconnect the axle from the springs by removing the U-bolts on both sides. The axle can now be withdrawn sideways through the lefthand wheel arch.

If it is required to remove the axle from the right, the same instructions apply except that in operation 6 the left hand brake plate has to be removed.

To remove the rear axle complete on models **TD** and **TF** proceed as follows:

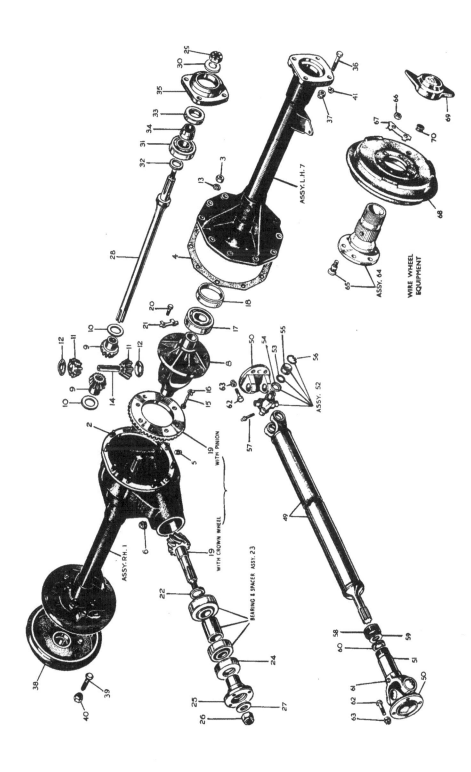

WIRE WHEEL
EQUIPMENT

WITH PINION

WITH CROWN WHEEL

BEARING & SPACER ASSY. 23

ASSY. R.H. 1

ASSY. L.H. 7

ASSY. 52

ASSY. 64

FIG 7:9 Exploded view of rear axle and propeller shaft TD, TF

Key to FIG 7:9

1 Axle tube assembly—R/H 2 Stud—cover 3 Nut—axle cover stud 4 Joint 5 Drain plug 6 Oil filler plug 7 Axle tube assembly—L/H 8 Cage—differential 9 Gear—differential
10 Washer—gear 11 Pinion—differential 12 Washer—pinion 13 Washer—cover stud 14 Pin—pinion 15 Locking bolt—pinion pin 16 Tab washer—locking bolt
17 Bearing—differential 18 Distance collar—bearing 19 Crown wheel and pinion 20 Bolt—crown wheel 21 Locking tab—crown wheel bolt 22 Distance washer—pinion—rear
23 Bearing and spacer assembly 24 Oil seal—pinion—front 25 Flange—universal joint 26 Castle nut—pinion 27 Washer—castle nut 28 Rear axle shaft 29 Nut—axle shaft
30 Washer—axle shaft nut 31 Bearing—rear hub 32 Distance washer—hub bearing 33 Oil seal—hub 34 Collar—oil seal 35 Support—brake plate 36 Bolt for support
37 Nut 38 Hub and brake-drum assembly (Disc wheels) 39 Wheel stud (Disc wheels) 40 Nut—wheel stud (Disc wheels) 41 Grease plug—axle tube
49 Tubular shaft assembly 50 Flange yoke 51 Sleeve yoke assembly 52 Journal assembly less greaser 53 Gasket—journal 54 Retainer—gasket 55 Needle bearing assembly
56 Snap ring 57 Grease nipple 58 Dust cap 59 Steel washer 60 Cork washer 61 Grease nipple 62 Bolt—coupling 63 Nut—coupling bolt
64 Hub assembly—L/H (Wire wheels) 65 Stud—hub (Wire wheels) 66 Nut—hub (Wire wheels) 67 Locking tab (Wire wheels) 68 Brake-drum (Wire wheels)
69 Hub cap—L/H (Wire wheels) 70 Plug—rubber (Wire wheels)

1 Raise the rear of the car and support it under the chassis just forward of the rear spring front mountings. Remove both rear wheels and release the handbrake.

2 Disconnect the flexible brake hose at its junction to the bracket on the chassis. See special note in **Section 10:4** on brake hoses.

3 Disconnect the brake cable casings from the spring brackets. Disconnect the brake cables from the brake shoe actuating levers by removing the clevis pins. Disconnect the damper arms at their lower ends.

4 Disconnect the propeller shaft from the rear axle having marked the two flanges to ensure refitting in the same relative positions. Support the rear end of the shaft through the aperture in the rear seat which gives access to the axle filler plug.

5 Undo all the rear spring U-bolts so that the axle rests on the check straps. Take the weight of the axle on a jack or stand.

6 Lower the exhaust pipe. Remove the check straps and the axle can now be withdrawn sideways.

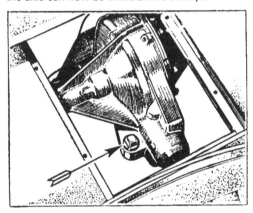

FIG 7:10   Rear axle filler plug TD, TF

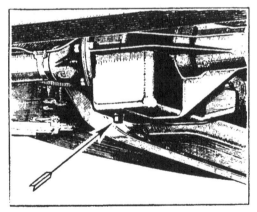

FIG 7:11   Rear axle drain plug TD, TF

7:6 Axle refitting

Refitting the rear axle is carried out by reversing the removal procedure but the following points should be noted:

1 The axle casing must be correctly positioned on the rear springs before the U-bolts are finally tightened.

2 Ensure that marks on flanges are in line when connecting the universal joint.

3 After connecting brake hoses the hydraulic system must be bled as described in **Chapter 10**.

4 Do not omit to refill the axle with the correct grade of lubricant.

7:7 Axle shafts, rear hub bearings

On models **TA**, **TB** and **TC**, to remove an axle shaft it is only necessary to remove the rear wheel and after removing the ring of bolts attaching the brake drum to the hub, remove the brake drum. Refit the wheel nut and by hitting one of the 'ears' of the nut with a copper or hide hammer the shaft can be driven out. **FIG 7:7** shows a shaft partially withdrawn. To examine the bearing, tap back the tab washer locking the bearing securing nut, undo the nut and withdraw the bearing housing complete with bearing. The assistance of a suitable puller may be needed. The bearing should be examined and renewed if it shows signs of play or roughness. The oil seal behind the bearing should also be examined and renewed if defective. Leakage at this point may allow grease to reach the brake drums and impregnate the friction linings. When reassembling ensure that the bearing locknut is really tight before locking it with the tab washer.

On models **TD** and **TF**, contrary to previous MG practice, the axle shafts can only be withdrawn after removing the wheel, the hub and brake drum, the brake back plate assembly and the wheel bearing housing. On cars fitted with disc wheels the brake drums are either permanently attached to the hubs by countersunk screws riveted at the ends or are cast in one piece with the hubs. In the case of the former no attempt must be made to separate the two parts. On **TF** models fitted with the optional **wire wheels** the brake drums 68 in **FIG 7:9** are detachable, being secured to the hubs 64 by six nuts 66 with three locking tabs 67. The drums however should not be removed from the hubs unless it becomes necessary and in this case they should be marked so that they are refitted in the same relative positions to ensure concentricity.

To remove the brake drum and hub on disc wheel models proceed as follows:

1 Jack up the wheel concerned and chock the remaining wheels as the handbrake must be fully released during the operation.

2 Remove the wheel .Remove the axle shaft nut which is secured by a split pin. Both shafts have righthand threads.

3 The hub is locked to the axle shaft by means of a tapered split collar in addition to the splines, so that an extractor of the type shown in **FIG 7:19** must be used. Note that the extractor bolts must have the correct internal threads to fit the wheel studs. On some cars these are $\frac{1}{2}$ inch BSF, on other cars they are $\frac{1}{2}$ inch UNF, as described in **Section 7:12**.

When refitting the hub ensure that the tapered split collar is fully home against the inner race. It can be tapped into position using a hide hammer, but care must be taken not to damage it in any way. The parallel portion of the collar engaging the oil seal must be undamaged. The oil seal should be renewed if its condition is in doubt.

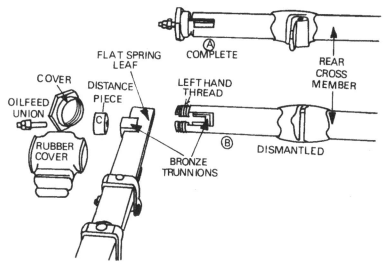

FIG 7:12 Rear spring trunnion bearing TA, TB. The rear ends of the front springs are similarly mounted

To remove the hub on **TF** models fitted with **wire wheels** a special hub drawer No. AJG 5031 is necessary. This is threaded internally to fit the right and lefthand hubs of the knock on type.

To remove the brake plate assembly on **TD** and **TF** models remove the hubs as described and undo the four nuts and bolts securing the brake back plate to the axle casing flange. If the brake hose is to be disconnected refer to **Chapter 10** and do not forget to bleed the brakes after refitting.

To remove an axle shaft from model **TD** or **TF**:
1 Remove the wheel, hub and brake drum assembly, and brake plate assembly, as already described.
2 Withdraw the split collar from the axle shaft.
3 Fit the special tool (Part No. 18G 374 for BSF or Part No. 18G 284 for UNF threads, see **Section 7:12**) to the end of the axle shaft.
4 Using the sliding impact weight on the tool, release the axle shaft complete with bearing, housing and oil seal.
5 The axle shaft can then be pressed out of the bearing. Reassembly is a reversal of the dismantling procedure, but the following points should be noted:
1 When fitting an oil seal in the wheel bearing housing, see that the sealing edge of the bore is towards the bearing. It should be a good press fit in the axle end cap.
2 Ensure that the split collar is clean and free from blemish, especially on its parallel portion, and pushed well home against the bearing inner race before refitting the wheel hub. It is advisable to tap it lightly into contact with the axle bearing with a hide hammer, taking the utmost care not to damage it in the process.

7:8 Description of suspension system

All cars in this series are fitted with semi-elliptic leaf springs at the rear. Driving and braking torque is taken by the spring leaves which are therefore pivoted at their front ends in fixed anchorages attached to the chassis frame side members. On all models Silentbloc bushes are used for these pivots. At the rear ends the springs are

allowed longitudinal movement by being mounted in early models on sliding trunnions and on later models in swinging shackles with rubber bushes.

On models **TA** and **TB**, the rear chassis frame is straight and the axle mounted above it as shown in the illustration of the **TC** model in **FIG 7:7**, but the rear ends of the springs are mounted in trunnions as shown in detail in **FIG 7:12**. This type of mounting was used on all MG Midgets and Magnettes up to 1939. The tubular chassis crossmember is extended as shown at B. The bronze trunnions are slotted so as to be a sliding fit on the spring main leaf and are free to rotate in the crossmember. The crossmember has wider slots than those in the trunnions, allowing a limited rotary movement as well as a sliding movement to the rear end of the spring. The trunnions are retained by a hexagonal cover nut threaded on to the end of the crossmember with a distance piece to limit side clearance. The whole is enclosed in a rubber cover and lubricated through a flexible feed from a nipple on the chassis frame.

On model **TC** the axle is also mounted above the chassis and the layout of the suspension is as shown in **FIG 7:7**. The front end of the spring is pivoted on a fixed anchorage with a Silentbloc bush, the rear end being mounted in an inverted shackle which is shown in section in **FIG 7:13**. The lower end of this shackle pivots on a pin secured to a lug on the tubular crossmember of the chassis.

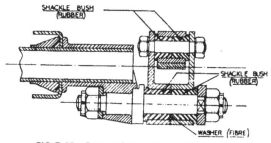

FIG 7:13 Rear spring rear mounting TC only

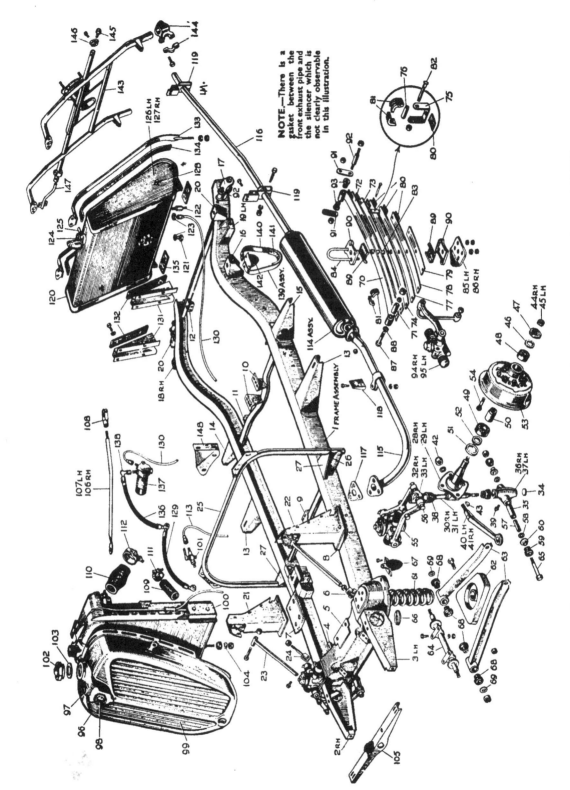

NOTE.—There is a gasket between the front exhaust pipe and the silencer which is not clearly observable in this illustration.

FIG 7:14 Exploded view of chassis, suspension, radiator, fuel tank and exhaust system components, model TD

Key to FIG 7:14

1 Chassis frame—complete 2 Extension—front R/H—frame 3 Extension—front L/H—frame 4 Bracket—engine steady 5 Bracket—engine mounting support
6 Anchor—stay tube 7 Bracket—frame stiffener R/H 8 Bracket—frame stiffener L/H 9 Bracket—engine mounting rear 10 Bracket—propeller shaft tunnel 11 Bracket—exhaust pipe
12 Bracket—exhaust pipe 13 Bracket—centre—body mounting 14 Bracket—front—rear spring R/H 15 Bracket—front—rear spring L/H 16 Bracket—rear—body mounting
17 Stiffener bracket—L/H 18 Mounting bracket—rear wing R/H 19 Mounting bracket—rear wing L/H 20 Mounting bracket—rear (valance) 21 Stiffener bracket R/H
22 Stiffener bracket—L/H 23 Stay tube assembly 24 Fork end 25 Dash stiffener assembly 26 Gusset plate—dash stiffener 27 Gusset plate—top—dash stiffener
28 Steering knuckle—L/H 29 Steering knuckle—R/H 30 Swivel pin—L/H 31 Swivel pin—upper R/H 32 Link—swivel pin—upper R/H 33 Link—swivel pin—upper L/H
34 Plate—link 35 Bush—link 36 Link—swivel pin—lower R/H 37 Link—swivel pin—lower L/H 38 Seal—swivel pin 39 Grease nipple ($\frac{1}{8}$ inch × 90°)—link
40 Steering lever—L/H 41 Steering lever—R/H 42 Nut—Simmonds thin. $\frac{3}{8}$ inch B.S.F. 43 Key—Woodruff No. 8 44 Nut—steering knuckle—R/H
45 Nut—steering knuckle—L/H 46 Felt washer—hub 47 Grease retainer—hub 48 Bearing hub—inner 49 Bearing hub—outer 50 Distance-piece—hub
51 Distance washer—hub 52 Oil seal—hub 53 Hub and brake-drum assembly—front 54 Wheel studs 55 Damper complete—front 56 Bolt—wishbone to link
57 Link—distance tube 58 Thrust washer—link 59 Seal—link 60 Support—link 61 Spring coil 62 Spring pan assembly 63 Bottom wishbone assembly
64 Fulcrum pin 65 Bolt—wishbone to link 66 Spigot for spring 67 Check rubber 68 Bush—bottom wishbone 69 Washer—wishbone 70 Main leaf complete with bush
71 Bush—Silentbloc 72 Second leaf 73 Third leaf 74 Fourth leaf complete with clips 75 Leaf clips 76 Distance tube 77 Fifth leaf 78 Sixth leaf 79 Seventh leaf
80 Rubber pad 81 Rubber—spring clip 82 Bolt—$\frac{1}{4}$ inch B.S.F. 83 Locating bolt 84 Clip—rear spring 85 Bracket—L/H (damper to rear spring)
86 Bracket—R/H (damper to rear spring) 87 Pin—rear spring front end 88 Washer—Silentbloc 89 Seating pad—rear spring 90 Locating plate—rear spring 97 Radiator false nose
92 Shackle pin 93 Bush 94 Damper complete—R/H 95 Damper complete—L/H 96 Radiator case (with medallion, grille and false nose)
98 Medallion—M.G.—radiator 99 Radiator grille 100 Radiator film block complete (with tanks) 101 Drain tap 102 Filler cap—radiator 103 Yoke end—stay tube
104 Packing washer—radiator mounting 105 Support member—radiator 106 Stay tube—radiator R/H 107 Stay tube—radiator L/H 108 Yoke end—stay tube
109 Hose—bottom—radiator 110 Hose—top—radiator 111 Clip—bottom hose 112 Clip—top hose 113 Drain pipe 114 Exhaust system complete (welded assembly)—later models
115 Front exhaust pipe only 116 Silencer and rear pipe assembly 117 Gasket—exhaust pipe flange 118 Bracket—front support 119 Support—tail pipe
120 Fuel tank complete 121 Drain plug—fuel tank 122 Main feed pipe 123 Washer (drain plug and main feed) 124 Filler cap (Westwood) complete 125 Trigger—cap
126 End cover—fuel tank L/H 127 End cover—fuel tank R/H 128 Special bolt—tank end cover 129 Pipe (between carburetters)
130 Pipe (tank to pump) complete with washer and union washer 131 Mounting bracket 132 Rubber for mounting bracket 133 Strap—fuel tank 134 Packing—tank strap
135 Rubber packing—tank to frame 136 Pipe—pump to carburetters 137 Fuel pump 138 Elbow—fuel pump 139 Check strap assembly—rear axle 140 Check strap
141 Buffer—checkstrap 142 Rebound rubber—rear axle 143 Spare wheel carrier bracket assembly 144 Clamp bracket—lower—carrier 145 Plug—spare wheel carrier
146 Clamp—rear number-plate 147 Mounting bracket—rear number-plate 148 Attachment plate—dash stiffener

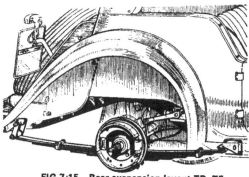

FIG 7:15   Rear suspension layout TD, TF

On models **TD** and **TF** the axle is carried below the chassis frame, which is upswept at the rear to accommodate it. **FIG 7:14** shows the chassis and suspension components in exploded view. The rear springs are carried at their front ends by pins 87 with Silentbloc bushes 71 in the brackets attached to the chassis frame 14 and 15. The spring leaves are interleaved with rubber and a rubber seating pad 89 is interposed between the main leaf 70 and the locating plate 90. The rear ends of the springs are carried in pendant shackles 91 with rubber bushes 93. The shackles are also shown in section in **FIG 7:16**.

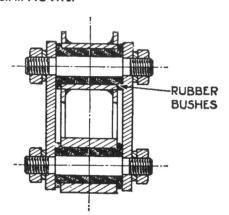

RUBBER BUSHES

FIG 7:16   Rear spring shackle TD, TF

7:9 Spring removal, servicing pivots and springs

On models **TA** and **TB**, remove the rear springs as follows:

1 Jack up and support the rear end of the car under the chassis frame and remove the road wheel.
2 Support the centre of the spring with a small jack. Remove the nuts from the U-bolts securing the spring to the axle. Lower the jack and remove the U-bolts.
3 Disconnect the oil feed pipe from the rear end of the spring.
4 Remove the hexagon cover nut shown in **FIG 7:12** which has a lefthand thread. Remove the nut from the pivot pin at the front end of the spring. The spring, complete with rubber cover and one trunnion, can then be removed from the car.

On models **TC, TD** and **TF,** remove the rear springs as follows:

1 Jack up the rear end of the car and support the chassis just in front of the rear spring front anchorage.
2 Take the weight of the axle on a small jack. Remove the nuts from the U-bolts securing the spring to the axle, lower the jack and remove the U-bolts.
3 (a) On models **TC** only, remove the split pin and the lower nut on the outside of the rear shackle, shown in section in **FIG 7:13**.
   (b) On models **TD** and **TF,** referring to **FIG 7:16**, remove the rear shackle pin nuts and outer shackle plate, then remove the inner plate with shackle pins. Lower the rear end of the spring to the ground.
4 Remove the pivot pin nut from the front end of the spring. On model **TC,** both ends of the spring can now be withdrawn at the same time. On models **TD** and **TF** the front end of the spring can now be removed.

To adjust the trunnions on models **TA** and **TB,** remove the rear spring as already described. The remaining trunnion can then be easily withdrawn from the chassis crossmember. Check the fit of the trunnion slots on the spring leaf. If the slots are worn, the trouble may possibly be cured by fitting new trunnions. If however a recess has also been worn in the spring leaf, a new spring or main leaf will have to be fitted. If the trunnions are still serviceable, side play can be taken up by removing just sufficient metal from the inner or split face of one trunnion to allow the joint to slide freely without side play when the cover nut is fully tightened. This work is best carried out by facing the trunnion in a lathe. If wear is considerable, remove equal amounts from the faces of both trunnions.

On models **TC, TD** and **TF,** the shackles at the rear end of the rear springs are fitted with rubber bushes each of which is in two halves. When the shackle pin nuts are slackened the bushes will be found to be a loose fit on their pins, but the action of tightening expands them into their housings and contracts them on to the pins. The Silentbloc bushes fitted to the front ends of the rear springs work on the same principle, but are housed in a metal sleeve which can be pressed out of the spring eye. The Silentbloc is renewed as a unit. Reassembly will be described in the following section, but it should be noted that **neither rubber bushes nor Silentbloc bushes must be lubricated.**

On early models the leaf springs are built up so that there is a metal to metal contact between the leaves. The leaves can be separated after removing the spring clamps, cleaned in paraffin and reassembled after impregnating with a suitable grease. If it is not desired to dismantle the springs, they can be lubricated by means of the high pressure equipment used by a service station. On models **TD** and **TF** the springs are interleaved with rubber as shown in **FIG 7:14** and must on **no account be lubricated or sprayed with paraffin or cleaning fluids.** If the springs are dismantled each leaf should be cleaned and dried and inspected for cracks or breakage. Check the centre bolt for wear or distortion. This bolt locates the spring on the axle pad and must be in good condition. Reassemble the springs and rubber interleaving pads as shown in **FIG 7:14.** When fitting new leaves it is important that they should be of the same curvature as the remaining leaves and of the correct length and thickness. If the original springs have lost their camber due to settling, the fitting of new springs is advisable.

7:10 Spring refitting

The refitting of rear springs follows a reversal of the removal procedure, but the following points should be noted. Pivots or shackles with rubber or Silentbloc bushes must be tightened with the weight of the car on the springs. This is because the pin does not revolve in the bush, the angular movement being taken up torsionally in the bush itself. If the bush is compressed without the weight being on the springs, the torsion will not be equally divided between bump and rebound movements and rapid wear of the bush will take place.

It is also essential in the case of the rear shackle bushes to ensure that each half bush projects equally from its housing, so that equal expansion takes place when the nuts are tightened. Some difficulty may be experienced in the case of the rear shackle on the **TC** model as shown in **FIG 7:13**, owing to the fact that the lower pin can only be tightened from the outside. Centralization of the bush can only be achieved by trial and error.

When refitting U-bolts, tighten the nuts evenly and diagonally. It is advisable to check the tightness of these nuts after 500 miles. If new U-bolts have been fitted this check is essential.

7:11 Damper maintenance, removal and testing

The dampers fitted to front and rear axles of the **TA** models are of the Girling vane type. Every 10,000 miles remove the filler plug on top of the case and replenish with Girling Shock Absorber Fluid. The chamber should be filled three quarters full. This is to allow for expansion of the fluid due to temperature increase. These dampers are adjustable. To increase the amount of damping, the regulator screw beneath the filler plug must be turned to the right, thus closing the valve. To decrease the amount of damping it is turned to the left thus opening the valve and permitting a freer flow of fluid. A very fine degree of adjustment can be obtained but the regulator screw should only be turned a quarter of a turn at a time. Care must be taken to make the adjustment so that the damping action of both dampers is equal. If the original setting has been entirely lost, disconnect the bottom end of the damper connecting link and balance the two dampers by checking by hand. The total amount of damping necessary can only be checked by road test with the dampers reconnected. Each regulator should then be turned the same amount to preserve the balance. The connecting link is fitted with a tilting bearing consisting of round blocks of rubber which grip the bearing portion of the link, thus obviating the need for ball joints. The bearing must not be lubricated.

On models **TC** and **TD** Luvax-Girling piston type dampers are fitted as shown in **FIG 7:17**. These are non-adjustable and require no maintenance other than topping up with Girling Piston Type Damper Fluid every 12,000 miles. Before removing the filler plug which is indicated by an arrow in the illustration, remove any dirt from the surrounding parts to ensure that none enters the damper. If it is suspected that the dampers

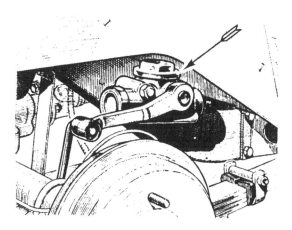

FIG 7:17 Rear damper model TD showing position of filler plug

are not functioning, check by bouncing each corner of the car up and down. A more positive check can be made by disconnecting the damper connecting link and moving the lever by hand up and down a few times through its full stroke. A uniform resistance should be felt throughout the stroke in both directions. Erratic resistance with free movement may indicate lack of fluid. To expel air which may be present in the operating chambers, add fluid while the lever arm is being worked up and down. This attention will be carried out more easily if the damper is removed from the car and held in a vice as shown in **FIG 7:18.** If it is not possible to move the arm by hand this indicates a broken internal part or seized piston, and a replacement damper should be fitted.

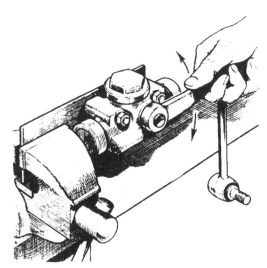

FIG 7:18 Testing hydraulic damper mounted in vice

TF cars are fitted with Armstrong dampers. Those at the rear are of the double acting type. These work on the principle of forcing oil through valves from one cylinder to another, the two cylinders being side by side in the damper body. The amount of fluid passing is controlled by the valves but these are pre-set before leaving the factory and should not be disturbed. The dampers should be topped up when necessary with Armstrong Damper Oil No. 549 through the filler cap on top of the damper body. All dirt should be cleaned from the area of the filler cap before removal. When servicing, the fixing bolts should be checked for tightness.

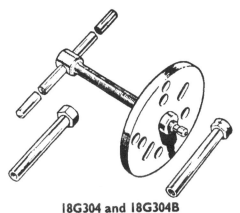

18G304 and 18G304B
or 18G304A

FIG 7:19 Hub extractor for TD and TF models fitted with disc wheels

7:12 Modifications

A production modification on the hypoid rear axles as fitted to **TD** and **TF** models affects the interchangeability of all threaded parts such as nuts, bolts and studs. Originally, BSF threads were used, but on later axles either ANF or Unified threads will be found. It should be noted that while for all practical purposes ANF and Unified are interchangeable with one another, neither is interchangeable with BSF. All components with the Unified threads, which are now being standardized on all BMC cars, are marked in the following manner:
Nuts: A circular groove in the end face of the nut or connected circles stamped on one flat of the hexagon.
Bolts and set screws: A circular depression turned on the head or connected circles stamped on one flat of the hexagon.
Wheel stud nuts: A notch cut in all corners of the hexagon.

These marks are shown in **FIG 7:20.** As an interim measure, certain axles were fitted with parts having the ANF thread. There is no identification mark for ANF threads, but these axles have been fitted with wheel stud nuts with the notches as on Unified and it is by this means only that they can be identified. It should also be borne in mind that BSF or Whitworth spanners will not fit ANF or Unified bolts and nuts, spanners of the correct dimensions being required.

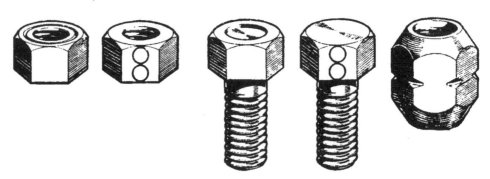

FIG 7:20 Unified Threads identification marks

7:13 Fault diagnosis
(a) Noisy axle
1 Insufficient or incorrect lubricant
2 Worn bearings
3 Worn gears

(b) Excessive backlash
1 Worn gears, shaft bearings or bearing housings
2 Worn axle splines
3 Loose or broken wheel studs
4 Worn hub splines

(c) Oil leakage
1 Defective oil seals in hub
2 Defective pinion shaft seal
3 Defective seals on universal joints

(d) Vibration
1 Propeller shaft out of balance
2 Worn universal joint bearings

(e) Rattles
1 Rubber bushes in damper links worn
2 Dampers loose
3 Spring U-bolts loose or rubber pad defective
4 Loose spring clips
5 Defective rubber or Silentbloc bushes
6 Worn trunnions, models TA, TB
7 Broken spring leaves
8 Defective rubber interleaving pads, models TD, TF

(f) 'Settling'
1 Weak or broken spring leaves
2 Badly worn rubber or Silentbloc bushes or pins.

CHAPTER 8

FRONT SUSPENSION AND HUBS

8:1 Description of system
8:2 Removal, dismantling and refitting front axle, TA, TB, TC
8:3 Removal, overhaul and refitting leaf springs, TA, TB, TC
8:4 Dismantling and reassembling front suspension TD, TF

8:5 Front hub bearings, seals and kingpins
8:6 Damper removal and refitting, topping-up, testing
8:7 Suspension geometry
8:8 Modifications
8:9 Fault diagnosis.

8:1 Description of system

On models **TA, TB** and **TC** the front beam axle is carried on semi-elliptic leaf springs, the front ends of which are attached to the chassis frame by hardened steel anchorage pins running directly in the spring eyes. On models **TA** and **TB** the rear ends of the springs are carried in sliding trunnions similar to those fitted to the rear springs and described in detail in **Section 7:8.** On model **TC** the rear ends of the front springs are carried in rubber-bushed swing shackles which are shown in section in **FIG 8:2.** The kingpins or pivot pins are located in the axle beam eyes by cotters, the kingpin bushes being pressed into the steering knuckles.

Models **TD** and **TF** are fitted with independent front suspension (i.f.s.) of the unequal wishbone type incorporating coil springs. The action of the system is shown diagramatically in **FIG 8:1.** The component parts are shown in **FIG 7:14** to which reference should be made. The lower wishbones 63 are mounted at their inner ends by rubber bushes 68 on the fulcrum pins 64 bolted to the chassis frame member. The upper wishbones form the operating arms of the hydraulic dampers

55, thus dispensing with separate linkage for the dampers. At the outer ends of both upper and lower wishbones the swivel pins 30 and 31 are threaded into the swivel pin links 32, 33, 36 and 37. The latter are pivoted on the wishbones by the bolts 56 and 65 and the bushes 35. Each of the four swivel links is provided with a grease nipple and with seals to retain the lubricant.

8:2 Removal, dismantling and refitting front axle, TA, TB, TC

To remove the front axle proceed as follows:
1 Jack up the front of car until the tyres are just clear of the ground and support it under the chassis frame. Remove the front wheels.
2 Disconnect the lower arms of the dampers from the spring brackets and disconnect the hydraulic brake hoses from the copper pipes on the chassis. Refer to the note on brake hoses in **Chapter 10.** On model **TA** disconnect the torque cables. Disconnect the drag link at the axle end.

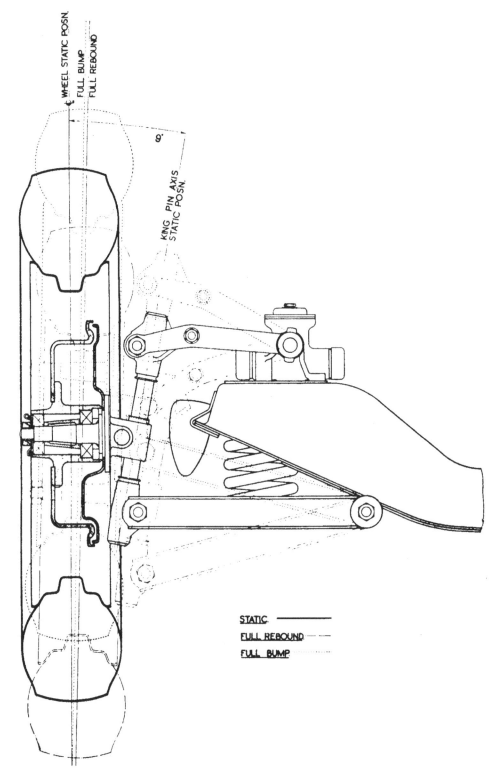

WHEEL STATIC POSN.

FULL BUMP

FULL REBOUND

9°

KING PIN AXIS
STATIC POSN.

STATIC.

FULL REBOUND

FULL BUMP

FIG 8:1   Front suspension system TD and TF showing effect of movement on camber

3 Remove the anchorage pins from the front ends of the springs. On models **TA** and **TB** disconnect the oil feed pipes from the trunnions. Remove the hexagon nut and withdraw the rear end of the spring sideways with the rubber cover and the outer half of the trunnion. On model **TC** undo the shackle pin nuts at the rear end of the springs and remove the shackle plates. The axle can now be withdrawn.

To dismantle the axle remove the track rod and steering arms, also remove the brake drums, hubs, brake back plates and kingpins as will be described in **Section 8:5**. The stub axles can then be withdrawn from the axle beam. The axle beam should be examined for obvious signs of damage, but accurate checking for truth is best carried out by the makers using the original jig or by a service agent specializing in this type of repair work. The removal and overhaul of the springs will be covered in the next Section.

The reassembly and refitting of the front axle is largely a reversal of the dismantling procedure. The wheel alignment should be checked as will be described in **Chapter 9** and the hydraulic system will need to be bled in accordance with instructions in **Chapter 10**.

On model **TA** torque cables are fitted on the front axle to absorb the torque reaction when the front brakes are applied. They should be adjusted so that with the steering in the straight ahead position there is $\frac{3}{4}$ to 1 inch free up and down movement when finger pressure is applied midway between the fulcrum pins. Tighten the locknuts on the cable yoke ends to maintain the adjustment.

8:3 Removal, overhaul and refitting leaf springs, TA, TB, TC

To remove a front spring without removing the axle from the car, proceed as follows:

1 Jack up the front of the car and support it under the chassis frame. Remove the road wheel. Support the centre of the spring with a small jack. Remove the nuts from the four bolts securing the axle beam to the spring. Lower the jack and remove the four bolts.
2 On models **TA** and **TB** disconnect the damper arm from the bracket on the spring. Disconnect the oil feed pipe from the trunnion at the rear end of the spring. Remove the hexagon nut and also the front anchorage pin. The spring is then withdrawn sideways with the rubber cover and the outer half of the trunnion. On model **TC** remove the shackle pin nuts and washers and the shackle plates, pins and rubbers at the rear end of the spring, shown in section in **FIG 8:2**. Lower this end of the spring to the ground. Remove the front anchorage pin and the spring can now be withdrawn from the car.

To dismantle the springs, remove the spring clips and the centre bolt. Each leaf should be thoroughly cleaned and examined for wear or cracks. The centre bolt should also be examined for wear and the holes in the leaves through which it passes should be checked for ovality. Leaves which are defective should be renewed, but springs which have lost their camber through settling are best renewed complete. Before reassembling spring leaves coat them with a suitable grease. To lubricate the springs when in service without removal from the car, remove the spring clips and separate the leaves with a

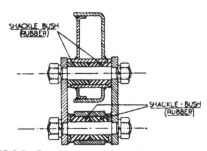

FIG 8:2   Front spring rear shackle model TC

screwdriver blade so that each can be smeared with grease. Alternatively they can be lubricated by means of high pressure equipment at a service station.

On models **TA** and **TB** the front spring eyes have renewable brass bushes, but on model **TC** the hardened anchorage pins work directly in the spring eyes. In this case renewal of the pins is usually sufficient to take up wear at this point. Otherwise a new main leaf must be fitted. The trunnion mountings at the rear ends of the front springs on models **TA** and **TB** are similar to those fitted to the rear springs and reference should be made to **Section 7:8** for the method of adjustment.

On model **TC** a swing shackle is fitted at the rear end of each front spring, as shown in section in **FIG 8:2**. Four special rubber bushes are fitted into the spring eye and the chassis frame tube and are clamped by the shackle plates. These bushes are quite a loose fit, but expand when clamped into their housings by the tightening of the shackle pin nuts. The bushes do not rotate on their surfaces, the torsional movement being taken up in the rubber itself. For this reason, **final tightening of the nuts should be carried out with the weight of the car on the springs.** When assembling the bushes they must be located so as to project an equal amount each side, both before and after tightening the shackle plates. This ensures that the clamping effect is equal in each bush.

Routine maintenance of the front suspension is confined to lubrication of the spring front anchorage pins which should be greased every 500 miles and the injection of oil into the nipples on the chassis frame for lubrication of the trunnions on models **TA** and **TB**. The front spring rear shackles on model **TC** are fitted with rubber bushes **and must on no account be lubricated.**

8:4 Dismantling and reassembling front suspension, TD, TF

Referring to **FIGS 8:1** and **8:3** it will be seen that the suspension units are entirely independent and either righthand or lefthand units can be removed separately. In the following description of the dismantling procedure the numbering of the parts refers to **FIG 7:14**.

1 Jack up the car and support it under the front crossmember so that the front wheels are just clear of the ground. Remove the front wheels.
2 Jack up under the spring pans as shown in **FIG 8:4** until the hydraulic damper arms are just clear of the rebound rubbers.
3 Disconnect the hydraulic brake hoses, referring to **Chapter 10** for the precautions to be observed.

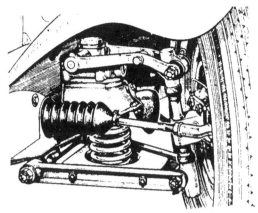

FIG 8:3   Front suspension assembly models TD and TF

Slacken the steering tie-rod nuts and screw the tie-rods out of the outer ball joints by means of the flats on the rods.

4 Remove the locknuts from the bolts 56 and 65 which connect the wishbones to the swivel links and withdraw the bolts. Withdraw the front hub and swivel pin units complete. If the swivel links are not to be removed from the swivel pins, ensure that they remain in the same positions relative to one another and to the swivel pins, wiring them if necessary, This will greatly facilitate reassembly. If the swivel links are to be removed, unscrew them from the ends of the swivel pins, noting that on the lefthand side of the car both threads are lefthand, while those on the righthand side are righthand. **The stub axle should not be removed from the swivel pin unless it is absolutely necessary.** It is held in place by the steering lever.

5 Release the jacks from under the spring pans. Press down the lower wishbone assemblies and remove the coil springs. Unbolt the wishbone arms from the spring pans.

6 Remove the nuts from the fulcrum pins 64 and slide off the wishbone arms with their rubber bushes. Remove the four bolts holding each of the fulcrum pins to the chassis crossmember.

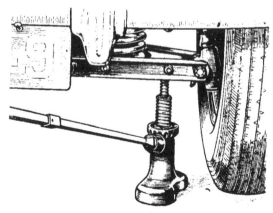

FIG 8:4   Jacking up front suspension

7 Remove the hydraulic dampers from the cross-member.

8 Remove the spring spigots 66 which will be found inside the outer ends of the crossmember, each being secured by a small bolt.

Before reassembly all parts should be examined for wear or damage. If the fulcrum pin bushes are split or perished, eccentric or oil soaked they should be renewed. **FIG 8:5** shows the dimensions of a bush in new condition. Examine the end holes in the lower wishbones for elongation and the assembly for looseness. If there is any sign of slackness between the wishbone arms and the spring pans, separate the components and check the bolt holes for elongation. The bolt holes should be $\frac{21}{44}$ inch in diameter.

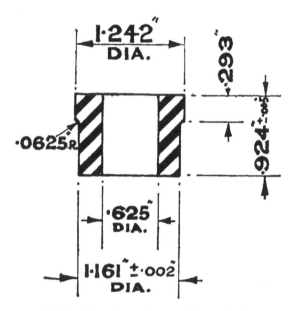

FIG 8:5   Dimensions of lower wishbone bushes

Examine the coil springs for cracks and check for free length and compression to the following figures:

Free length   9.59 $\pm \frac{1}{16}$ inch
Loaded to 1095 lb   6.44 $\pm \frac{1}{32}$ inch

Check the swivel links. The dimensions across the thrust faces should be 2.327 $\pm$ .0015 inch. If these are appreciably worn the assembly of link and bush should be renewed. If the bush only is worn, a new one should be pressed in and reamed and burnished to .750 $\pm$ .0005 inch. When pressing in the bush ensure that the hole in the bush faces the threaded bore.

Check the threaded bores on the swivel pins. When new, these are a free turning fit without slack. An appreciable amount of slack is permissible in these threaded bearings and they do not need renewal unless very slack.

Check the fulcrum pin distance tubes for scoring or wear. These should be 2.337 $\pm$ .0015 inch long by .7485 to .7480 inch diameter, Examine the case-hardened thrust washers for ridges. The faces should be flat and parallel within .0005 inch. The thickness should be .066 to .068 inch, the bore .505 to .510 inch and the outside diameter 1.25 inch.

When the swivel links, distance tubes and thrust washers are assembled as shown in **FIG 8:6** the total clearance between the link and the thrust washers should be .008 to .013 inch. Check that all grease nipples are clear and their joint faces undamaged. Examine the rubber seals and renew if perished or split.

Reassemble the front suspension as follows:

1 Bolt the spring spigots inside the chassis cross-member. Bolt the dampers to the crossmember, The dampers are interchangeable from side to side.

2 Bolt the fulcrum pins to the crossmember. Note that the rear inner bolts are fitted with their nuts uppermost.

3 Fit the rubber bushes into the lower wishbone arms These bushes will be found to be quite a loose fit in the arms, but when clamped by the fulcrum pin nuts will expand into their housings. The bushes must be assembled so that they are centrally located as shown in **FIG 8:7**. Note that they do not rotate on their surfaces, the torsional movement being taken up by the rubber itself. **It is essential therefore to clamp the bushes when the lower wishbone arms are parallel to the ground,** thus ensuring equal torsion on upward and downward movement of the suspension. After tightening the fulcrum pin nuts, check that the bushes still project equally on each side as shown in **FIG 8:7**. Secure the nuts with split pins.

4 Fit the spring pans between the wishbone arms, with the heads of the bolts inside the pans. Leave the nuts half a turn slack at this stage.

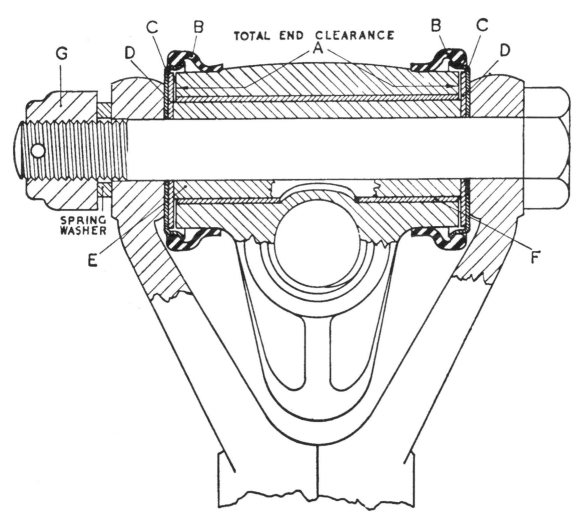

FIG 8:6 Sectional view of swivel pin link

Key to FIG 8:6
A Total end clearance   B Seal   C Seal support   D Thrust washers   E Distance piece   F Bush   G Locknut

EQUIDISTANT

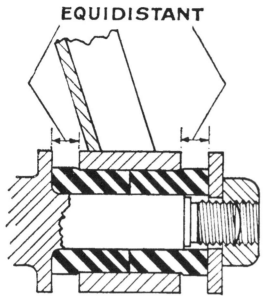

FIG 8:7 Sectional view of bushes, lower wishbone

5 Press down the lower wishbones. Smear each end of the coil springs with grease to prevent any slight squeaking in operation. Insert the tops of the springs so as to engage the spigots in the crossmember and fit the lower ends to the recesses in the spring pans. Jack up the lower wishbones so that they are parallel to the ground.

6 Fit the swivel pin and hub assemblies to the outer ends of the upper and lower wishbones. The right-hand assembly has righthand threads on the stub axle and on the swivel pin, that on the lefthand side of the car having lefthand threads. Ensure that the swivel link bushes are correctly assembled with the thrust washers, rubber seals and retainers as shown in FIG 8:6. Lubricate the bolts on assembly and again afterwards with the grease gun. Leave the nuts half a turn slack at this stage.

7 If the swivel pin links have been removed from the swivel pins, they must be correctly positioned on the pins before inserting the bolts which attach them to the wishbones. Referring to FIG 8:6 it will be seen that the swivel pin threads are waisted at their centres to avoid fouling the bolts. Screw the upper link on to the swivel pin until the waisted portion lines up with the bolt hole. Place the bolt in position and screw the link on as far as it will go, which will be found to be about three turns. Unscrew the link about one and a half turns to allow the maximum clearance for the bolt in each direction. Fit the lower link in same way.

8 Connect up the hydraulic brake hoses and bleed and adjust the brakes as described in **Chapter 10**.

9 Connect the steering tie-rods to the outer ball joints, screwing the rods right in and then slackening off five complete turns. Tighten the locknuts. This adjustment will give a rough wheel alignment. Detailed instructions for checking wheel alignment will be found in **Chapter 9**.

10 Fit the front wheels and remove jacks and supports. Bounce the front of the car up and down a few times to allow the suspension joints to settle down. Tighten the spring pan bolts, then tighten the fulcrum pin and upper and lower swivel link bolts and secure with split pins.

If it is required to renew a front spring, it is not necessary to dismantle the complete suspension. The work is carried out as follows:

1 Jack up the front of the car and support under the centre of the front crossmember so that the wheels are just clear of the ground. Remove the front wheels on the side affected.

2 Jack up under the spring pan as shown in FIG 8:4 until the hydraulic damper arm is just clear of the rebound rubber.

3 Remove the bolt securing the swivel pin link to the outer end of the lower wishbone. Swing up the hub and swivel pin unit and support it on a suitable block.

4 Release the jack from under the spring pan, press down the lower wishbone assembly and remove the coil spring.

5 Refitting is carried out in the reverse manner to that described for removal. Ensure that the swivel link components are correctly assembled as shown in FIG 8:6. Lubricate these parts during assembly and afterwards with the grease gun. Smear both ends of the spring with grease.

Routine maintenance of the front suspension is confined to lubrication of the four swivel pin links. The grease nipples shown in FIG 8:8 should be given a few strokes of the grease gun every 500 miles using a recommended grease. Lubrication will be more effectively carried out if the front of the car is jacked up so as to take the weight off the swivel pins. The remaining suspension points have rubber bushes and must not be lubricated.

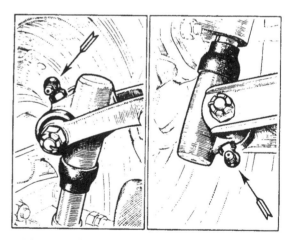

FIG 8:8 Position of grease nipples on upper and lower swivel links

8:5 Front hub bearings, seals and kingpins

To remove the front hub bearings on models **TA**, **TB** and **TC**:

1 Remove the road wheel and brake drum and remove the grease from inside the hub.

2 Removal of the plug from the small hole in the splined portion of the hub gives access to the split pin in the castellated nut which secures the hub. Undo the nut with a box spanner and remove the outer washer.

3 Using a suitable extractor withdraw the hub from the stub axle, complete with both bearings. The outer ball race is smaller than the inner one and can be easily withdrawn from the hub, but before removing the inner race the oil seal must be withdrawn.

On reassembling, the bearings and distance piece will go together without any difficulty, but after tightening the castellated nut it is advisable to spin the hub to ensure that it rotates freely. Fit the split pin and the steel plug. Pack the inside of the hub with grease and smear the external splines with graphite grease.

On **TD** and **TF** models the front brake drums are either permanently attached to the hubs or in later cars are cast in one piece with the hubs. The procedure for removal of the front hub bearings is as follows.

1 Remove the road wheel. Prise off the grease-retaining cap, where fitted. Remove the split pin from the castellated stub axle nut and remove the nut, remembering that the stub axle on the lefthand side of the car has a lefthand thread. Remove the grease-retaining disc and washer fitted to early models.

2 Place the hub extractor, tool No. 18G 304 shown in **FIG 7:19**, in position over the wheel studs and refit the wheel nuts to hold the extractor plate. The extractor centre screw is then tightened to withdraw the hub and brake drum assembly. In the absence of the specified tool it may be possible to improvise a suitable puller to fix on the wheel studs.

3 The outer ball race will be withdrawn with the hub, but the inner race may remain on the stub axle. It must then be withdrawn, using either the special extractor No. 68895 or a standard claw-type puller. Care must be taken to see that the claws do not damage the oil seal behind the bearing.

If the grease is cleaned from the hub and the bearings washed for examination, ensure that they are repacked with grease before reassembly. **Note that the inner bearing and oil seal must be removed from the stub axle.** If the hub is pressed on to the axle without first fitting the bearing and oil seal to it, the inner oil seal will be displaced. Fit the bearing spacer with the chamfered end towards the outer bearing and then press the inner bearing into the hub. Fit the oil seal and distance washer, the metal face of the oil seal and the recessed side of the distance washer facing away from the bearing. Fit the hub on the stub axle. On early **TD** models fitted with a grease nipple on the hub, fit a new felt washer and refit the grease-retaining disc. Tighten the castellated nut and secure with a new split pin.

Hubs on later **TD** and **TF** models, instead of having a grease nipple, are fitted with grease caps which are a push fit on the hubs. The caps have to be carefully prised off every 6000 miles and the bearings packed with a recommended grease. This production modification was introduced to overcome a tendency on earlier models for grease to leak on to the outside of the hub. Details of a conversion suitable for earlier models will be found in **Section 8:8.**

On cars fitted with wire wheels, remove the front wheel locknuts every 6000 miles and pack the hubs with a recommended grease. On cars with disc wheels fitted with grease nipples, one stroke of the grease gun should be given every 6000 miles.

To renew the kingpins and bushes on models **TA, TB** and **TC**:

1 Jack up the front of the car and support it under the chassis frame. Remove the road wheel and brake drum. Remove the hub as described earlier in this Section. Disconnect the brake hose at the chassis end, referring to **Chapter 10** for precautions to be observed.

2 Remove the bolts securing the brake backplate to the stub axle and remove the backplate complete with brake gear.

3 Remove the cotter securing the kingpin in the axle beam eye and press out the kingpin. Remove the stub axle.

4 Press out the top and bottom kingpin bushes from the stub axle.

5 Press the new kingpin bushes into the stub axle. They must now be reamered to size using a reamer long enough to pass through both bushes, thus ensuring that they are in line. Do not fit a kingpin too tightly. It should be just possible to press it into the bushes by hand pressure. Lubricate the bushes with a recommended grease before fitting the kingpin.

6 When assembled, there should be a slight up and down play between the stub axle and axle beam eye, but this should not exceed .004 inch measured with a feeler between the steel thrust washer and the flange of the bush.

7 The reassembly of the remaining parts is carried out in the reverse order to that of dismantling. Bleed and adjust the brakes as described in **Chapter 10.**

Routine maintenance of kingpins and bushes on models **TA, TB** and **TC** consists of lubricating by means of the four grease nipples, two on each side of the car, every 500 miles. **It is essential for each of the front wheels to be jacked up so as to take the weight of the car off the kingpins when carrying out this operation, otherwise the bushes will not be fully lubricated.**

8:6 Damper removal and refitting, topping-up, testing

On models **TA, TB** and **TC** the front dampers are similar to those fitted on the rear axle, for which instructions have already been given in **Section 7:11.** In the case of the **TD** and **TF** models, the procedure for topping up and testing the front dampers is the same as for those fitted to the rear, but as the front dampers form part of the independent suspension system, the method of removal differs:

1 Jack up under the spring pan as shown in **FIG 8:4** until the wheel is clear of the ground. Remove the wheel.

2 Remove the bolt from the upper swivel link, item 56 in **FIG 7:14.** Swing the hub and swivel pin unit clear of the damper arms and support it so as not to strain the brake hose. Do not turn the swivel link in relation to the swivel pin.

3 Unscrew the four bolts securing the damper assembly 55 to the chassis frame.

4 Refitting is a reversal of the removal procedure, but care must be taken to ensure that the swivel link components are correctly assembled as shown in **FIG 8:6.**

The Andrex TE1/N damper illustrated in **FIG 8:10** is fitted as supplementary equipment to the **TD Midget Mark II** and is in principle a development of the Hartford friction damper. The moving and fixed plates, interleaved with discs of specially impregnated wood, are under the pressure of a plate spring and are enclosed in an oil-filled casing.

The spring pressure is adjusted by means of a small set screw and locknut which can be seen in **FIG 8:10.** Use two spanners, one on the set screw and one on the locknut. Approximately $2\frac{1}{2}$ turns of the set screw covers the full range of adjustment, $\frac{1}{4}$ turn being equivalent to a difference of 3 lbs in loading. The dampers are pre-set by the makers at 16 lbs measured at the end of the operating arm. When fitted to the **TD Mark II** the front dampers are set to 24 lbs and the rear dampers to 22 lbs. Turn the set screw clockwise to increase the loading, anticlockwise to decrease. The casing should be filled with a heavy oil such as Esso Cantona LK 190.

FIG 8:10 Andrex friction damper

On models **TA, TB** and **TC,** weakness and settling of the front springs or excessive wear of the shackle bushes can affect castor angle. Worn kingpins and bushes will reduce the camber. On models **TD** and **TF** with independent suspension, reference to **FIG 8:1** shows that the camber varies slightly on the upward and downward movement of the suspension. A weak coil spring will decrease the camber in the static position, while excessively worn suspension joints will have the effect of giving a permanent negative camber.

8:8 Modifications

On earlier **TD** models fitted with disc wheels and a grease nipple on each front hub, grease has been found to leak past the felt sealing washer on to the outside of

FIG 8:9 Grease cap on front hubs, later TD, TF

8:7 Suspension geometry

Three dimensions relating to the front suspension which can effect the steering are camber, swivel pin or kingpin inclination and castor angle. Camber is an outward inclination of the top of the front wheels to facilitate cornering. Swivel pin inclination indicates that the swivel pins are inclined in the opposite direction, so that the line of the pin, if continued downwards, would strike the ground near the point of contact of the tyre. Castor angle is effected by inclining the swivel pins towards the back of the car at their upper ends.

No adjustments are provided for the correction of these angles and departures from specification are due to damage or excessive wear in the suspension joints. Dimensions for the various models are given in Technical Data in the Appendix, but accurate measurement is only possible with the aid of specialized checking equipment which is unlikely to be available to the owner.

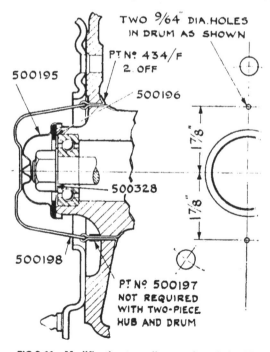

FIG 8:11 Modification to earlier type front hubs, TD

the hub. Later **TD** and **TF** models have a modified grease retaining cap fitted to the hub, as shown in **FIG 8:9**, which eliminates this trouble. **FIG 8:11** illustrates a conversion which can be carried out to the front hubs of earlier cars, consisting of a grease cap with a rubber sealing gasket and held in place by a spring clip.

The parts required for this conversion are as follows:

500196	Seal	2 off
500195	Grease retainer cap	2 off
500198	Spring clip	2 off
434/F	Split pin ($\frac{1}{8}$ inch × $1\frac{1}{8}$ inch) ...	4 off
500328	Washer	2 off
500197	Distance tube	2 off
	(for one-piece hub and drum only).	

The modified hub is packed with a recommended grease every 6000 miles.

8:9 Fault diagnosis
(a) Wheel wobble
1 Worn hub bearings
2 Broken or weak front springs
3 Uneven tyre wear
4 Worn suspension linkage
5 Loose wheel fixings

(b) 'Bottoming' of suspension
1 Check 2 in (a)
2 Rebound rubbers worn or missing
3 Dampers not working

(c) Heavy steering
1 Neglected swivel pin lubrication
2 Wrong suspension geometry
3 Front tyres under-inflated

(d) Excessive tyre wear
1 Check 4 in (a), 3 in (b) and 2 in (c)

(e) Rattles
1 Check 2 in (a)
2 Pivot lubrication neglected, rubber bushes worn
3 Shackle pins, bushes or sliding trunnions worn
4 Torque cable slack (model TA)
5 Damper mountings loose

(f) Excessive 'rolling'
1 Check 2 in (a) and 3 in (b)

CHAPTER 9

THE STEERING GEAR

9:1 Operating principles
9:2 Routine maintenance and adjustment, TA, TB, TC
9:3 Removing, dismantling and refitting steering, TA, TB, TC
9:4 Routine maintenance, TD, TF
9:5 Removing, dismantling and refitting steering TD, TF
9:6 Removing and refitting steering wheel and column, TD, TF
9:7 Steering connections and wheel alignment
9:8 Fault diagnosis

9:1 Operating principles

Models **TA**, **TB** and **TC** are fitted with Bishop cam steering gear in conjunction with the beam type axle. The steering box is shown in part section in **FIG 9:1**. A cam, in which a spiral groove is cut, is mounted on the shaft carrying the steering wheel. A peg or follower runs in the cam groove and transmits the movement of the cam to the rocker shaft, the other end of which carries the drop arm. The whole of the mechanism is carried in an oiltight steering box with detachable end and top covers. The cam is mounted in ballbearings which also take the end thrust, shims being fitted under the end cover to allow adjustment for wear in the bearings. The rocker shaft is carried in a plain bush, the thrust on this shaft being taken directly on the top cover plate. Shims are also fitted under this cover to provide adjustment for the meshing of the follower in the cam groove.

The steering box is attached to a bracket bolted to the chassis frame and is mounted with the splined end of the rocker shaft pointing downwards. The drop arm is thus nearly horizontal and moves in an arc to left and right across the car. The steering arms attached to the wheel stub axles extend towards the rear. A transverse drag link connects the drop arm with the steering arm on the opposite wheel, that is to say the lefthand wheel on a righthand drive car. The two steering arms are connected by a single track rod, both drag link and track rod being situated behind the axle beam.

Models **TD** and **TF** are fitted with rack and pinion steering gear in conjunction with independent front suspension. **FIG 9:2** shows the steering gear components in exploded form. The rack housing 1 is attached to the front of the chassis frame by four bolts. The rack 2 slides in the housing and is engaged by the pinion 3 the shaft of which is attached by a flexible coupling to the lower end of the inner steering column 45. Both the rack and the pinion shaft run in plain bearings in the oiltight housing, no adjustment for bearing wear being provided, other than the renewal of worn parts.

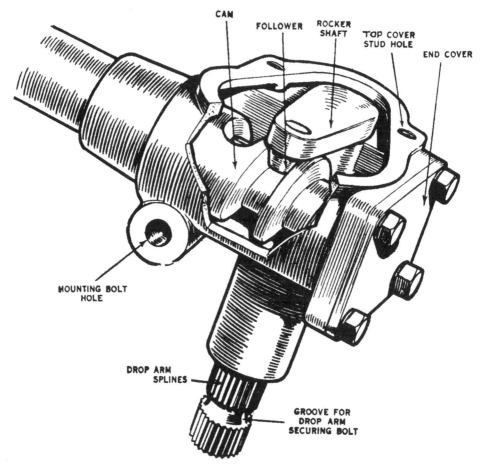

FIG 9:1 Bishop cam steering box, TA, TB, TC

Each end of the rack is connected by a tie rod 16 to the corresponding steering lever attached to the wheel stub axle. The inner ends of the tie rods have adjustable ball joints, while the the outer ball joints are non-adjustable. **FIG 8:3** in the previous Chapter shows the lefthand tie-rod and the method by which the ball joints allow for the up and down movement of the front suspension.

9:2 Routine maintenance and adjustment, TA, TB, TC

Every 3000 miles the steering box should be replenished with oil. A suitable grade is SAE.140.EP and an oil-gun nipple is provided on the box for the purpose. The only adjustment likely to be necessary is to take up play which may have developed between the follower on the rocker shaft and the cam groove, which are shown in **FIG 9:1**. This play will have the effect of lost motion between the steering wheel and the drop arm. It can be taken up by the removal of one or more shims from the top cover and the work can be carried out without removing the steering box from the car. The cam track is slightly relieved from the centre towards each end, and adjustment must be made so that there is no play when the wheels are in the straight-ahead position. On the other hand no stiffness must be evident in this position. The shims under the top cover are of varying thicknesses so that a very fine adjustment is possible. Adjustment should be carried out with the drag link disconnected from the drop arm and before refilling the steering box with oil.

9:3 Removing, dismantling and refitting steering, TA, TB, TC.

The steering column and steering box are removed as an assembly as follows:

1 Remove the drop arm from the rocker shaft, ensuring that the two parts are marked so that the arm can be refitted in the same position relative to the splined rocker shaft. On the type of rocker shaft illustrated in **FIG 9:1**, the arm is secured by a bolt passing through the arm and locating in a groove in the shaft. After removing the bolt, no difficulty should be experienced in withdrawing the arm from the splines. Earlier cars have a rocker shaft which is threaded at the end, the arm being held in place by a nut secured by a split pin. After removal of the nut, a drawer may be necessary to

pull the arm off the splines. If a suitable tool is not available, remove the top cover from the steering box and tap the rocker shaft upwards out of the arm.

2 Withdraw the steering wheel by slackening the pinch bolt which secures it to the column.

3 Remove the baffle board after undoing the screws that hold it in position. Remove the bolts securing the metal foot ramp.

4 Disconnect the steering column support bracket under the scuttle. Remove the bolts holding the steering column bracket to the frame and withdraw the column complete with bracket from the car.

5 To dismantle the steering box, remove the top cover, noting the number of shims fitted. Withdraw the rocker shaft.

6 The cam and mainshaft are mounted on ballbearings which take the thrust from the rocker shaft, and shims of various thicknesses are fitted under the end cover so that the cam can be adjusted for end play. It should not normally be necessary to alter this adjustment, but if the steering box is further dismantled for cleaning or inspection, note the number of shims fitted. On reassembly the shaft should spin freely but there must be no end play.

Reassembly and refitting are carried out in the reverse order from dismantling. Instructions for adjustment of the meshing of the follower with the cam groove have been given in the previous Section. The only difficulty which may arise is in refitting or renewing a drop arm where marks are not available to show the correct position in relation to the rocker shaft. In such cases, after fitting the steering column and steering box assembly and securing the steering wheel, proceed as follows:

1 Attach the end of the drop arm to the drag link, but at this stage do not fit the drop arm on its shaft. Jack up the front wheels and set them in the straight ahead position.

2 Rotate the steering wheel slowly. It will be found that its travel is limited in each direction by internal stops in the steering box. Count the number of turns needed to turn the steering wheel from one end of its travel to the other. Divide this figure by two and thus set the wheel in its central position.

3 Fit the drop arm to the rocker shaft, but do not finally tighten the securing nut until the following check has been carried out:

4 With the front wheels still jacked up, turn the steering wheel to its limit in one direction. With the steering wheel and the front wheels in this position, remove the drop arm from the shaft. It should now be possible to turn the steering wheel a little further, indicating that it is the lock stop on the axle which is limiting the travel. Repeat the procedure on the opposite lock. If free movement of the steering wheel is obtained on both left and right locks, the adjustment is in order and the drop arm should be finally secured to the rocker shaft.

5 If on disconnecting the drop arm further movement of the steering wheel is not available it indicates that the axle lock stops are not coming into action and further adjustments must be made as follows:

6 If movement of the steering wheel is available on one lock but not on the other, fitting the drop arm on to the next spline may effect a cure.

7 If no position of the drop arm on the splines will give free movement of the steering wheel at both locks, the axle lock stops must be adjusted accordingly. The amount of free movement of the steering wheel should be the same on both locks.

9:4 Routine maintenance, TD, TF

FIG 9:3 shows the position of the lubrication nipple for the rack and pinion steering gear. Every 12,000 miles this should be lubricated using one of the special hypoid gear oils recommended for the gearbox and hypoid rear axle of this model. Ten strokes of the hand operated gun supplied in the toolkit will be sufficient. There is also one grease nipple on each of the two outer steering ball joints. These will be lubricated with grease when servicing the other chassis lubrication points every 500 miles. The inner ball joints of the tie rods are enclosed in the steering box and receive oil from the rack. The rubber boots or seals, item 28 in FIG 9:2 should be examined periodically. If perished or damaged they should be renewed at the earliest opportunity. To renew the seals it is not necessary to remove the steering box from the car, but the outer ends of the tie rods 16 will have to be detached from the steering levers. The ball joints 23 are next unscrewed from the tie rods, noting their exact position for reassembly. If the rubber boots have been defective for a considerable time, it is in any case advisable to dismantle the steering box for inspection.

Felt bushes 43 and 44 in FIG 9:2 are fitted to the steering column. These are impregnated with oil and graphite and no lubrication should be necessary, but if after long periods a dry squeak develops, this may be cured by a small application of oil.

9:5 Removing, dismantling and refitting steering, TD, TF

1 Raise the front of the car and support it under the chassis. Remove the front wheels. Referring to FIG 9:2, disconnect the two outer ball joints 23 from the steering levers. Detach any electric cables from the steering box.

2 Unscrew the outer ball joint on the same side of the car as the steering column, taking care not to alter the position of its locknut 17.

3 Undo the engine steady rod and remove its mounting bracket from the chassis.

4 Remove the three bolts 47 from the steering column coupling. Detach the steering box from the chassis frame by removing the four bolts and nuts.

5 Slide the unit to one side until the tie rod from which the outer ball joint has been removed can be withdrawn through the large hole in the chassis front extension. The whole steering box unit can then be lifted away to the front.

Before dismantling the steering gearbox it should be noted that while a visual examination of its components can be made for damage or scoring, measurement of wear involves dimensions having a tolerance of .0005 inch for which vernier micrometers will be necessary. These dimensions will be found in the Technical Data Section of the Appendix. Adjustment of the inner ball joints and of the steering damper assembly, however, are carried out by means of shims, the latter adjustment

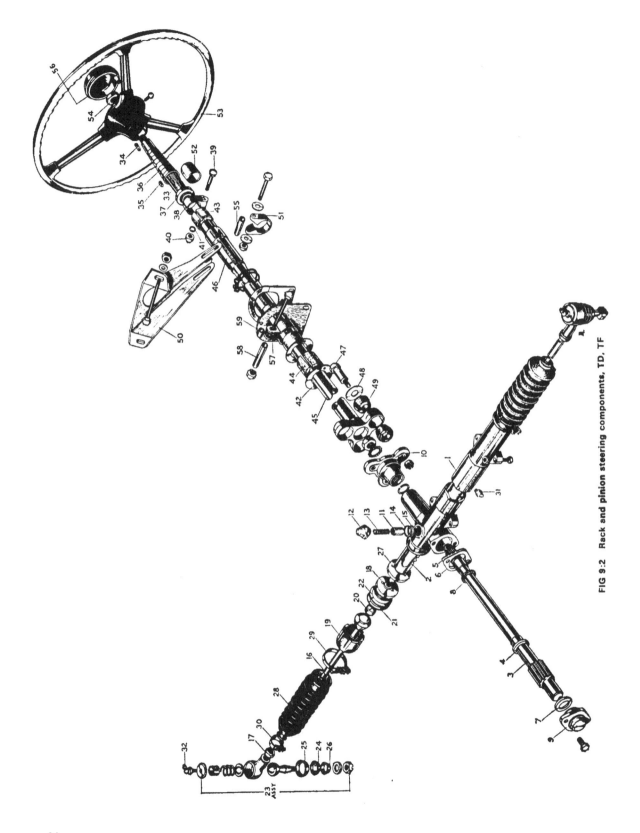

FIG 9:2 Rack and pinion steering components, TD, TF

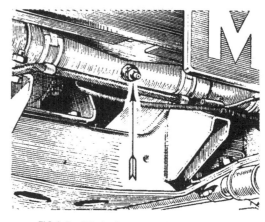

FIG 9:3   Oil nipple, rack and pinion steering

being possible with the steering in position on the car. To dismantle the steering box proceed as follows:

1 Referring to **FIG 9:2**, undo the clips 29 and 30 and remove the rubber boots 28.
2 Unscrew the damper housing cap 12 and remove the damper spring 13. The damper pad 11 can then be removed. A number of shims 14 and 15 will be found under the cap. These should be retained. The damper assembly is shown in detail in **FIG 9:4**.
3 Referring again to **FIG 9:2**, remove the bolts securing the pinion tail bearing 9 and remove the bearing. Remove the nut from the other end of the pinion shaft and remove the coupling flange 10. Remove the circlip behind the flange.
4 Withdraw the pinion shaft 3 by holding the steering box with the pinion upwards and leaving the thrust washer 4 behind, this washer being trapped behind the rack teeth.
5 Hold the rack bar 2 in a vice, knock back the lock washers and unscrew the ball joint cap 19, using the special C-spanner 18.G.311. The ball seat 20 and shims should now drop out. Next screw out the ball seat housing 18, using the special peg spanner 18.G.315 If the ball seat cap comes away complete

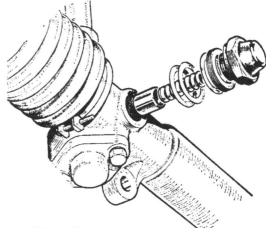

FIG 9:4   Rack and pinion steering gear damper

Key to FIG 9:2
1 Rack housing—steering 2 Rack—steering 3 Pinion—steering 4 Thrust washer—top—pinion 5 Shim (.005 inch thick)—pinion 6 Shim (.007 inch thick)—tail bearing
7 Thrust washer—bottom—pinion 8 Seal—pinion 9 Tail bearing—pinion 10 Flange—pinion 11 Tie-rod 12 Housing cap—damper pad 13 Spring—damper pad
14 Shim (.003 inch)—damper pad housing 15 Shim (.020 inch)—damper pad housing 16 Tie-rod 17 Locknut for tie-rod 18 Ball seat housing 19 Ball joint cap
20 Ball seat 21 Shim—ball seat adjuster (.005 inch) 22 Shim—ball seat adjuster (.003 inch) 23 Ball socket assembly—outer 24 Cap—inner—grease retaining
25 Cap—outer—grease retaining 26 Pressure ring—for caps 27 Lock washer—ball seat housing 28 Rubber boot—ball joint 29 Clip—large 30 Clip—small
31 Grease nipple ($\frac{1}{8}$ inch straight)—rack housing 32 Grease nipple ($\frac{1}{8}$ inch × 90°)—steering arm 33 Telescopic extension 34 Key—steering wheel 35 Key—connector
36 Spring cover 37 Cover cup 38 Clamp—steering column 39 Bolt—clamp 40 Nut—clamp bolt 41 Washer—clamp bolt 42 Plate—bottom bush 43 Bush—top
44 Bush—bottom 45 Inner column—welded—complete 46 Outer column 47 Bolt—column flange to box flange 48 Washer—column flange bolt 49 Rubber bearing—column
50 Support bracket—top 51 Clamp—steering column 52 Distance tube—column adjustment 53 Steering wheel 54 Nut—steering wheel
55 Distance-piece—steering column clamp 56 M.G. medallion 57 Clip—steering column steady 58 Distance tube—long 59 Distance tube—short

with the ball seat housing the extractor 18.G.312 will be necessary to separate the parts.

6 Remove the rack bar from its housing.

When reassembling the steering box the following points should be noted:

1 When refitting the pinion shaft ensure that the thrust washers have their chamfered sides towards the pinion. End float should be from .002 to .005 inch. This is controlled by means of the shims which are available in .005 and .007 inch thicknesses.

2 With the rack in the central position, engage the pinion with the arrow uppermost. Refit the coupling with one of the coupling bolts in line with the arrow on the pinion shaft. This will ensure that the steering wheel spokes are in the correct position on the car.

3 Oil all parts on assembly and refill the steering box with $\frac{3}{4}$ pint of the recommended grade of hypoid gear oil as used for the gearbox and rear axle.

The inner steering ball joints are adjusted as follows:

1 Fit the lock washer 27 and shims and screw home the ball seat housing 18 on the rack bar.

2 Insert the ball seat 20.

3 Insert the ball end of the tie rod 16 and screw the ball joint cap 19 against its shoulder. The ball should now be a free rolling fit but without end play. Adjustment is carried out by varying the shims which are supplied in .003 and .005 inch thicknesses.

The rack damper is shown in **FIG 9:4** and as items 11 - 15 in **FIG 9:2**. Its purpose is to ensure the required amount of damping in the steering tie rods and to maintain the minimum of backlash in the rack and pinion teeth. The damper should be adjusted in the following manner:

1 Check the damper spring, which should have a free length of approximately 1.024 inch and should give a load of 80 lb when compressed to .75 inch.

2 When the steering box is completely assembled, fit the damper plunger, spring and cap, but omit the shims. Screw down the cap until the plunger just locks the rack bar in the housing. This can be felt by rotating the pinion shaft or steering wheel if the adjustment is being made with the steering assembled in the car. With feeler gauges measure the gap left under the damper cap.

3 Add .051 inch to this measurement and insert shims equal to the total amount under the cap.

4 This gives the correct standard pre-load. If on testing on the road the damping is found to be too slack or too tight, the added measurement of .051 inch can be decreased to .030 inch or increased to .070 inch respectively.

9:6 Removing and refitting steering wheel and column, TD, TF

Models **TD** and **TF** have a steering column which is adjustable for length to suit the driver. **FIG 9:5** shows the position of the adjusting nut. Slacken off the nut, raise or depress the steering wheel to the required position and securely lock the nut.

If it is required to remove the steering wheel, this is removed complete with the telescopic extension. **FIG 9:6** shows the telescopic extension and its keyways, the steering wheel and spring cover having been removed for clarity of illustration only. Referring again to **FIG 9:2**,

proceed as follows:

1 Remove the clamp nut 40 and clamp bolt 39. Lift the steering wheel to its fullest extent and compress the spring cover 36 upwards against the wheel.

2 This will reveal the connector key 35, which engages in a slot in the steering column 45 and can slide throughout the length of the long keyway cut in the telescopic extension 33. This key prevents the splined extension from being pulled right out of the steering column. Lift the key by sliding a thin strip of metal along the keyway. Withdraw the key and lift out the steering wheel and telescopic extension complete.

3 It will not normally be necessary to separate the steering wheel from the extension, but if this assembly has to be dismantled, remove the 'MG' medallion which is secured by a countersunk screw in the side of the boss, remove the steering wheel nut 54 and pull the steering wheel off the extension using an extractor. The key 34 locates the wheel on the extension. On reassembly tighten the nut 54 to a torque of 500 inch lb.

To remove the steering column on model **TD**:

1 Remove the steering wheel and extension as described in previous operations 1 and 2.

2 Remove the bolt and nut from the support clamp 51 under the dash. Remove the bolt and nut holding the steering column to the body steady bracket, on the engine side of the bulkhead.

3 Remove the three bolts 47 from the steering column universal joint, retaining the rubber inserts. This will enable both inner and outer steering columns to be withdrawn forwards through the space between the radiator and the wing.

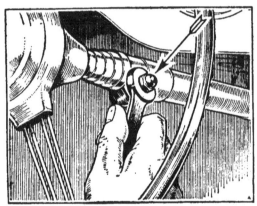

FIG 9:5 Adjustable steering column, TD, TF

To remove the steering column on model **TF**, proceed as for model **TD** but first remove the radiator, also the carburetters and air cleaner(s) on righthand drive cars, or the generator on lefthand drive cars.

Refitting the steering column involves a reversal of the removal instructions. When connecting the universal joint ensure that the bolts 47 are fully tightened against their shoulders.

To renew the steering column felt bushes, remove the steering wheel and extension as described. The top bush 43 in **FIG 9:2** can then be picked out. Coat the new bush with graphite grease on the face which contacts the inner column and feed it into place. Access to the lower bush 44 is obtained by removing the screws from the plate 42.

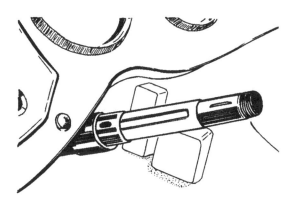

FIG 9:6 Steering column telescopic extension showing keyways

9:7 Steering connections and wheel alignment

On models **TA, TB** and **TC,** adjustable ball joints are fitted at each end of both the track rod and the drag link. These are lubricated every 500 miles by means of the grease nipples provided. To adjust the ball joints the split pin is removed and the slotted end plug screwed up tightly and then released half a turn before fitting a new split pin. If the joints are dismantled for cleaning and inspection, make sure the parts are reassembled in the correct order. In the case of the drag link the order of the parts at the drop arm end is: ball seat, ball, ball seat, spring, plug and split pin. At the outer end the order is: spring, cup, ball, end plug and split pin.

On models **TD** and **TF** the inner tie rod ball joints form part of the rack and pinion steering box assembly and their adjustment has been dealt with in **Section 9:5.** The outer ball joints however are of the non-adjustable type and if worn, the complete ball joint assembly must be renewed. The rubber boots or dust excluders can be

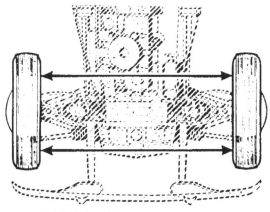

FIG 9:7 Checking front wheel alignment

renewed separately. Each of the outer ball joints is provided with a grease nipple for lubrication at 500 mile intervals.

Commencing at chassis Nos.TF4910(LH) and TF4760(RH) modified steering ball end assemblies are fitted incorporating 'Unified' threads for the ball pin nut and for the grease nipple. The threaded bore for the steering tie rod, however, remains a BSF thread, so that the new assembly may be fitted in place of the old.

FIG 9:7 illustrates the alignment of the front wheels. If the front measurement is less than that at the rear of the front wheels when in the straight ahead position, they are said to have toe-in. In practice the alignment is measured as follows:

1 Ensure that the car is on a level floor and that the tyres are correctly inflated.
2 Set the front wheels in the straight ahead position.
3 Using a suitable trammel gauge, measure the width of track at the rear of the front rims at wheel centre height. Mark the tyre with chalk at this point.
4 Push the car forward one half turn of the wheels and take the front reading at the point already marked on the tyre.
5 Subtract the front measurement from the rear measurement to obtain the amount of toe-in. This should be:

Models TA, TB . . . . . . $\frac{1}{2}$ inch.
Model TC . . . . $\frac{1}{16}$ to $\frac{1}{4}$ inch.
Models TD, TF . . . . . Nil (i.e., front wheels parallel).

The checking of both steering and suspension geometry can be carried out more accurately by a service agent using specialized measuring equipment.

On models **TA, TB** and **TC** the toe-in is adjusted by lengthening or shortening the track rod. The track rod ends have right and lefthand threads. Slacken the clamp bolt at each end of the track rod and rotate the rod until the necessary adjustment is obtained. **Ensure that both ball joints are in the same plane and tighten the clamp bolts securely.**

On models **TD** and **TF,** slacken the locknut at the outer end of each of the two tie rods. Both rods have righthand threads and are adjusted by rotating them using a spanner on the flats provided. It is essential that the two rods should be adjusted to the same length. Turn each rod by an equal amount and check their lengths by measuring the distance from the ends of the flats to the locknuts. Tighten the locknuts securely when the adjustment is complete.

9:8 Fault diagnosis

(a) Wheel wobble
1 Unbalanced wheels and tyres
2 Slack steering connections
3 Incorrect steering geometry
4 Excessive play in steering gear
5 Broken or weak front springs
6 Worn hub bearings

(b) Wander
1 Check 2, 3, 4 in (a)
2 Front suspension and rear axle mounting points out of line
3 Uneven tyre pressures

4 Uneven tyre wear
5 Weak dampers or springs

(c) Heavy steering
1 Check 3 in (a)
2 Very low tyre pressures
3 Neglected lubrication
4 Wheels out of track
5 Steering gear maladjusted

6 Steering column bent or misaligned
7 Steering column bushes tight

(d) Lost motion
1 End play in steering column
2 Loose steering wheel, worn splines or keyway
3 Worn or incorrectly adjusted steering box
4 Worn ball joints
5 Worn suspension system

CHAPTER 10

BRAKES, WHEELS AND TYRES

10:1   Description of brake layout
10:2   Routine maintenance, brake shoe adjust-
         ment
10:3   Removing master cylinder
10:4   Dismantling brakes, note about flexible
         hoses
10:5   General instructions on servicing hydrau-
         lic internals
10:6   Dismantling and servicing master and
         wheel cylinders

10:7   Reassembly, brake shoe linings
10:8   Bleeding
10:9   Pedal clearance
10:10   Handbrake adjustment
10:11   Modifications
10:12   The Dunlop Centre Lock Wheel
10:13   Rebuilding and trueing wire wheels
10:14   Removing and refitting disc wheels
10:15   Tyre fitting and wheel balancing
10:16   Fault diagnosis

10:1 Description of brake layout

All models in this series are fitted with Lockheed 9 inch hydraulic brakes on all four wheels. The hydraulic operating system comprises a combined fluid supply tank and master cylinder in which the hydraulic pressure is generated, and wheel cylinders which operate the brake shoes. Copper or steel pipe lines with unions and flexible hoses convey the hydraulic pressure from the master cylinder to each wheel cylinder.

On models **TA, TB** and **TC** the layout of the pipe lines is as shown in **FIG 10:1**. Each of the four brakes has a single fixed wheel cylinder with two opposed pistons operating the leading and trailing shoes as shown in **FIG 10:2**, with a snail-cam adjuster for each shoe.

On models **TD** and **TF,** which have independent front suspension, the layout of the pipe lines is somewhat different, as will be seen in **FIG 10:3**. The front brakes are of the two leading shoe type, each shoe being operated by a fixed wheel cylinder with a single piston, as shown in **FIG 10:4**. An adjuster, indicated by arrow in the illustration, is provided for each shoe. The rear brakes on these models are of the leading and trailing shoe type in order to provide sufficient braking power in reverse. Each rear brake has a single wheel cylinder with a single piston, mounted between the two shoes as shown in **FIG 10:5**. The cylinder is not rigidly attached to the brake backplate but is free to float so that cylinder and piston apply equal pressure to the two shoes. A single adjuster, indicated by an arrow in the illustration, is provided for the adjustment of the two shoes.

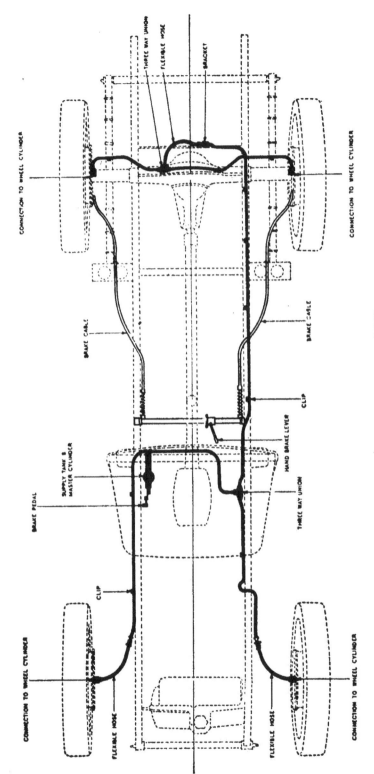

FIG 10:1 Brake layout, model TC

10:2 Routine maintenance, brake shoe adjustment

Every 1000 miles, or monthly if the car is covering smaller mileages, the fluid level in the supply tank attached to the master cylinder should be checked. This will be found under the floorboards just behind the brake pedal. On models **TA**, **TB** and **TC** the barrel type supply tank has a filler cap which can be unscrewed by hand. On models **TD** and **TF** a small inspection cover in the floorboard gives access to the hexagonal filler plug 21 in **FIG 10:3**. In either case, carefully clean around the filler before removal, to avoid the possibility of dirt entering the system. Ensure that the vent hole in the filler cap or plug is clear. The fluid should be maintained at a level 1 inch below the filler cap on models **TA**, **TB** and **TC** and $\frac{1}{4}$ inch below the filler plug on models **TD** and **TF** as shown in **FIG 10:8**. These levels should not be exceeded in order to allow for expansion of the fluid when warm. On the other hand, if the level is allowed to drop air may be drawn into the hydraulic system.

It is essential to use only the genuine Lockheed Brake Fluid, for two reasons. Firstly, the fluid must be of the correct consistency to suit the system, and secondly its composition must be such that it is not detrimental to the type of seals used. Vessels used for hydraulic fluid must be scrupulously clean and must not have been used for petrol, mineral oils or cleaning fluids, all of which are injurious to the seals and flexible hoses. If very frequent topping up is found necessary, the hydraulic system should be examined for leaks.

The brakes should be adjusted periodically to compensate for wear in the brake linings, which will allow excessive travel in the pedal before the brakes function. Adjustment is provided for bringing the brake shoes closer to the drums. On models **TA**, **TB** and **TC** each brake has two snail cam adjusters as shown in **FIG 10:2**.

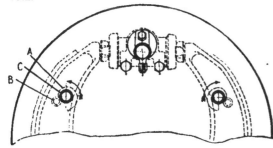

FIG 10:2 Brake shoe adjustments, model TC

All four brakes should be adjusted as follows:

1 Jack up the wheel, scotching two of the other wheels as a precaution against moving the car. In the case of the rear brakes, the handbrake must be off.
2 The two adjusting nuts C in **FIG 10:2** will be found at the back of the brake backplate. Turn the nut in the direction of the arrow until the cam A pressing on the peg B brings the shoe into contact with the drum and locks the wheel.
3 Slacken the nut just sufficiently to free the wheel. Note that one complete turn of the nut is sufficient to take up all lining wear, so that only a partial turn will be needed for adjustment.

4 Adjust the other shoe, noting that the nut rotates in the opposite direction. Adjust the other three brakes in the same manner.

To adjust the brakes on models **TD** and **TF**, proceed as follows:

1 Jack up a front wheel, scotching the others as a precaution. Remove the wheel and rotate the brake drum until the two adjusters can be reached through the holes provided in the drum as shown in **FIG 10:6**. The position of the adjusters can be seen in **FIG 10:4**.
2 With a screwdriver turn both adjustment screws as far as they will go in a clockwise direction until the drum is locked solid, then turn them in an anticlockwise direction one notch only. The brake drum should then be free to rotate without the shoes rubbing and the adjustment on this wheel is complete.
3 Adjust the other front brake in the same manner.
4 In the case of the rear brakes, each has only a single adjuster as shown in **FIG 10:5**. Ensure that the handbrake is in the off position when adjusting the rear brakes.

10:3 Removing master cylinder

On models **TA**, **TB** and **TC**, drain the supply tank by disconnecting the pipe connection at the master cylinder and depressing the brake pedal slowly by hand. Allow the expelled fluid to flow into a clean container until the tank is empty. Detach the pushrod from the brake pedal, remove the nut securing the master cylinder to the chassis and withdraw the cylinder.

On models **TD** and **TF**, remove the floorboard and disconnect the union nut connecting the pipe line to the master cylinder. Remove the two nuts and bolts securing the master cylinder to the chassis frame. Disconnect the brake pedal return spring from the frame. Lift out the brake pedal with pushrod, rubber boot and pedal return spring. The master cylinder complete with main supply pipe is then removed.

Refitting of the master cylinder is a reversal of the removal procedure in all cases, but after fitting it will be necessary to bleed the hydraulic system as will be described in **Section 10:8**.

10:4 Dismantling brakes, note about flexible hoses

To remove the brake shoes on models **TA**, **TB** and **TC**:

1 Remove the wheel and brake drum.
2 Unhook the brake shoe pull-off spring and remove the split pins and washers on the shoe steady pins protruding through the webs of the shoes. Remove the horseshoe circlip retaining the shoes on the anchor pin.
3 In the case of rear brakes, unhook the handbrake cable from the lever behind the brake shoe.
4 The shoes are now free and can be withdrawn from the anchor pin.
5 Precautions should be taken to prevent the brake pedal being depressed when the shoes have been removed, as the pistons may be forced out of the wheel cylinders and air drawn into the system. It is a common practice to secure the pistons by means of rubber bands or wire to prevent this happening.

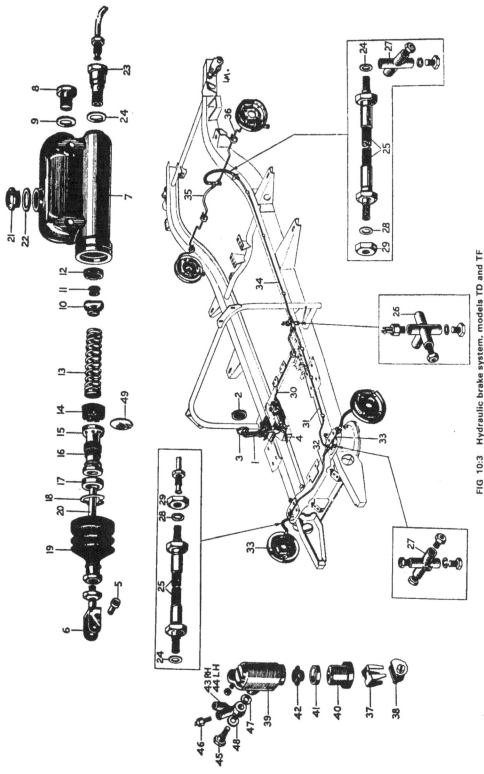

FIG 10:3   Hydraulic brake system, models TD and TF

Key to FIG 10:3

1 Brake pedal and bush   2 Brake pedal rubber pad   3 Brake pedal pad   4 Brake pedal return spring
5 Brake pedal pin   6 Master cylinder fork end   7 Master cylinder and tank assembly   8 Drain plug   9 Drain plug gasket
10 Valve assembly   11 Valve cup   12 Valve washer   13 Piston return spring (with retainer)   14 Piston cup
15 Master cylinder piston   16 Piston secondary cup   17 Piston stop   18 Circlip   19 Master cylinder boot
20 Master cylinder push-rod   21 Filler plug assembly   22 Filler plug gasket   23 Master cylinder adaptor   24 Master cylinder gasket
25 Hose assembly   26 Four-way piece   27 Three-way piece   28 Lock washer   29 Hose locknut   30 Pipe (master cylinder to 4-way)
31 Pipe (4-way to 3-way)   32 Pipe (front 3-way to RH front hose pipe)   33 Pipe (front 3-way to front hose)   34 Pipe (4-way to rear hose)
35 Pipe (axle hose bracket to LH rear)   36 Pipe (axle hose bracket to RH rear)   37 Shoe adjuster mask   38 Brake-shoe adjuster
39 Body with studs and abutment   40 Piston and dust cover assembly   41 Piston cup   42 Cup filler   43 Banjo connection, forward RH
44 Banjo connection, forward LH   45 Bolt   46 Bleeder screw   47 Banjo bolt gasket, small   48 Banjo bolt gasket, large   49 Washer

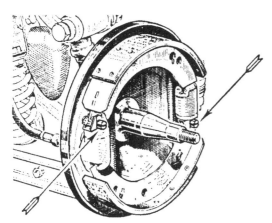

FIG 10:4 Front brake shoes showing adjusters, TD, TF

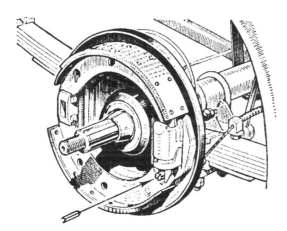

FIG 10:5 Rear brake shoe with single adjuster, TD, TF

FIG 10:6 Method of brake shoe adjustment, TD, TF

To remove the brake shoes on models **TD** and **TF**:

1 Remove the wheel. Remove the hub and brake drum. Detailed instructions will be found in **Sections 7:7** and **8:5**.

2 Draw the brake shoes apart until they can be removed from the brake backplate.

3 Observe the same precautions against pistons being forced out of cylinders as described for models **TA**, **TB** and **TC**.

Before describing the removal of wheel cylinders it will be convenient at this stage to describe the general method of disconnecting flexible hoses on hydraulic systems. The hose must on no account be disconnected from the brake backplate until it has been released at the union with the copper or steel pipeline at its inner end. **FIG 10:7** shows a type of fitting which is common to all models. First unscrew the union 1 on the metal pipeline. Hold the hexagon on the flexible hose and unscrew the locknut 2 which secures the hose to its mounting bracket. With its inner end now free, the hose can be unscrewed from its outer end on the brake backplate. Always refit in the reverse order.

To remove the wheel cylinders on models **TA**, **TB** and **TC**:

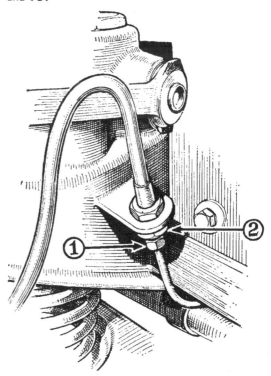

FIG 10:7 Inner end of flexible hose showing union nuts
Key to FIG 10:7   1 Union nut   2 Locknut

1 Remove the brake shoes as described.

2 In the case of front brakes, disconnect the inner ends of the flexible hoses. Unhook the brake shoe return spring. Remove the two screws holding the cylinder to the backplate and withdraw the cylinder complete with flexible hose.

3 In the case of rear brakes, the procedure is similar except that the copper tubing must be disconnected from the backplate.

To remove the wheel cylinders on models **TD** and **TF**:

1 Remove the brake shoes as described.
2 To remove the front brake cylinders, disconnect the flexible hoses at their inner ends, then referring to **FIG 10:3** remove the union bolt 45 from the wheel cylinder. Note that the copper washers 47 and 48 on either side of the banjo union 43/44 are of different sizes, the smaller of the two being next to the cylinder. Remove the two $\frac{1}{4}$ inch nuts securing the cylinder and remove the cylinder from the backplate. The other cylinder is removed in the same manner.
3 To remove the rear brake cylinders, release the metal feed pipe from the cylinder by undoing the $\frac{7}{16}$ inch union nut. Remove the $\frac{7}{16}$ inch adaptor securing the bleed screw banjo union to the wheel cylinder, observing that the smaller of the two copper washers is next to the cylinder. Remove the clevis pin from the handbrake cable yoke and disconnect the cable from the wheel cylinder lever. Remove the rubber boot and withdraw the lower half of the piston from the wheel cylinder. Extract the cylinder from the backplate.

10:5 General instructions on servicing hydraulic internals

Before describing the dismantling of the various hydraulic components, a few general points will be mentioned here. Leakage past the pistons in master and wheel cylinders is prevented by rubber seals. These have a raised lip which presses firmly against the polished cylinder bore. As the lip faces fluid pressure, the greater the pressure the stronger the seal. From this it will be appreciated that the seals and bores must be in perfect condition and also spotlessly clean. To ensure this, it is essential to remove all outside dirt before dismantling any hydraulic parts. After dismantling, wash the rubber parts in clean brake fluid and no other liquid. If metal parts are washed in solvent liquids such as petrol, all traces must be dried off before reassembling.

It is advisable to renew all seals, especially if there has been leakage. To avoid damage, remove and refit the seals with the fingers. Start reassembly by lubricating all parts with the correct brake fluid and assemble wet. When refitting the rubber seals in the cylinder bores, enter the raised lip first and make sure that it is not trapped or turned back on itself.

FIG 10:8 Part-sectioned view of master cylinder, TD, TF

10:6 Dismantling and servicing master and wheel cylinders

The combination barrel type master cylinder fitted to models **TA**, **TB** and **TC** differs only in constructional detail from the later type fitted to models **TD** and **TF**. A description of the latter will therefore suffice to cover all models. **FIG 10:8** shows the master cylinder in section. **FIG 10:3** includes an exploded view of the cylinder with numbered items.

Within the master cylinder 7 is the piston 15 with the cup 14, normally held in the off position by the spring 13. Immediately in front of the cup when in this position is a bypass port connecting the cylinder with the supply tank. This compensates for any temperature changes by allowing fluid to flow into the tank when it expands or to be supplemented by fluid flowing from the tank when it cools and contracts, thus maintaining a constant volume of fluid in the system. Brake pedal pressure is applied to the piston by means of the pushrod 20. This is adjustable and must have a slight clearance, corresponding to $\frac{1}{8}$ inch free movement at the pedal pad, when the system is at rest. Without this clearance, the piston will not return to contact the stop 17 and the piston cup will cover the bypass port, causing pressure to build up within the system and producing binding brakes on all wheels. The reduced skirt of the piston forms an annular space which is filled with fluid from the supply tank by way of the feed hole. Leakage of fluid from the open end of the cylinder is prevented by the secondary cup 16 fitted to the flange end of the piston. The combination inlet and outlet valve 10 in the cylinder is provided to allow the passage of fluid under pressure into the pipelines and to control its return into the cylinder so that a small pressure of approximately 8 lb/sq inch is maintained in the pipelines to ensure that the cups of the wheel cylinders are kept expanded. It also prevents fluid pumped out from the cylinder when bleeding the system from returning to the cylinder, thus ensuring that a fresh charge is pumped out at each stroke of the pedal.

On releasing the brake pedal after application, the piston is returned quickly to its stop by the return spring, thus creating a vacuum in the cylinder. This vacuum causes the main cup to collapse and pass fluid through the small holes in the piston head from the annular space provided by the piston skirt. This additional fluid finds its way back to the reserve supply under the action of the brake return springs, when the system finally comes to rest, through the outlet valve and compensating orifice.

To dismantle the master cylinder on models **TA**, **TB** and **TC**, remove the rubber boot and pushrod, the piston retaining spring clip and washer and withdraw the piston from the panel. Remove the cup, spring and valve. To remove the secondary cup from the piston, carefully stretch it over the end flange, using the fingers only.

On models **TD** and **TF**, remove the main feed pipe, union and copper washers, push the piston down the cylinder bore and remove the circlip. Remove the piston, piston cup, return spring, valve assembly and valve seating washer. To remove the secondary cup from the piston, carefully stretch it over the end flange, using the fingers only.

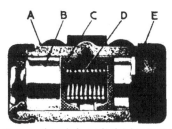

FIG 10:9 Part-sectioned view of wheel cylinder, model TC
Key to FIG 10:9   A—Cylinder   B—Piston   C—Rubber cap
D—Spring   E—Rubber boot

On models **TA, TB** and **TC** each brake has a single fixed wheel cylinder with opposed pistons as shown in part section in **FIG 10:9**. To dismantle, remove the rubber boots E, and withdraw the pistons B, rubber cups C and the spring D together with the cup fillers.

FIG 10:10 shows the front and rear wheel cylinders as fitted to models **TD** and **TF**. To dismantle the front wheel cylinders, of which there are two for each brake, withdraw the piston, piston cup and cup filler. In the case of the single rear wheel cylinders, first tap out the handbrake lever pivot pin and withdraw the lever. Withdraw the upper half of the piston, the piston cup and the cup filler. On later models the centre of the cup filler has a spigot which engages a spiral spring.

Examine all master cylinder and wheel cylinder components for wear or distortion. The fitting of new cups and seals is advised in any case and these are supplied as sets. If the cylinder bores are scored, however, leakage past the pistons will not be cured by the fitting of new cups, and a service replacement unit should be fitted. It should also be noted that perished cups and seals usually indicate the presence of mineral oil or other contamination in the fluid, and in such cases the whole of the system must be flushed out with brake fluid. Brake hoses will also be suspect as they may have been contaminated in the same way.

10:7 Reassembly, brake shoe linings

Reassemble the master cylinder as follows:
1 Clean all parts thoroughly with Lockheed Brake fluid. All traces of petrol, paraffin or solvents used for cleaning metal parts must be removed before assembly. Dip all the internal parts in brake fluid and assemble them wet.
2 Referring to **FIG 10:3**, stretch the secondary cup 16 over the end flange of the piston 15 with the lip of the cup facing towards the opposite end of the piston. When the cup is in its groove, work it round gently with the fingers to ensure it is correctly seated.
3 Fit the valve 10, valve cup 11 and washer 12 on the return spring 13 and insert the spring valve first into the cylinder 7. See that the spring retainer is in position.
4 Insert the piston cup 14, lip first, taking care not to damage or turn back the lip and press it down on to the spring retainer.
5 Place the dished washer 49 on the end of the piston cup, **with its concave face in contact with the cup.** It is essential that this washer should be fitted in all cases.
6 Insert the piston, taking care not to damage or turn back the lip of the secondary cup. Push the piston down the bore slightly and insert the circlip 18 in its groove in the bore.
7 Test the master cylinder by filling the tank and pushing the piston down the bore and allowing it to return. After one or two strokes fluid should flow from the outlet.
8 Refitting of the master cylinder is a reversal of the removal procedure described in **Section 10:3**. Ensure that there is sufficient clearance in the pushrod to provide approximately $\frac{1}{2}$ inch free travel at the brake pedal pad. When the hydraulic system has been assembled bleed the brakes as described in **Section 10:8**.

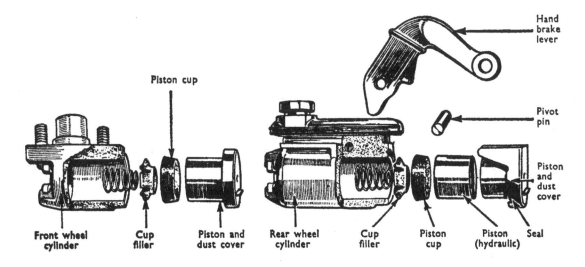

FIG 10:10   Front and rear wheel cylinder components, TD, TF

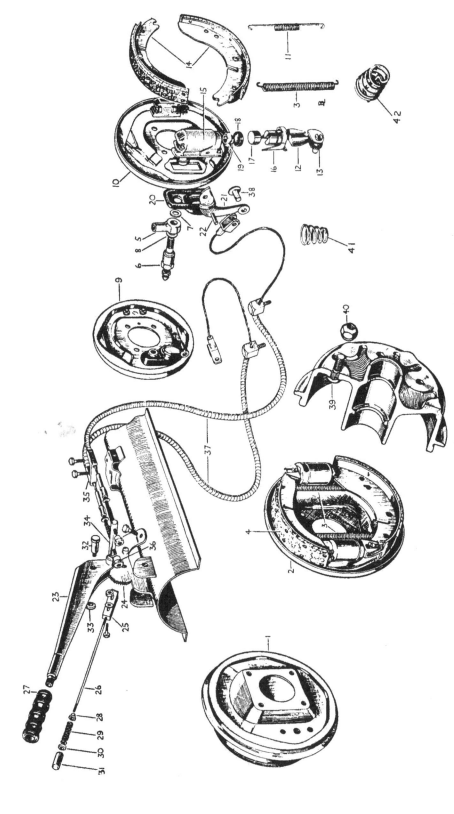

FIG 10:11 Handbrake and brakeshoe components TD, TF

Key to FIG 10:11
1 Brake gear (front axle) back plate assembly, RH   2 Brake gear (front axle) back plate assembly, LH
3 Shoe pull-off spring   4 Front brake-shoe—lined complete   5 Banjo connections   6 Bolt   7 Banjo bolt gasket, small
8 Banjo bolt gasket, large   9 Brake gear (rear axle) back plate assembly, RH   10 Brake gear (rear axle) back plate assembly, LH
11 Shoe tension spring   12 Shoe adjuster mask   13 Brake shoe adjuster   14 Rear brake shoe—lined complete
15 Body and abutment strip   16 Piston and dust cover   17 Piston (hydraulic)   18 Piston cup   19 Cup filler   20 Wheel cylinder boot
21 Hand brake lever   22 Pivot pin, hand brake lever   23 Lever assembly   24 Ratchet assembly   25 Hand brake pawl
26 Hand brake pawl rod   27 Hand grip   28 Bush for rod   29 Spring, lever knob   30 Spring washer   31 Pawl rod knob
32 Fulcrum pin   33 Fulcrum pin washer   34 Hand brake trunnion   35 Twin cable abutment   36 Brake cable adjuster nut
37 Hand brake cable   38 Clevis pin   39 Wheel stud   40 Wheel nut   41 Spring, wheel cylinder piston   42 Spring, brake shoe steady

To assemble the wheel cylinders on models **TA**, **TB** and **TC**:

1 Dip all parts in Lockheed brake fluid and assemble wet.
2 Referring to **FIG 10:9** insert one piston, flat face first, and insert one rubber cup, also flat face first but from the opposite end of the cylinder.
3 Insert the spring complete with cup fillers. Insert the second cup, lip first, taking care not to damage or turn back the lip. Insert the second piston, flat face first and press down on to the rubber cup.
4 Fit the rubber boots into the groove on the ends of the pistons and then over the ends of the cylinders.

To assemble the wheel cylinders on models **TD** and **TF**:

1 Dip all parts in Lockheed Brake Fluid and assemble wet.
2 Referring to **FIGS 10:10** and **10:11** place the spring 41 with its small end engaging in the spigot of the cup filler 19, on which it should be a push fit.
3 Insert the cup filler, **shallow side and spring first,** and the rubber cup 18 concave side first.
4 Refit the piston 17 and in the case of the rear brake cylinders, insert the hand brake lever 21 and its pivot pin 22.

Refitting of wheel cylinders on models **TA**, **TB** and **TC** is a reversal of the removal procedure. On models **TD** and **TF**, however, the following points should be noted:

The front brake wheel cylinders are interchangeable, but the link pipe banjo unions must be fitted so that the flexible hose is connected to the forward cylinder and the bleed screw to the rear cylinder. The front brake shoes are interchangeable but the recessed ends must engage the adjusters and **the pull-off springs must be fitted between the shoes and backplates** as shown in **FIG 10:4**. The rear wheel cylinder must be fitted on the forward side of the axle casing with the bleed screw vertical. The shoes are interchangeable, but the recessed end of the lower or leading shoe must engage the adjuster. The other shoe is also fitted with its recessed end against the wheel cylinder. The light brake shoe pull-off spring is fitted away from the wheel cylinder and both springs are fitted between the shoes and the backplate as shown in **FIG 10:5**. On completing assembly of the hydraulic system, the brakes must be bled as described in **Section 10:8** and the shoes adjusted as detailed in **Section 10:2**.

If brake shoe linings are worn the brakes must be relined. Owing to variations in driving conditions no hard and fast mileage can be stated for this service, but the rivets are recessed well below the surface of the lining material. If the latter shows signs that it is wearing down anywhere near the rivet heads it is essential to reline. Scored linings will indicate a scored brake drum which will have to be refaced or renewed. Oil-soaked linings will cause considerable unevenness in braking and must be renewed. At the same time the source of contamination, such as a defective hub oil-seal, must be traced and rectified.

Relined brake shoes are available on an exchange basis and should always be used in preference to attempting to reline the existing shoes. Exchange shoes

and linings are carefully checked by the manufacturers for concentricity and are ready for fitting to the car. When the brakes are relined the shoe adjustment must be slackened completely before fitting the brake drums, and then adjusted as described in **Section 10:2**. Re-adjustment will become necessary after a small mileage to allow the linings to bed down. **It is important to avoid contamination of the linings by oil or grease.**

10:8 Bleeding

This operation is necessary if any of the hydraulic pipelines or unions have been disconnected, or if the level of fluid in the supply tank has fallen so low that air has entered the system. The presence of air is usually indicated by a 'spongy' feeling of the brake pedal and loss of braking power. After dismantling the complete system, more than one tankful of fluid may be needed, so that sufficient fluid must be at hand to keep the supply tank topped up throughout the process. The services of an assistant will also be needed.

1 With every hydraulic connection secure and the supply tank topped up with Lockheed Brake Fluid, start with the brake with the longest pipeline from the master cylinder. On models **TA** and **TB**, remove the set screw from the end of the bleeder screw and screw in the bleeder drain tube, which is a screwed brass nipple fitted with a rubber tube. On models **TC**, **TD** and **TF**, remove the rubber cover from the wheel cylinder bleeder screw (46 in **FIG 10:3**), or if the cover is missing thoroughly clean the outside of the screw. Attach the bleeder tube, allowing the free end to be immersed in a small quantity of fluid in a clean jar.
2 Unscrew the bleed nipple one turn. Depress the brake pedal slowly through a complete stroke. Fluid and air bubbles will be seen coming out of the tube in the jar, Continue the slow steady strokes, pausing when the pedal is right back to allow the master cylinder to fill. When fluid without a trace of air bubbles is seen to emerge into the jar, tighten the bleed screw while the pedal is held at the bottom of a stroke.
3 The supply tank must be kept topped up throughout the series of operations, otherwise air will be drawn into the system and a fresh start will have to be made.
4 Repeat the operation on the other three brakes, finishing with the one nearest to the master cylinder. Finally, top up the supply tank to the correct level. Fluid drained into the jar will probably be dirty as well as aerated and its re-use is not recommended.

10:9 Pedal clearance

The correct amount of free movement between the master cylinder pushrod and piston is set during assembly of the car and should not need alteration. In the event however of the adjustment having been disturbed, adjust the effective length of the rod connecting the cylinder to the pedal until the pedal pad can be depressed approximately $\frac{1}{2}$ inch before the piston begins to move. The clearance can be felt if the pedal is depressed by hand. Note that before making any alteration it is important to ensure that neither the floorboard nor the floor carpet obstructs the pedal, and that the piston has not stuck in the master cylinder bore.

10:10 Handbrake adjustment

On all models the handbrake is of the 'fly-off' type, the ratchet knob being depressed to hold the brake in the 'on' position, while a slight pull on the lever releases the ratchet without depressing the knob. The brake operates on the rear wheels through encased cables. On models **TA**, **TB** and **TC** the handbrake is adjusted by means of a thumb nut at the base of the lever. When adjusting, ensure that the adjustment is not too tight or the brake shoes may be in contact with the drums with the handbrake in the 'off' position.

Details of the handbrake arrangements on models **TD** and **TF** are shown in **FIG 10:11**. Although the handbrake operates the rear brakes by means of cables, adjustment of the hydraulic brake shoes automatically adjusts the handbrake. No separate adjustment is necessary and **if the two brass nuts 36 on the lever are moved, the whole braking system will be upset.** Sufficient movement is allowed at the lever to deal with full wear at the linings. If the wheel cylinder operating cables 37 have been disconnected, they should be readjusted in the following manner:

1 Return the handbrake lever to the fully released position.
2 Remove the splitpin and clevis pin 38 retaining the brake cable to each wheel cylinder lever 21.
3 Adjust the brake shoes as described in **Section 10:2**.
4 Screw up the cable adjusting nuts 36 by equal amounts until the cable clevis pins 38 will fall into position in the cable forks without moving the wheel cylinder lever 21. Replace the split pins.

10:11 Modifications

Cases have occurred where the rear brake pipes lying along the axle rub against the rear axle strap on models **TD** and **TF**, or against the damper arms on the **Mark II** Competition Model. The pipes are adequately clipped, and care should be taken to see that the pipe is set to allow at least 1 inch clearance at these points.

10:12 The Dunlop Centre Lock Wheel

All MG Midgets up to and including model **TC** were fitted with Dunlop Centre Lock Wheels, popularly known as 'knock-ons'. These were also available as optional equipment on model **TF**. They provide the most rapid method of changing road wheels, but like all mechanical devices must be properly treated in order to ensure satisfactory service.

FIG 10:12 shows a righthand wheel and the direction of unscrewing the locknut. The nuts on the lefthand wheels undo in the opposite direction. A copper hammer of the type provided in the original toolkit must be used for unscrewing or tightening the nuts. The following points should also be noted:

1 When the car or the wheels and hubs are new, after the first 50 miles jack up each wheel and hammer the nuts to ensure they are tight.
2 When changing wheels, wipe the serrations and cones on the hub, wheel and locknut to remove any foreign matter which would prevent the wheel from seating properly. Lightly coat these surfaces with fresh grease. Hammer the locknuts tight with the

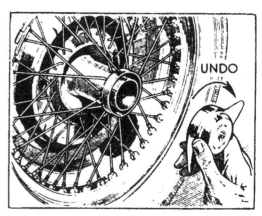

FIG 10:12 Dunlop Centre Lock Wheel. A righthand wheel is shown. Lefthand wheels undo in the opposite direction

wheel jacked up, and after 50 miles, again check for tightness.
3 Every twelve months remove the wheels for examination and regreasing. After any work involving stripping of front or rear axles check that the inscription on the wheel locknuts corresponds with the side of the car to which they are fitted.

10:13 Rebuilding and trueing wire wheels

Wire wheels of the 'knock-on' type were fitted to models **TA**, **TB** and **TC** and were supplied as optional equipment on model **TF**. The trueing or rebuilding of wire wheels is a skilled job which should preferably be entrusted to the specialist. However, the following instructions are included for the owner wishing to undertake the work:

In wheel building, the rim, hub shell, spokes and nipples should be loosely assembled to bring the rim into as true a running position with the hub as practicable, while ensuring that the outside dish is maintained. Outside dish is the distance from the edge of the rear rim flange to the flange of the hub shell. **FIG 10:13** shows the inset dimension of ¾ inch applicable to model **TF**. When this condition is reached, and not before, the wheel should be mounted on a running hub. Each

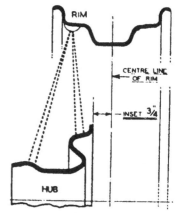

FIG 10:13 Outside dish of wire wheel TF

pair of spokes should then be tensioned carefully a small amount at a time using a nipple key, working from one pair of spokes and thence to the diametrically opposed pair; afterwards repeating the process with the opposed pairs which are at right angles to the original pair tensioned, and so on.

At each stage of the tensioning the truth of the wheel should be checked carefully both for lateral and up and down movement, correcting any error by giving a slight additional tension to the appropriate spoke or sets of spokes.

It is important that as little additional tension as possible should be given when pulling the rim true in this manner, the ideal condition to aim at being that all spokes are as nearly as possible at the same tension when the rim is true. If excessive tension is required to bring the rim true, the opposing spokes must be loosened slightly. The experienced wheel-builder will generally be able to gauge when the correct tension has been reached, either by the general feel of the spokes or the ringing note which the spoke gives when lightly struck with the nipple key.

When building is completed, any spoke ends which project into the rim well should be carefully filed flush with their nipples.

10:14 Removing and refitting disc wheels

Pressed steel disc wheels are fitted to models **TD** and **TF**. **FIG 10:14** shows the correct method of removing the hub disc or embellisher. This should be levered off with a sideways movement as shown, using the flattened end of the wheel brace. A radial movement of the spanner will strain the disc with the result that it may become detached when on the road. To refit the disc, fit its rim over two of the three securing buttons on the wheel centre and give a sharp blow with the fist to spring it over the third button.

When removing a wheel, slightly slacken the five wheel securing nuts before jacking up. All are fitted with righthand threads. Raise the car to lift the wheel clear of the ground and remove the nuts. When refitting, reverse the procedure, finally tightening the nuts alternately a little at a time. Use the wheel brace which is carried in the car for tightening the nuts as use of more powerful hand or pneumatic tools may lead to difficulty in changing a wheel on the road. Check the tightness of wheel nuts every 1000 miles or 50 to 100 miles after any wheel change.

10:15 Tyre fitting and wheel balancing

In order to obtain good steering it is of importance to ensure that the wheels, with tyres fitted, are in good balance. To assist this, tyre manufacturers are now marking their tyres with a white spot or spots near the bead at the lightest point of the cover. Tubes are marked with similar spots at their heaviest point. When tyres are assembled the spots on cover and tube should therefore coincide as shown in **FIG 10:15**.

In some cases special balancing discs are fitted to the inside of the cover and these should not be removed or mistaken for repair patches. Special balance weights are also available for attachment to the wheel rim, in steps of $\frac{1}{4}$ ounce from $\frac{1}{2}$ to $3\frac{1}{2}$ ounces. The owner can balance a wheel and tyre statically by these means, but a tyre service station will balance a wheel and tyre dynamically using specialized equipment for the purpose.

A point often overlooked when fitting tyres is the necessity of the cover bead rising fully out of the well in the rim all round. A ring is moulded at the base of the cover wall for the purpose of checking this point. The pattern of this ring varies in different makes but it is essential for the same width to be visible all round the rim, otherwise the tyre cannot run true.

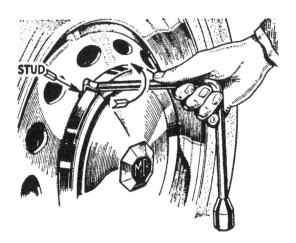

FIG 10:14   Correct method of removing hub disc TD, TF

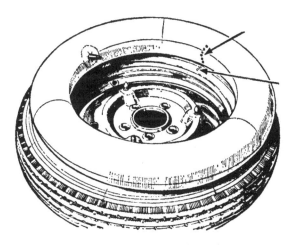

FIG 10:15   Balance marks on tyre and tube

10:16 Fault diagnosis

(a) 'Spongy' pedal
1 Leak in the system
2 Worn master cylinder
3 Leaking wheel cylinders
4 Air in the system
5 Gaps between shoes and undersides of linings

(b) Excessive pedal movement
1 Check 1 and 4 in (a).
2 Excessive lining wear.
3 Very low fluid level in supply tank.
4 Too much free movement of pedal.

(c) Brakes grab or pull to one side
1 Brake backplate loose.
2 Scored, cracked or distorted drums.
3 High spots on drum.
4 Unbalanced shoe adjustment.
5 Wet or oily linings.
6 Worn or loose rear spring fixings.
7 Front suspension or rear axle anchorages loose.
8 Worn steering connections.
9 Mixed linings of different grades.
10 Uneven tyre pressures.

(d) Brakes bind
1 Seized handbrake cable.
2 Shoes incorrectly adjusted.
3 Weak or broken shoe springs.
4 Pedal spring weak or broken.
5 Wheel cylinder piston seized or cups swollen.
6 Blocked pipeline.
7 Filler cap vent choked.
8 No free movement on pedal.
9 Compensator port in master cylinder covered by swollen rubber cup.

CHAPTER 11

THE ELECTRICAL EQUIPMENT

11:1   The electrical system
11:2   Battery maintenance and testing
11:3   Generator routine maintenance, electrical tests
11:4   Removing and dismantling generator
11:5   Brush and commutator servicing, field coil testing
11:6   Starter motor tests in situ
11:7   Removing, testing and dismantling starter

11:8   The control box, regulator adjustment
11:9   Cut-out adjustment, fuses
11:10   Headlamp dismantling, focusing, beam setting
11:11   Warning lights and flasher units
11:12   Horn adjustment
11:13   Windscreen wiper servicing
11:14   Modifications
11:15   Fault diagnosis

11:1 The electrical system

All models covered by this manual have 12-volt electrical systems in which the positive side of the battery is earthed. The pre-war models **TA** and **TB** have two 6-volt batteries connected in series but all other models have a single 12-volt battery. On models **TA** and **TB** the generator has the third-brush system of control, with a full- and half-charge switch. The post-war models **TC, TD** and **TF** have two-brush generators with constant voltage regulators.

The starter is of basically similar type on all models and is mounted on the righthand side of the engine. On models **TA, TB** and **TC** the starter switch is attached to the starter body, while on models **TD** and **TF** it is mounted on the bulkhead. In both cases it is mechanically-operated by a cable from the dashboard knob.

TA and **TC** cars built for the home market were originally fitted with 'dip-and-switch' headlamps. To comply with recent UK regulations these must now be converted to 'double-dipping' as described in **Section 11:14. TC** models intended for the USA and all **TD** and **TF** cars were fitted with double-dipping headlamps and conversion will not be necessary. Pre-focus were introduced on the **TD** model. Late **TD, TF** and all USA models have provision for flashing indicators. Late **TD** and **TF** models have a foot-operated dipswitch and the **TF** model has a redesigned instrument panel.

Wiring diagrams are given in the Appendix to enable those with some electrical experience to trace and correct wiring faults. The diagrams cover each of the principal types of circuit used, but it should be noted that detailed production modifications may have been introduced from time to time. In the case of early cars the wiring may also have been modified at a later date to bring the lighting system into line with newer regulations.

Serious mechanical and electrical defects in the generator and starter motor are best cured by fitting new units on an exchange basis, but instructions for adjustments which can be carried out by a reasonably competent engineer have been included in this Chapter. It must be emphasized that electrical tests of such units call for the use of accurate measuring instruments and that unreliable instruments will make accurate adjustments impossible.

11:2 Battery maintenance and testing

The batteries are of the lead acid type, using dilute sulphuric acid as an electrolyte. Pre-war models use two 6-volt batteries in series, while all other models have a single 12-volt battery. The life of a battery is a hard one and will be considerably shortened by lack of regular maintenance.

The outside of the battery should be kept clean and dry, and in particular any corrosion at the terminals should be dealt with. Disconnect both terminals and remove the battery. Clean all affected parts of the terminals and battery support with a brush dipped in dilute ammonia or soda solution. Flush off the solution with clean water when it has stopped foaming and dry thoroughly. Paint the affected areas of the battery support with acid-resting paint and smear the terminals with petroleum jelly before reconnecting. Note that on pre-war models acid spilling from the two batteries may attack the chassis side members and the rear silencer.

The level of the electrolyte in the cells of the battery should be checked regularly and topped up with distilled water. This is because it is only the water which evaporates as a result of charging and discharging. Electrolyte which has been spilled, however, must be replaced by dilute sulphuric acid of the same specific gravity as that in the cell concerned. Acid can be obtained ready diluted, but if strong sulphuric acid is used, remember when diluting always **add acid to the water. The reverse procedure is highly dangerous.**

The specific gravity of the electrolyte in the battery can be checked by using a hydrometer and gives an indication of the state of charge of each cell. At a temperature of 16°C or 60°F the indications are as follows:

Fully charged . . . . 1.280 to 1.300
Half charged . . . . 1.210 approximately
Discharged . . . . 1.150 or under

Add or subtract .002 respectively for a rise or fall of 3°C (5°F) in temperature.

If the battery is unused for long periods it should be recharged at least once a month or its condition will deteriorate rapidly.

11:3 Generator routine maintenance, electrical tests

The generator bearings are packed with grease on assembly, but where the rear bearing is fitted with a lubricator of the type shown in **FIG 11:1**, this should be removed every 12,000 miles and the cap half-filled with high melting point grease. On generators fitted with an oil hole, two or three drops of engine oil should be given at regular intervals. Do not over-lubricate. The grease nipple on the revolution-counter (tachometer) drive at the rear end of the generator, also shown in **FIG 11:1** should be lubricated with chassis grease every 3,000 miles.

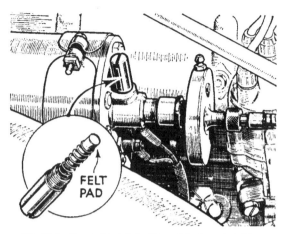

FIG 11:1   Generator lubricator and tachometer drive

The generator is driven by the same belt as the fan and water pump. Belt slip will cause lowered generator output and the belt should be adjusted as described in **Section 4:2**. Another frequent cause of low output is a deposit of greasy carbon dust on the commutator. Detailed instructions on brush and commutator servicing will be found in **Section 11:5**. All cars in this series have 'window' type generators allowing access to the brushes without dismantling the generator.

The pre-war **TA** and **TB** models employ the third brush system of generator output control, in conjunction with the Lucas PLC type lighting and charging switch. This system differs considerably from those used on post-war cars, so that a brief description will not be out of place at this stage. Instead of the field being connected across the output leads from the two main brushes, it is connected between one of the main brushes and a third brush. The position of this third brush relative to the main brush has the effect of regulating the output current so as to keep it nearly constant at varying engine speeds. For details of the circuitry, reference should be made to **FIG 13:1** in the Appendix. The generator output, however, does not vary according to the state of the battery. This disadvantage is to some extent overcome by the use of the PLC switch, the wiring of which can be seen in **FIG 11:2**. Two additional resistances are inserted in the field circuit by turning the switch to HALF CHARGE. One resistance only is in circuit on FULL CHARGE, thus allowing a discharged battery more current, while both resistances are shortcircuited when the switch is in the HEAD position, bringing the generator output up to its maximum. Note that the L terminal is isolated when the switch is in this position, being only used if sidelamps are to be extinguished when headlamps are on, in accordance with the regulations in some countries. Normally both side and tail lamps should be connected to the T terminal.

The position of the third brush is set when the instrument leaves the factory and in the event of generator output being low, check for belt slip, dirty commutator or faulty connections before attempting to regulate the output by moving the third brush. This is the small brush

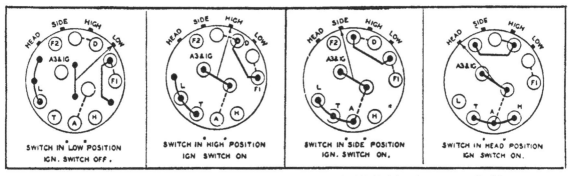

FIG 11:2   Connections of lighting and charging switch used with third-brush generator, TA, TB

and it will be found that on slackening the clamp screw the brush can be moved. To check and adjust the output proceed as follows:

1 Run the engine at about 1500 rev/min.
2 Switch on all lamps and other electrical equipment to provide maximum load. The ammeter on the dashboard should register a small charge, say 1 amp.
3 If the ammeter shows a discharge, move the third brush in the direction of rotation of the armature until a charge is shown.
4 Switch off all lamps and accessories. If the ammeter now registers a charge of more than 12 amps, move the third brush in the opposite direction until 12 amps is shown.
5 Repeat operation 2. If this now shows a slight discharge, adjust the brush to give a zero reading.
6 Tighten the third brush clamp screw.

On models TC, TD and TF the generator is of the two-brush type. The output can be checked without removing the generator, as follows:

1 Check the belt tension as described in **Section 4:2.**
2 Verify generator connections, terminals D and F on the generator being connected to the respective terminals D and F on the control box.
3 Switch off all lights and accessories. Disconnect the cables from generator terminals D and F and join the two terminals with a short piece of wire.

4 Clip the negative lead of a 0-20 volt moving coil voltmeter to one generator terminal and the positive lead to a good earth on the generator body.
5 Start the engine at idling speed and gradually increase speed. The voltmeter reading should rise rapidly without fluctuations. Do not allow the reading to reach 20 volts and do not race the engine in an attempt to increase the reading. A fast idling speed should be sufficient.
6 If there is no reading, check the brush gear.
7 If the reading is about $\frac{1}{2}$ to 1 volt, the field windings may be faulty.
8 If the reading is about 4 to 5 volts the armature windings may be faulty.

11:4 Removing and dismantling generator

To remove the generator:

1 Disconnect the battery.
2 Disconnect the two cables from the generator.
3 Disconnect the revolution counter (tachometer) drive from the rear end of the generator.
4 Slacken the three attachment bolts and swing the generator towards the engine as far as possible. Carefully free the belt from the generator pulley.
5 Supporting the generator, completely remove its attachment bolts and lift it from the engine.

FIG 11:3 is an exploded view of the generator fitted

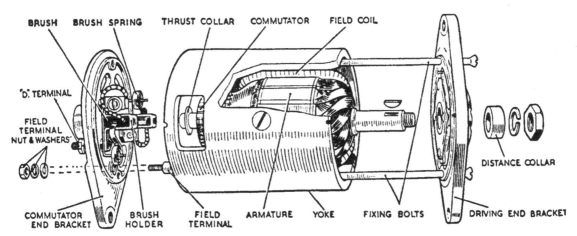

FIG 11:3   The generator components, post-war cars

to **TD** cars. All other types, including the pre-war third-brush generator, are of basically similar construction and the dismantling instructions will apply:

1 Remove the generator pulley.
2 Remove the cover band, hold back the brush springs as shown in **FIG 11:4** and remove the brushes from their holders.
3 Unscrew the nuts from the fixing bolts at the commutator end. Withdraw the bolts from the driving end,
4 Remove the nut, spring washer and flat washer from the smaller terminal on the commutator end, this being the field terminal. Remove the commutator end bracket from the yoke.
5 Remove the driving end bracket together with the armature and ballbearing from the yoke. It is not necessary to separate the driving end bracket from the armature unless the ballbearing has to be renewed, in which case the shaft must be pressed out in a hand press.

Reassembly and refitting of the generator are carried out in the reverse order to that for removal and dismantling.

11:5 Brush and commutator servicing, field coil testing

To obtain access to the generator brushes it is not necessary to dismantle the generator, although on some models it is better to remove it from the car. All cars in the series have 'window' type generators and the brushes are exposed by removal of the spring cover band.

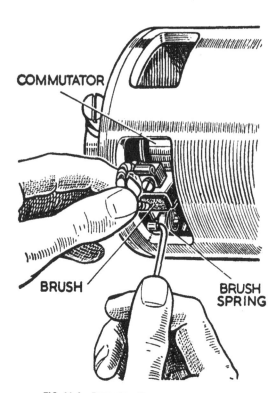

COMMUTATOR

BRUSH

BRUSH SPRING

FIG 11:4   Releasing the generator brushes

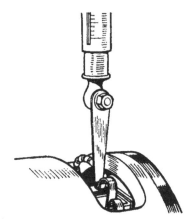

FIG 11:5   Testing the tension of brush springs

Take care not to lose the securing screw nut as the band flies open. To remove a brush, hold back the spring as shown in **FIG 11:4**. If there are signs of the brush sticking in its holder, clean the brush with a rag moistened in petrol, or if necessary, ease the sides of the brush by polishing with a smooth file.

After removing brushes for cleaning or other purposes, care must be taken to replace them in their original positions, otherwise they will not bed properly on the commutator. If brushes are so badly worn that they need to be renewed, always use the manufacturer's genuine replacement parts. On early models the brushes have to be bedded in to the commutator. This is carried out by fitting them and sliding a strip of fine glasspaper round the commutator and under the brushes, then working to and fro. Brushes for later models are supplied pre-formed so that bedding-in is not necessary. Test the brush springs with a spring balance as shown in **FIG 11:5**. The tension should be 20 to 25 oz and weakened springs should be renewed.

A commutator in good condition will be smooth and free from pits or burned spots. It should be cleaned with a cloth moistened in petrol. Take care not to soak the armature windings as this will affect the insulation. A badly worn commutator can be skimmed in a lathe, removing as little metal as possible. The insulation between the commutator segments must then be squarely undercut to a depth of $\frac{1}{32}$ inch. The work however should preferably be entrusted to a service agent. Some recent generators have moulded segments and **these must not be undercut**.

Field coils can be tested in the following manner:

1 Referring to **FIG 11:3**, connect a 12-volt battery between the field terminal and the generator body, with an ammeter in series. The reading should be about 2 amps.
2 A much higher reading indicates that the field coil insulation has broken down.
3 No reading indicates a break in the field coil circuit. This could be in the windings themselves, in the connection between the two windings or in the connections to the field terminal and earth.

Renewal of defective field coils entails removal of the pole-pieces, for which a special tool is required. This work is best carried out by a service agent.

11:6 Starter motor tests in situ

The same basic type of starter is fitted to all cars in this series and maintenance instructions will therefore apply to all models. **FIG 11:6** shows an exploded view of the components of the **TD** starter.

If the starter will not operate, first make sure that the battery is fully charged. If the lights go dim when the starter control is pulled, but there is no sound from the starter, the pinion may be jammed. Turn the squared end of the starter armature shaft with a spanner as shown in **FIG 11:7** to free the pinion. The shaft end is normally protected by a metal cap. Another method is to rock the car backwards and forwards in top gear until the pinion is heard to free itself. At the first opportunity the starter motor should be removed for inspection.

The starter switch is mounted on the starter body on models **TA**, **TB** and **TC**, and on the bulkhead on later cars. The switch is operated mechanically by cable from the dashboard control. The electrical connections from battery to switch and from switch to starter should be checked. A faulty connection in a battery lead may set up sufficient resistance to prevent the heavy current necessary for starter operation from passing, although lamps and accessories may still function. On pre-war models fitted with two 6-volt batteries the connection between the batteries should not be overlooked.

11:7 Removing, testing and dismantling starter

On models **TD** and **TF**, to facilitate starter removal,

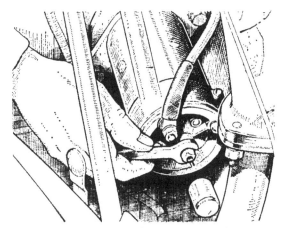

FIG 11:7   Freeing a jammed starter pinion

first disconnect and remove the exhaust system from the manifold, the gearbox and the third and rear cross-members. On all models, disconnect the battery. On models **TA**, **TB** and TC disconnect the heavy cable from the starter switch. On models **TD** and **TF** disconnect the cable from the commutator end of the starter. Remove the set pins securing the starter to the flywheel housing and withdraw the starter.

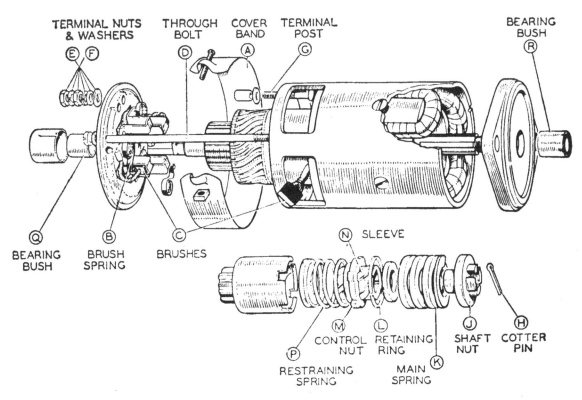

FIG 11:6   The starter components

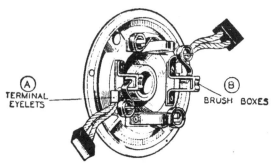

FIG 11:8   The starter end cover showing connections

To test the starter motor when removed from the car, secure the body of the starter firmly in a vice and connect it by heavy cables to a 12-volt battery. One cable should be connected to the starter terminal and the other held against the starter body. Under these light load conditions the starter should run at a very high speed.

To dismantle the starter:

1 Referring to **FIG 11:6**, remove the cover band A at the commutator end, hold back the brush springs B and take out the brushes C.
2 Remove the two through bolts D and withdraw the armature complete with the driving end bracket.
3 Remove the terminal nuts and washers E, F from the terminal post G and remove the commutator end bracket.

Examine the brushes as was described for the generator brushes in **Section 11:5**. The correct tension for starter brush springs is 30 to 40 oz. If starter brushes have to be renewed, the procedure differs from that applicable to generator brushes. The two insulated brushes shown in **FIG 11:8** have their leads soldered to the terminal eyelets A on the brush boxes B. The leads can be unsoldered from the eyelets and the new brush leads soldered in place. The two earthed brushes shown at A in **FIG 11:9** have their leads soldered to tappings B on the field coils, and in this case it is better to entrust the work of renewal to a service agent. The pole-pieces have to be removed, calling for a special tool for refitting, and great care is necessary in unsoldering and renewing

the leads. Excessive heat will damage the field coil insulation, while some later type starters have aluminium field coil windings to which the connections cannot be soldered directly. In this case the old leads have to be cut and the new leads soldered to them.

The field coils can be tested for an open circuit by connecting a 12-volt battery, with a 12-volt bulb in one of the leads, to the tapping point of the field coils to which the brushes are connected, and the field terminal post. If the lamp does not light there is an open circuit in the wiring of the field coils.

Every 12,000 miles the starter drive should be examined. Its components are shown in exploded form in **FIG 11:6**. When the starter is operated, the rotation of the armature screws the pinion assembly along the sleeve N to mesh with the flywheel teeth, the main spring K absorbing the initial shock as the starter turns the engine. As soon as the engine fires and turns faster than it is being driven by the starter, the pinion will be screwed back along the sleeve and out of mesh with the flywheel teeth. The light restraining spring or control spring P is placed between the splined washer and the control nut M to prevent the pinion from being vibrated into mesh when the engine is running.

If the pinion is found to be tight on the screwed sleeve wash away dirt and congealed oil with paraffin. To dismantle the drive:

1 Remove the split pin H and the shaft nut J. Lift off the main spring K and remove the retaining ring L.
2 Slide off the control nut M, the sleeve N and the restraining spring P. The splined washer and pinion can now be removed.

Reassembly and refitting of the starter are carried out in the reverse sequence to dismantling and removal.

11:8 The control box, regulator adjustment

FIG 11:10 shows the control box, comprising voltage regulator, cut-out and fuses, of the type fitted to earlier **TD** models. Later **TD** and **TF** models have a basically similar control box, but the fuses are contained in a

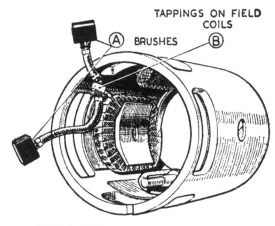

FIG 11:9   Field coil connections of starter motor

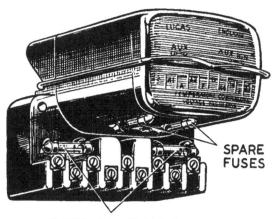

FIG 11:10   Control box with fuses, TC and early TD models

separate fuse box. The purpose of the regulator is to control the output of the generator in accordance with the load on the battery and its state of charge. Note that models **TA** and **TB** are not fitted with a voltage regulator, having generators with the third-brush system of control described in **Section 11:3**.

The regulator should not normally need adjustment, and if the charging rate is too low or the battery does not keep fully charged, first make sure that these conditions are not due to a slipping generator belt, a dirty commutator or battery defects, before suspecting the regulator. **The regulator electrical setting** is checked as follows:

1 Without removing the control box cover, disconnect the cables from the A and A1 terminals and join the cables together. Connect the negative lead of a 0-20 moving coil voltmeter to the D terminal on the generator and connect the other lead to a good earth.
2 Start the engine and slowly speed up until the voltmeter needle flicks and steadies. This should occur at a reading between the limits shown for the appropriate temperature of the regulator as follows:

Temperature	Voltage
10°C (50°F)	16.1 to 16.7
20°C (68°F)	15.8 to 16.4
30°C (86°F)	15.6 to 16.2
40°C (104°F)	15.3 to 15.9

3 If the voltage at which the reading becomes steady is outside these limits, stop the engine, remove the control box cover and adjust the setting accordingly. Referring to **FIG 11:11**, hold the adjusting screw B while releasing the locknut A. Turn the screw clockwise to increase the voltage or anticlockwise to reduce. Note that only a very small movement of the adjusting screw is needed and the output should be checked again after locking the nut A.
4 Do not run the engine at more than half throttle as high engine speeds will give a false reading. Note also that the tests and adjustments should be completed as quickly as possible as the rapid temperature rise in the regulator coils will also give false readings.

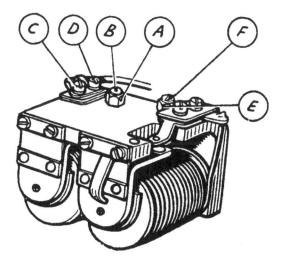

FIG 11:11   Regulator (left) and cut-out, TC, TD and TF

The mechanical setting of the regulator will only need adjustment if the armature has been removed for any purpose. Referring to **FIG 11:12**, adjustment is carried out as follows:

1 Slacken the two armature fixing screws E. Insert a .018 inch feeler between the back of the armature A and the regulator frame B.
2 Press the armature back against the frame and down on to the top of the bobbin core C with the gauge in position. Lock the armature by tightening the two fixing screws.
3 Check that the gap between the under side of the armature and the bobbin core is between .012 and .020 inch. If the gap is outside these limits correct by adding or removing shims F at the back of the fixed contact D.
4 Press the armature down on to the bobbin core and check that the gap between the contacts is between .006 and .017 inch.

To clean the regulator contacts, referring now to **FIG 11:11**, slacken the screw C a little more than the screw D so that the contact plate can be swung outwards. Clean the contacts with fine carborundum stone or fine emery cloth and wipe away all traces of abrasive or dirt. Finally tighten the two securing screws.

11:9 Cut-out adjustment, fuses

The cut-out acts as an automatic switch to prevent the battery discharging through the generator when the latter is running slowly or is stationary. On early models with third-brush generator there is a cut-out and fuse assembly, while on post-war cars the cut-out is enclosed in the control box together with the voltage regulator, as shown in **FIGS 11:10** and **11:11**.

An electrical check for the cut-out on models **TC, TD** and **TF** is carried out as follows:

1 Connect a voltmeter between the terminals marked D and E on the control box cover. These are shown in **FIG 11:10** only.
2 Start the engine and slowly increase its speed. When the voltmeter reads between 12.7 and 13.3 volts the contacts should close.
3 If the contacts operate outside these limits they must be reset. Remove the control box cover and referring now to **FIG 11:11** slacken the locknut E and turn the adjusting screw F clockwise to increase the operating voltage or anticlockwise to reduce it. Tighten the locknut after making the adjustment.

Models **TA** and **TB** are fitted with a cut-out and fuse box containing six fuses. These protect the generator field, headlamps, side and tail lamps, electric horn and auxiliary equipment.

Later model cars fitted with the RF 91 or RF 95 type control boxes have two fuses, one protecting auxiliary circuits taken directly from the ammeter, the other protecting auxiliary circuits controlled by the ignition switch. Late TD and TF models have similar fuses but these are mounted in a separate fuse box.

When a fuse blows, always find the cause of the failure before replacing it. Always replace with the fuse of the correct value, which is marked inside the glass tube.

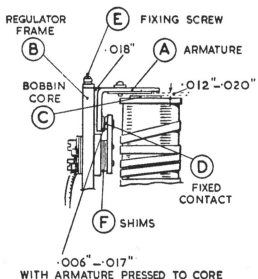

REGULATOR FRAME **B**

E FIXING SCREW

·018" **A** ARMATURE

BOBBIN CORE **C**

·012"–·020"

D

FIXED CONTACT

F SHIMS

·006"–·017"
WITH ARMATURE PRESSED TO CORE

FIG 11:12 Regulator mechanical adjustments, TC, TD and TF

11:10 Headlamp dismantling, focusing, beam setting

TA and **TC** cars built for the home market were originally fitted with 'dip-and-switch' headlamps. To comply with recent UK regulations these must now be converted to 'double dipping' as described in **Section 11:14.** On these models the headlamp front is secured by a small screw and catch underneath the rim. If focusing is necessary this is achieved by slackening the clamp screw which holds the bulbholder in the reflector. The holder can then be slid forward or back as necessary.

On model **TD** the headlamp rim is secured by a screw as shown in **FIG 11:13,** both lamps being fitted with double filament bulbs of the pre-focus type as illustrated. To remove the bulb, twist the back shell in an anticlockwise direction to withdraw it and pull the bulb out of the light unit. The bulb has a slotted flange to engage with a projection in the light unit so that it cannot be fitted the wrong way up.

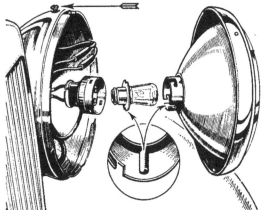

FIG 11:12   Headlamp as fitted to model **TD,** showing light unit attachment screw and pre-focus bulb

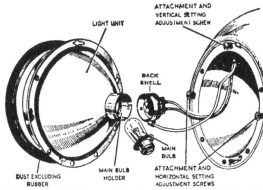

FIG 11:14   Built-in type headlamp of model TF showing pre-focus bulb and beam-setting screws

FIG 11:14 shows the components of the built-in headlamps fitted to model **TF.** These also have double-filament pre-focus bulbs but the method of fitting the light unit differs from previous models. To remove a bulb, unscrew the retaining screw at the bottom of the lamp rim and lift the rim away from the dust-excluding rubber. Remove the rubber, exposing three spring-loaded screws. **Do not turn these,** or the beam setting will be disturbed. Press the light unit inwards against the tension of the springs and turn it anticlockwise until the heads of the screws pass through the enlarged ends of the keyhole slots in the lamp rim. Remove the light unit. The pre-focus bulb is fitted as already described for the **TD** model. When refitting the light unit, ensure that keyhole slots pass between the heads of the three adjusting screws and their springs.

Setting of the headlamp beams is best undertaken by a good service agent possessing optical beam-setting devices giving a more efficient result than is possible by means available to the owner. If however the work has to be carried out in an emergency, there are two methods of adjusting the angle of the reflectors. On models other than **TF,** the stem-fitting lamps can be swivelled in any direction when the clamp nuts securing them are slackened. In the case of **TF** cars, remove the headlamp rim and the rubber ring as already described, but leave the light unit in position. The top screw is then used for adjusting the vertical setting of the reflector and the two side screws for horizontal adjustment.

11:11 Warning lights and flasher units

Models **TA, TB** and some **TC** cars were fitted with a 30 mile/hr warning lamp on the dashboard. A cable from the ammeter side of the panel light switch or the foglamp switch is led to the warning lamp, from which another cable leads to a contact unit in the speedometer head. When 30 mile/hr is reached the contacts close, completing the earth return and the lamp is illuminated. For cable colours reference should be made to the appropriate wiring diagram in the Appendix.

The petrol level warning lamp fitted to most cars is wired in a similar manner to the 30 mile/hr. warning lamp In this case the petrol tank unit completes the circuit to earth when the level of fuel drops to approximately 2 gallons. On later cars there is also a warning lamp to indicate when the main headlamp beams are in operation.

No direction indicators were fitted as original equipment to TA, TB, TC (home market) or early TD models. Flashing indicators combined with the sidelamps and with the stop and tail lamps were fitted to TC (USA export) and to later TD and all TF models. Two systems were used, the TC (USA) cars having two relays, one for lefthand indicators, the other for the righthand indicators, while on the TD and TF systems a single relay unit was used. The circuitry for these systems of indicators will be found in the wiring diagrams for the appropriate models given in the Appendix. Owners of earlier cars which were not originally fitted with indicators may fit these systems if desired, but the majority will prefer to install a set of four separate amber flashing indicators as now specified for new vehicles. These can be obtained complete with flasher unit and switch. Not only are these more effective but their system of operation is less complicated than earlier types.

11:12 Horn adjustment

The Lucas windtone horns, type WT 614 should give long periods of service without attention. If they fail to operate or become uncertain in action, first ensure that the fault is not due to a discharged battery, a loose connection, a faulty horn switch, or a blown fuse. In the latter case it is essential to locate the cause of the fuse blowing before fitting a replacement. The performance of a horn can be upset by its mounting having become loose, or by the vibration of a loose component nearby.

If adjustment should be necessary, remove the cover after removing the fixing screw. Disconnect and insulate the lead to the other horn, and short-circuit the fuse, otherwise it is liable to blow during adjustment. Slacken the locknut shown in FIG 11:15 and rotate the adjusting nut until the contacts are just separated, indicated by the horn failing to sound. Turn the adjustment half a turn in the opposite direction and tighten the locknut. If the horn note is still unsatisfactory, it should not be dismantled but returned to a Lucas service depot for examination.

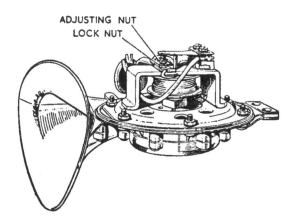

FIG 11:15   Lucas type WT 614 windtone horn

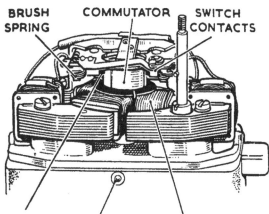

BRUSH SPRING   COMMUTATOR   SWITCH CONTACTS

BRUSH   LUBRICATOR   ARMATURE

FIG 11:16   Windscreen wiper motor type CW with cover removed to show switch contacts

11:13 Windscreen wiper servicing

The majority of cars in the series covered by this manual are fitted with the Lucas type CW windscreen wiper motor, the arm and blade on the driver's side being geared directly to the armature spindle. The motor is shown with the cover removed in FIG 11:16. The electrical feed to the wiper is taken from the ignition auxiliary circuit, so that the instrument only operates when the ignition is switched on. To start the wiper, pull the setting lever towards you and move the swich to the right. To park the wiper arms switch off the motor by moving the switch arm to the left, pulling the setting lever towards you and then turning it to engage the end of the switch arm.

If the wiper fails to operate, check whether current is passing through the instrument. This will be indicated by movement of the ammeter. If no current is indicated the trouble can be due to a faulty connection, a blown fuse or faulty switch contacts in the wiper itself. If the fuse has blown check for short-circuits in the wiring before renewing the fuse, If the fuse blows again the wiper motor should be removed for inspection. Faulty contacts, damage to the switch by a dented cover, or broken internal connections should be rectified. The brushes should receive attention similar to that advised for generator brushes in Section 11:5 and the commutator should be cleaned with a rag moistened in petrol. Stiffness in the action of the armature can be due to lack of lubricant in the bearings or in the gears. The bearings are lubricated with a few drops of machine oil through the lubricator shown in the illustration. Access to the gears and links is obtained by removing the backplate. Pack the gears with a high melting-point zinc-oxide grease. Remove any dirt between the armature and the pole shoes.

Model TF cars are fitted with a rack and cable type windscreen wiper. Electrical checks are carried out in the same way as for the earlier types. The cable is lubricated with medium engine oil and the gearbox packed with grease as used for chassis lubrication points.

11:14 Modifications

Under new lighting regulations which came into force on April 1 1968, the 'dip-and-switch' headlamp system, in which the righthand lamp is extinguished when the lefthand lamp is dipped became illegal. All **T series** Midgets produced for the home market up to 1949 must therefore be converted to the 'double-dipping' system shown in **FIG 13:4** in the Appendix, bringing them into line with the **TC** model produced for the USA.

Home models of the **TC** with lighting systems as in **FIGS 13:2** and **13:3** can be modified by fitting a double-filament holder and bulb to the righthand lamp, with an additional wire to the dip filament as shown at 2 in **FIG 13:4.** The existing dipswitch will then operate both headlamps.

FIG 13:1 shows the original wiring of the **TA** model with solenoid-operated dipping reflector. It does not appear practicable to retain the use of the dipping reflector. Both headlamps must be fitted with double-filament holders and bulbs. The existing 'one-way and off' dipswitch must be replaced by a modern two-way dipswitch. Wiring to the old dipswitch and headlamps should be removed and this part of the system rewired. From the headlamp fuse on the fuse-box run a wire to the centre terminal of the new dipswitch. Connect one contact terminal of the dipswitch to both main filaments and the other terminal to both dip filaments. The circuit will then be similar to that shown in **FIG 13:4.**

All cars not already modified to comply with post-war regulations must of course be fitted with twin rearlamps.

11:15 Fault diagnosis

(a) Battery discharged
1 Terminals loose or dirty
2 Lighting circuit shorted
3 Generator not charging
4 Regulator or cut-out not working properly
5 Battery internally defective

(b) Insufficient charging current
1 Loose or corroded battery terminals
2 Generator driving belt slipping

(c) Battery will not hold charge
1 Low electrolyte level
2 Battery plates sulphated
3 Electrolyte leakage from cracked casing or top sealing compound
4 Plate separators ineffective

(d) Battery overcharged
1 Voltage regulator needs adjustment
2 Incorrect use of charging switch (third-brush systems)
3 Incorrect third-brush setting

(e) Generator output low or nil
1 Broken or slipping driving belt
2 Regulator unit out of adjustment
3 Blown generator fuse (third-brush system)
4 Fault in charging switch circuit (third-brush system)

5 Incorrect third-brush adjustment
6 Worn bearings, loose pole pieces
7 Commutator dirty, worn, burned or shorted
8 Armature shaft bent or worn
9 Insulation proud between commutator segments
10 Brushes sticking, springs weak or broken
11 Field coil wires shorted, broken or burned

(f) Starter motor lacks power or will not operate
1 Battery discharged, loose cable connections
2 Starter pinion jammed in mesh with flywheel gear
3 Starter switch faulty or operating cable slack or broken
4 Brushes worn or sticking, leads detached or shorting
5 Commutator dirty or worn
6 Starter shaft bent
7 Engine abnormally stiff
8 Armature or field coils faulty

(g) Starter revolves but does not turn engine
1 Pinion sticking on screwed sleeve
2 Damaged pinion or flywheel teeth

(h) Noisy starter pinion when engine is running
1 Restraining spring weak or broken (pinion remains engaged)

(j) Starter rough or noisy
1 Mounting bolts loose
2 Damaged pinion or flywheel teeth
3 Main pinion spring broken

(k) Lamps inoperative or erratic
1 Battery low, bulbs burned out
2 Faulty earthing of lamps or battery
3 Fault in connection between two batteries (TA, TB only)
4 Faulty lighting switch, loose or broken wiring connections

(l) Windscreen wiper inoperative or sluggish
1 Faulty switch contacts
2 Brushes or commutator need attention
3 Faulty armature
4 Lack of lubrication of spindle or gears
5 Cable rack tight in housing (TF model)

(m) Wiper motor operates but does not drive arms (TF)
1 Wheelbox gear and spindle worn
2 Cable rack faulty
3 Gearbox components worn

(n) Petrol warning lamp does not operate
1 Bulb burnt out
2 Open circuit between battery and lamp or lamp and tank unit
3 Tank unit contacts faulty
4 Tank unit not earthed

CHAPTER 12

THE BODYWORK

12:1 Care and repair of bodywork
12:2 Hood and sidescreens
12:3 Front wing removal and refitting
12:4 Rear wing removal and refitting

12:5 Running-boards
12:6 Facia board and instrument panel
12:7 Body removal
12:8 Body refitting, door adjustment

12:1 Care and repair of bodywork

The open body is of normal coachbuilt construction with metal panels on a wooden framework. It is attached to the chassis frame by a series of bolts and is removed without difficulty by following the directions given at the end of this chapter. Many aspects of body maintenance are within the capabilities of the enthusiastic owner, but the removal of dents in body panels should only be attempted by a skilled panel beater. Amateur attempts to knock out dents usually result in raising a worse one. Very small dents, however, can be filled using one of the catalytic fillers supplied for this purpose.

The finish is cellulose and in refinishing after repair it is better to have a larger area sprayed, such as a complete wing, than to repaint a small section. If the car is still finished in one of the maker's original colours, supplies of the correct shade of cellulose enamel can be obtained from an agent's Service Parts Department in $\frac{1}{2}$-pint, 1 pint and gallon tins.

12:2 Hood and sidescreens

The hood should not be folded when it is wet or damp. Always wait until it dries. **FIG 12:1** shows the correct method of folding on models **TC, TD** and **TF**. Before folding the hood back, release the press buttons at each side. Referring to the numbered illustrations:

1 Make sure that no hood material is trapped between the hood-sticks and that the rear panel of the hood is pulled forward.
2 Fold the hood-sticks right down and gently pull the hood material out as shown.
3 Fold the two corners at right angles and fold the back in once.
4 Fold the hood material over again and the hood is then ready for the tonneau cover to be fitted over it.

The sidescreens are fitted to the doors by socket fittings and slotted brackets which engage locking screws. When not in use the screens are stored in the special compartment at the back of the body behind the seat. As this compartment has been kept to minimum dimensions it is essential that the sidescreens are packed carefully so as to prevent damage. **FIG 12:2** shows the method of stowing the earlier type of sidescreens fitted to Model **TD**. Referring to the numbered sections of the illustration, the operations are as follows:

1 Start with the righthand front sidescreen and lay it on a flat surface as shown, taking care that the stays are the right way up. Then place the lefthand front sidescreen on top of it, with its flap folded under and the stays at opposite ends.
2 Lay the righthand rear sidescreen on the other two as shown, tucking its front bracket under that of the

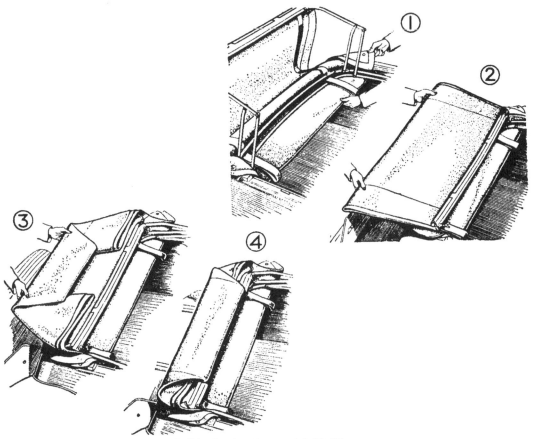

FIG 12:1   Folding the hood, TC, TD, TF

lefthand front sidescreen.

3 Lay the lefthand rear sidescreen on the others in the opposite direction with its bracket slipped under the cranked stay of the righthand front sidescreen with which the pile was started.

4 Transfer the complete pile of sidescreens to the compartment provided, inserting them brackets first as shown.

FIG 12:3 shows the method of stowing the deeper sidescreens which were fitted to later **TD** models. Procedure is as follows:

1 Place the lefthand rear sidescreen in the compartment as shown, with the attachment lugs facing the front of the car and the canvas part against the lefthand body panel.

2 Place the righthand rear sidescreen in front of the first one, again with the attachment lugs facing the front of the car, but with the canvas part against the righthand panel.

3 Insert the righthand front sidescreen with its lugs pointing downwards and its flap folded under towards the rear of the car. Make sure it is inserted as far down as it will go.

4 Insert the lefthand front sidescreen, again with its attachment lugs downwards and its flap folded under to the rear. The stowage compartment lid can now be

closed and secured by means of the two press studs.

FIG 12:4 shows the method of stowing the sidescreens on Model TF:

1 Start with the lefthand front sidescreen and stow it face downwards with the top edge against the rear of the stowage compartment and the front lower point against the lefthand wheel arch.

2 Place the righthand front sidescreen on top of the lefthand one with its face side uppermost and its rear edge against the righthand wheel arch.

3 Place the lefthand rear sidescreen on top of the other two, with the chromium-plated side uppermost and the front edge against the righthand wheel arch.

4 Place the righthand rear sidescreen with its chromium plated side uppermost and its front edge against the lefthand wheel arch. The lid of the stowage compartment should now close without difficulty.

12:3 Front wing removal and refitting

To remove the front wings from Model **TD** proceed as follows:

1 Disconnect the battery. Remove the headlamp and sidelamp fronts and disconnect and withdraw the cables through the wing clips and valance.

2 Remove the nuts, bolts and spring washers attaching the headlamp tie rod bracket to the radiator shell and

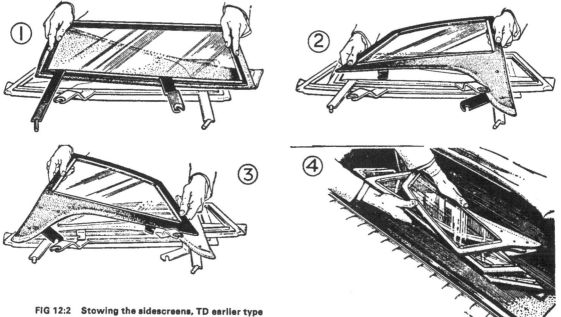

FIG 12:2 Stowing the sidescreens, TD earlier type

the nuts, locknuts and flat washers securing the tie rod bracket to the wings.

3 Remove the bolts and spring washers securing the sidelamp and sidelamp cable clips to the wings.

4 Withdraw the two Phillips screws and flat washers securing each side of the front valance to the wings, and the bolt securing the leading edge of the valance below each bumper attachment bolt.

5 Remove the two nuts, bolts and spring and flat washers forward of the suspension unit and the four bolts with spring and flat washers to the rear of it securing the wing to the chassis frame.

6 Remove the two Phillips screws securing the wing to the body and the three nuts, bolts and spring and flat washers securing the wing to the running-board. Lift the wing clear of the car.

FIG 12:3 Stowing the sidescreens, TD later type

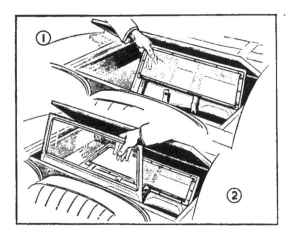

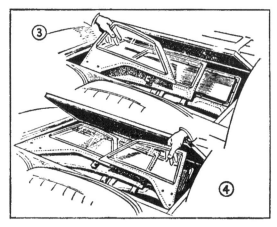

FIG 12:4   Stowing the sidescreens, TF

Refitting is carried out in the reverse order to that given for removal. Detailed descriptions have been given of washers used, as the omission of any of these will prevent the rattle-free attachment of wings. Where holes in sheet metal have become enlarged, additional large diameter washers may be inserted to rectify this trouble. Although the detailed description given applies to **TD** models only, the basic instructions apply also to earlier cars.

To remove the front wings from **TF** models:

1 Disconnect the battery.
2 Remove the bolt securing each front bumper bracket.
3 Disconnect the sidelamp and headlamp wires at the snap connectors on the engine side of the valances. Pull the wires through the clips in the valances.
4 Unscrew the line of bolts under each wing securing it to the valance and the bolts at the end flange securing it to the running-board.
5 Unscrew the nuts below the running-boards and release the tread strips. The wings can now be removed from the car.

Refitting is carried out in the reverse order to that given for removal.

12:4 Rear wing removal and refitting

To remove the rear wings from **TD** models:

1 Remove the nuts, screws and flat washers securing the stop- and tail-lamps to the wings. On later models Phillips screws with flat and spring washers are used. Disconnect the stop- and tail-lamp cables, noting the respective connections to ensure correct operation on reassembly.
2 Remove the nut, bolt and two washers securing each wing to the chassis frame and the five bolts with flat washers securing the wing to the body.
3 Remove the nut, bolt, flat washers and rubber packing securing the wing to the running-board and lift off the wing.

To remove the rear wings from **TF** models:

1 Disconnect the tail-lamp wires.
2 Unscrew the bolts securing the wings to the running-boards and the line of bolts and screws securing each wing to the body.   The wings can now be removed from the car.

Refitting is carried out in the reverse order to that given for removal. Detailed descriptions have been given of washers used, as the omission of any of these will prevent rattle-free attachment of the wings. The rubber packing between the wings and the running boards should be renewed if unserviceable.

12:5 Running-boards

To remove the running-boards from **TD** models:

1 Remove the three nuts, bolts and spring ane flat washers securing each running-board to the front wing.
2 Remove the nut, bolt, flat washers and rubber packing securing each running-board to the rear wing.
3 Remove the three bolts and flat washers securing each running-board to the body. The running-boards can now be lifted clear of the car.

Refitting is carried out in the reverse order to that described for removal.

To remove the running boards from **TF** models:

1 Unscrew the nuts securing the tread strips to the running-boards and front wings.
2 Unscrew the bolts securing the running-boards to the wings and body. The running-boards can then be lifted clear of the car.

Refitting is carried out in the reverse order to that described for removal. Renewal of worn or scuffed tread-strips will greatly enhance the appearance of the bodywork.

12:6 Facia board and instrument panel

The following instructions are for the removal of the facia board and instrument panel from the **TD** model, Earlier cars differ in having the speedometer on the lefthand side of the facia, a position occupied on the **TD** model by the glove box. Individual instruments on the central instrument panel are also mounted in a slightly different order, but the same basic instructions will apply:

1 Disconnect the battery.
2 Extract the screws from the brackets and the rubber stop securing the instrument panel undershield to the lower edge of the facia board.
3 Insert a hand through the aperture provided in the

undershield and disconnect the drives from the speedometer and revolution counter.

4 Withdraw the innermost screw from each hinge of the glove box lid. Remove the eight Phillips screws and cup washers securing the facia board.

5 Draw the facia board forward and disconnect the oil pressure gauge pipe and the instrument panel wiring.

Refitting is carried out in the reverse order to that described for removal.

To remove the facia board and instrument panel from **TF** models:

1 Disconnect the battery.

2 Remove the eight Phillips screws securing the panel undershield and remove the shield.

3 Disconnect the speedometer and revolution counter drives and all controls and wiring.

4 Unscrew the six nuts securing the instrument panel and remove the panel from the facia board.

5 Unscrew the securing bolt at each end underneath the facia board, which can now be removed.

Refitting is carried out in the reverse order to that described for removal.

12:7 Body removal

All the cars covered by this manual have a separate body and chassis and if complete restoration or major overhaul of the vehicle is contemplated, removal of the body presents little difficulty. A block and tackle should be used for lifting in conjunction with a rope sling. The following detailed instructions are for the removal of the body from **TD** models, but the basic procedure will apply to both earlier and later cars:

1 Remove the two round-headed screws securing the rear bonnet support to the bulkhead and lift the bonnet clear of the car.

2 Disconnect both battery leads. Remove the battery.

3 Remove the front wings as described in **Section 12:3** and remove the running-boards as described in **Section 12:5** .The rear wings may be left in position, but to avoid damage they should be removed as described in **Section 12:4**.

4 Remove the bolts securing the rear bumper bar to the chassis frame and withdraw the bumper bar assembly and distance tubes. Remove the spare wheel and remove the bolts and two Phillips screws to release the rear valance.

5 Drain the petrol tank, disconnect the delivery pipe and the fuel gauge wire. Slacken the nut and locknut on the lower end of each petrol tank strap and the bolts clamping the spare wheel carrier to the chassis rear crossmember. Remove the four domed nuts securing the spare wheel carrier and petrol tank straps to the body. Swing the spare wheel carrier to the left and lift off the petrol tank.

6 Remove the number plate lamp cover, disconnect the cables, withdraw the rubber sleeve and thread the cables through the carrier tube. By removing the clamp bolts the spare wheel carrier can then be removed.

7 Withdraw the sidescreens from their stowage. Undo the wingnut locating each side of the backrest and lift it clear of the car. Slide the seat cushions from their runners. Remove the carpets and underfelt.

8 Remove the steering wheel as described in **Section 9:6** and release the steering column from the support bracket.

9 Remove the screws from the brackets and rubber stop securing the instrument panel undershield to the lower edge of the facia board and remove the shield. Disconnect the starter pull cable from the switch and the mixture control cable from the carburetter. Disconnect the throttle pedal control and return spring from the carburetter and detach the revolution counter drive cable clip from the bulkhead. Disconnect the oil pressure gauge pipe, revolution counter and speedometer drive cables from the instruments.

10 Remove the innermost screw from each hinge of the glove box lid and the eight screws with cup washers securing the facia board and draw the facia forward. Disconnect the main wiring loom from the rear of the instrument panel and remove the facia board complete with instruments and starter and mixture control cables.

11 Remove the gearbox protecting cover, pedal draught excluder retaining plate and floorboards. Remove the trim panel beneath the scuttle. Slacken the draught excluder clip at the foot of the steering column and remove the three bolts securing the retainer plate to the toe-plate. Remove the bolts and nuts securing the toe-plate to the body, noting the position of the long bolt below the ignition coil.

12 Disconnect the horn leads and all cables from the starter motor switch and petrol pump. Remove the control box from the bulkhead. Draw all instrument panel wiring through the bulkhead and coil it over the engine, together with the control box and ignition coil.

13 Disconnect the flexible oil pipe from the engine and the revolution counter drive from the rear of the generator. Withdraw the speedometer cable from the bulkhead and coil it over the engine. Disconnect the pipes from the petrol pump. Slacken and remove the handbrake cable adjusting nuts and springs. Release the outer cables from the abutment bracket and thread them through the propeller shaft tunnel flange. Remove the five bolts securing the propeller shaft tunnel to the body and chassis frame.

14 Remove the two nuts and bolts from the attachment plates securing each side of the body to the stiffener tube below the bulkhead.

15 The body is secured to the chassis frame by eight bolts. The rear two are located in the rear corners of the sidescreen stowage compartment and the front two are inserted through the bulkhead flanges into the A brackets on the chassis frame. The four remaining bolts are inserted through the body floor.

16 Carry out a final check to ensure that no cables connecting body and chassis have been overlooked, especially if modifications to the wiring have been carried out since the car was new. The body can now be lifted clear of the chassis. Note the position of any cork or felt packing pieces between the body and chassis.

17 If the body is to be stored while work is carried out on the chassis, it should be supported carefully on suitably placed blocks to avoid distortion.

12:8 Body refitting, door adjustment

When refitting the body, the following procedure will enable it to be remounted so that the bonnet, wings and doors fit correctly:

1 Some insulating material must be placed between all body support brackets secured to the chassis frame and the body. Usually this consists of cork or felt pads.
2 Register the body in a central position on the chassis frame.
3 Refit any additional packings in the same position as they were before the body was removed. If this is not known refer to operations 8 and 9.
4 Locate and fit the securing bolts, but do not tighten any until all the bolts are in place.
5 Tighten all bolts around the scuttle.
6 Tighten all bolts on either side of the body.
7 Secure the rear end of the body.
8 The correct fitting of doors depends on correct positioning of the packing pieces referred to in operation 3, and adjustments are carried out as follows. If the door is too high, sufficient packing must be fitted under the front end of the body forward of the door. This will necessitate slackening all bolts around the scuttle.
9 If the door is low, packing must be inserted under the hinge pillar.
10 The packing used for adjustment can be in the form of large flat washers or steel plates of suitable size and thickness. The success of this operation can only be judged when all body securing bolts have been tightened so that a certain amount of trial and error may be necessary.

From time to time it is advisable to check the tightness of all body mounting bolts, as well as those securing the wings and running-boards.

APPENDIX

TECHNICAL DATA

Engine Details   Fuel System
Ignition System   Cooling
Clutch   Gearbox   Rear Axle
Front Suspension   Rear Suspension
Dampers   Steering   Braking System
Electrical Equipment   General Dimensions

WIRING DIAGRAMS

FIG 13:1   TA model 1938
FIG 13:2   TC 1945/8 Home model
FIG 13:3   TC 1948/9 Home model
FIG 13:4   TC 1948/9 Export model USA
FIG 15:3   TD model
FIG 13:6   Later TD model
FIG 13:7   TF model

HINTS ON MAINTENANCE AND OVERHAUL

GLOSSARY OF TERMS

TECHNICAL DATA

ENGINE DETAILS

Dimensions are in inches unless otherwise stated

Type: ... ... 4-cylinder in-line, overhead valve

Firing Order: 1–3–4–2
No. 1 Cylinder nearest to front of car

Capacity (cc):

		Bore (mm)	Stroke (mm)
MPJG engine, TA Midget: 1292		63.5	102
XPAG engine, TB, TC, TD, TF: 1250		66.5	90
XPEG engine, TF 1500: 1466		72	90

Compression ratio:

		bhp	rev/min
TA:	6.4/6.6	50	@ 4,500
TB, TC, TD, TD2:	7.25	54.4	@ 5,200
TD Mark II, TF:	8.1	57	@ 5,500
TF 1500:	8.3	63	@ 5,000

Number of main bearings: 3

Main bearing material:
TA: ... ... Whitemetal cast in situ
All other models: ... ... Steel-backed whitemetal shell type

Main bearing dimensions, model TA:
Journal diameter ... ... 52 mm
Length ... ... 33 mm

Main bearing dimensions all models except TA:
Journal diameter standard 2.047
First regrind diameter (except TF 1500) 2.027
Second regrind diameter (minimum) 2.007
(No regrinding is permissible on TF 1500 engines)
Main bearing length, front 1.496
                 centre 1.496
                 rear 1.575
Thrust taken on ... ... Centre bearing
Centre main bearing end clearance ... ... .0014 to .0037
Main bearing diametrical clearance ... ... .0008 to .003

Big-end bearing material:
TA ... ... White metal cast in situ
All models except TA ... ... Steel-backed whitemetal shell typc

Big-end dimensions, model TA:
Journal diameter ... ... 45 mm
Length ... ... 28 mm

Big-end dimensions, all models except TA:
Crankpin diameter, standard 1.772
Crankpin diameter minimum for regrind 1.722
(No regrinding is permissible on TF 1500 XPEG engines)
Diametrical clearance ... ... .0005 to .002
Side clearance ... ... .004 to .006

Connecting rod, length between centres:
TA ... ... 190 mm
TB, TC, TD, TF, TF 1500 ... ... 178 mm

Piston types:
Early TA engines ... ... Aluminium alloy, 4-ring

Piston types (cont.):
    Later TA, TB, TC, TD ... ... Aerolite, 3-ring
    Later TA, TB, TC, TD ... ... Hepolite replacement, 4-ring
    TF ... ... Aerolite tin-coated, 3-ring

Piston clearance:
    Early TA 4-ring piston ... ... .11 mm
    Aerolite 3-ring pistons ... ... .0021 to .0029 at pressure face below oil ring

First oversize rebore ... ... +.020

Second oversize rebore (maximum) ... ... +.040

Graded piston sizes (see SECTION 1: 12) TD, TF: STD, +.0005, +.0010, +.0015

    +.020 range ... ... +.0200, +.0205, +.0210 +.0215

    +.040 range ... ... +.0400, +.0405, +.0410 +.0415

Suitable for bore sizes ... ... Nominal bore + oversize piston marking −.0000 +.0004

Piston ring width, TA Hepolite 4-ring:
    Compression rings (two) ... ... 2 mm
    Scraper rings (two) ... ... 4 mm
TA, TB, TC, TD, Aerolite 3-ring:
    Compression rings (two) ... ... 2.25 mm
    Scraper rings (one) ... ... 4 mm
TF Aerolite 3-ring:
    Compression rings (two) ... ... 2.25 mm
    Oil control ring (one) ... ... 4 mm

Piston ring gap ... ... .006 to .010

Gudgeon pin diameter:
    TA ... ... 16 mm
    All other models ... ... 18 mm

Fit in piston ... ... Double thumb press

Fit in connecting rod ... ... Clamped

Valve head diameter:	Inlet	Exhaust
TB, TC, TD	33 mm	31 mm
TD Mark II, TF	36 mm	33 mm

Valve throat diameter:		
TA	30.5 mm	26 mm
TB, TC, TD	30 mm	26 mm
TD Mark II, TF	32.6 mm	28.5 mm

Valve seat angle:
    TA ... ... 45 deg.
    All other models ... ... 30 deg.

Valve stem diameter ... ... 8 mm

Valve timing: TA:
    Inlet opens ... ... 11 deg. before tdc
    Inlet closes ... ... 59 deg. after bdc
    Exhaust opens ... ... 56 deg. before bdc
    Exhaust closes ... ... 24 deg. after tdc
    Overlap ... ... 35 deg.

Valve lift	10 mm
Valve clearance, hot: inlet	.010
exhaust	.015

Valve timing, TB, TC and TD engines up to XPAG/TD2/24115:

Inlet opens	11 deg. before tdc
Inlet closes	57 deg. after bdc
Exhaust opens	52 deg. before bdc
Exhaust closes	24 deg. after tdc
Overlap	35 deg.
Valve lift	8 mm
Valve clearance, hot, inlet and exhaust	.019

Valve timing, engines from XPAG/TD2/24116 and TF:

Inlet opens	5 deg. before tdc
Inlet closes	45 deg. after bdc
Exhaust opens	45 deg. before bdc
Exhaust closes	5 deg. after tdc
Overlap	10 deg.
Valve lift	8 mm
Valve clearance, hot, inlet and exhaust	.012

Valve spring pressure:

		Shut	Open
Early TA		60 lb	108.5 lb
Later TA		101 lb	170 lb
TB, TC, TD...	Inner	31 lb	43 lb
	Outer	62 lb	80 lb
	Total	93 lb	123 lb
TD Mark II, TF	Inner	41 lb	55 lb
	Outer	73 lb	95 lb
	Total	114 lb	150 lb

Camshaft, TD, TF:

Number of bearings	Three
Material, front bearing	Whitemetal
rear and centre bearings	Zinc alloy
Bearing clearance, front	.0016 to .004
rear and centre	.0018 to .0037
Camshaft end float	.005 to .013

End thrust taken on front end.

Camshaft drive, all models	Endless duplex roller chain
Chain pitch, TB, TC, TD, TF	$\frac{3}{8}$
Chain length TB, TC, TD, TF	60 pitches (30 links)

Timing marks	White chain links and 'T' marks on chain wheels

Oil pump, all models	Gear type, driven by helical gears from camshaft

Oil pressure relief valve opens	50 to 70 lb/sq in

Oil pressure, normal	40 to 45 lb/sq in

Oil filter, all models	External full-flow type
Filter mounting TA, TB, TC, earlier TD	Separately mounted
Filter mounting later TD, TF	Attached to oil pump

Filter emergency bypass:

TA, TB	Incorporated in filter
TC, earlier TD	Bypass valve above oil pump
Later TD, TF	Bypass valve in filter head

Oil filter element types:

Owing to the number of different types of element fitted, it is essential to quote the engine number when ordering replacements.

Sump capacity:

TA	...	...	...	...	...	...	...	11 pints (13.2 US pints)
TB, TC, earlier TD ...	...	...	...	...	...	...		9 pints (10.8 US pints)
TD from engine 14948, TF...	...	...	...	...	...			10½ pints (12.6 US pints)

Flywheel:

	Diameter	Number of teeth on ring gear	Number of teeth on starter pinion	Ratio
TA	—	—	—	9.5 to 1
TB	—	93	10	9.3 to 1
TC	298.9 mm	93	10	9.3 to 1
TD	298.9 mm	120	9	13.33 to 1
TD2	—	—	—	13.33 to 1
TF	273 mm	120	9	13.33 to 1

Torque spanner data TD:

Cylinder head stud nuts	...	...	...	...	...	42 lb/ft
Connecting-rod big-end bolts (to next split-pin hole)		...	...	27 lb/ft
Main bearing cap nuts (to next split-pin hole)		...	...	...	62 lb/ft
Steering wheel attachment nut	...	...	...	...	42 lb/ft
Gudgeon pin clamp screw	...	...	...	...	33 lb/ft

Torque spanner data TF:

Cylinder head stud nuts (up to Engine No. XPAG/TF/31727)	...	50 lb/ft
Cylinder head stud nuts (from Engine No. XPAG/TF/31728)	...	40 lb/ft

Other torque spanner data as Model TD

FUEL SYSTEM

Fuel pump:

All models except later TF	...	...	...	...	...	SU electric type L
Position of pump	...	...	...	...	...	On scuttle or toolbox
Flow	...	...	...	...	...	7½ gallons per hour
Suction lift ...	...	...	...	...	...	36 inches
Diaphragm spring	...	...	...	...	...	Length 1 inch under load of 7½ to 8 lb

Fuel pump:

Later TF	...	...	...	...	...	SU electric, high pressure
Position of pump	...	...	...	...	...	On rear righthand chassis member
Flow	...	...	...	...	...	10 gallons per hour
Suction lift	...	...	...	...	...	33 inches
Output lift	...	...	...	...	...	48 inches
Carburetters: ...	...	...	...	...	...	Twin SU semi-down-draught

TA:

Bore	...	...	...	...	...	1 inch
Needle (standard)	...	...	...	...	...	AC
Needle (rich)	...	...	...	...	...	MI
Needle (weak)	...	...	...	...	...	5

TB, TC, TD:

Bore	...	...	...	...	...	1¼ inch
Needle (standard)	...	...	...	...	...	ES
Needle (rich)	...	...	...	...	...	EM
Needle (weak)	...	...	...	...	...	AP

TD Mark II, TF, TF 1500:

Bore	1½ inch
Needle (standard)	GJ
Needle (rich)	HI
Needle (weak)	GL

Piston damper (dashpot) fitted to later TC, TD, later TF

Air cleaner:

Oil-wetted type	Clean in petrol and re-oil every 5000 miles
Oil-bath type	Clean element in paraffin, clean and refill oil-bath every 3000 miles
'Pancake' type, TF	Clean element in petrol and re-oil every 3000 miles with SAE 20 engine oil.

Petrol tank capacity:

Early TA	15 gallons (18 US gallons) including 3 gallons (3.6 US) reserve
Later TA, TB, TC	13½ gallons (16.2 US gallons) including 2½ to 3 gallons reserve
TD	12½ gallons (15 US gallons)
TF	12 gallons (14.4 US gallons) including 2 gallons reserve.

IGNITION SYSTEM

Type	12 volt coil and distributor
Coil:	
TA, TB, TC, early TD	Lucas model Q12
Late TD, TF	Lucas LA12, fluid filled
Distributor drive	From camshaft
Distributor rotation	Anticlockwise
Distributor:	
Early cars	Lucas DK4A–DA27
Earlier TD	Lucas D2A4–40162–A to D (with symmetric or asymmetric low-lift type cams)
Later TD	Lucas D2A4–40162–E onwards (high-lift cams) or Lucas D2A4–40367 (high-lift cams)
TF	Lucas D2A4–40367A
Contact point gap:	
Early cars and all distributors with low-lift cams	.010 to .012
Distributors with high-lift cams	.014 to .016
Ignition timing	TDC
Automatic advance (centrifugal)	32 deg. on crankshaft
Timing marks	Pointer or arrow on timing cover. Mark or hole in crankshaft pulley (Timing marks in line give TDC on Nos 1 or 4 cylinders).

Sparking plugs ... ... 14 mm

Sparking plug types:

Engine:	Champion type	Reach	Gap
TA	L10	½ inch	.018
TB, TC, TD up to XPAG/TD2/22734	L10S	½ inch	.020 to .022
TD from XPAG/TD2/22735 and TF	NA8	¾ inch	.020 to .022

Owing to its longer reach, the NA8 plug must on no account be fitted to earlier engines

COOLING SYSTEM

TA	Water pump on cylinder head
All other models	Water pump on cylinder block

Models TF, TF 1500 have pressurized cooling systems

Cooling system, capacity:

TA	15 pints (18 US pints)
TB, TC	14 pints (16.8 US pints)
TD	12 pints (14.4 US pints)
TF	10¼ pints (12.3 US pints)

Radiator filler cap:

TA, TB, TC, TD	External
TF, TF 1500	Under bonnet

CLUTCH

Type:

TA	Single wet-plate. Oil feed from engine
TB, TC, TD	Borg & Beck 7¼ inch single dry-plate
TD2, TF	Borg & Beck 8 inch single dry-plate

Clutch fork shaft diameter for identification:

7¼ inch clutch	⅝
8 inch clutch	¾

Lining material:

TA	Cork inserts
TB, TC, TD	Woven yarn, type RYZ
TD2, TF	Woven yarn or moulded type.
Competition clutch...	Ferodo RAD 41, cemented

Clutch springs:

TA	12 per set. Pressure, pedal free 652.2 lb
TF, 8 inch standard clutch	Colour brown, 150/160 lb Free height 2 inch Assembled height 1.56
TF, 8 inch competiton clutch	Colour light grey 195/205 lb Free height 2.27 Assembled height 1.56

Free movement measured at clutch pedal pad:

TA	1 inch minimum
All other models	¾ inch minimum

GEARBOX

Gear ratios

TA (to engine MPJG 683):

	Gearbox	Overall (with 8/39 axle)
Top	1	4.875
Third	1.42	6.923
Second	2.2	10.725
First	3.715	18.111
Reverse	4.78	23.303

TA (from engine MPJG 684):

	Gearbox	Overall (with 8/39 axle)
Top	1	4.875
Third	1.32	6.435
Second	2.04	9.945
First	3.454	16.838
Reverse	4.44	21.645

TB, TC:

	Gearbox	Overall (with 8/41 axle) (standard)	Overall (7/38 axle)	Overall (8/39 axle)
Top	1	5.125	5.429	4.875
Third	1.36	6.95	7.383	6.630
Second	1.95	10.00	10.587	9.506
First	3.38	17.32	18.350	16.478
Reverse	3.38	17.32	18.350	16.478

TD:

	Gearbox	Overall (8/41 axle) (standard)	Overall (8/39 axle)	Overall (9/41 axle)
Top	1	5.125	4.875	4.555
Third	1.385	7.098	6.752	6.309
Second	2.07	10.609	10.09	9.429
First	3.5	17.938	17.06	15.942
Reverse	3.5	17.938	17.06	15.942

TF:
Ratios as TD except that 8/39 axle ratio fitted as standard.

Synchromesh:
TA   ...   .   Third and top only
All other models   ...   .   Second, third and top

Gear box oil capacity:
TA   ...   .   2 pints (2.4 US pints)
TB, TC, TD, TF   ...   .   1¼ to 1½ pints (1.5 to 1.8 US pints)

REAR AXLE

Type:

TA, TB, TC	Three-quarter floating, spiral bevel, 4-star differential in detachable carrier. 'Banjo' type axle casing.
TD, TF	Semi-floating, hypoid bevel 1 inch offset, in unit-construction axle casing

Axle ratios:

	Standard	Alternatives	
TA	8/39 (4.875/1)		
TB, TC	8/41 (5.125/1)	7/38 (5.429/1)	8/39 (4.875/1)
TD	8/41 (5.125/1)	8/39 (4.875/1)	9/41 (4.555/1)
TF	8/39 (4.875/1)	8/41 (5.125/1)	9/41 (4.555/1)

Oil capacity:

TA, TB, TC	2 pints (2.4 US pints)
TD, TF	$2\frac{1}{4}$ pints (2.7 US pints)

FRONT SUSPENSION

Type:

TA, TB	Half-elliptic leaf springs, sliding trunnions
TC	Half-elliptic leaf springs, swing shackles
TD, TF	Independent. Wishbones and coil springs

Front spring dimensions:

TA:

Length (spring eye centre to rear end of main leaf)	$27\frac{5}{16}$
No. of leaves	7
Thickness of leaves	$1...\frac{5}{32}$
	$5...\frac{3}{16}$
	$1...\frac{7}{32}$
Camber	1.5 (flat at 515 lb)

TB:

Length	As model TA
No. of leaves	7
Thickness of leaves	$\frac{7}{32}$
Camber	1.24
Working load	515 lb

TC:

Length	$26\frac{3}{4}$
Width	$1\frac{1}{4}$
No. of leaves	6
Thickness of leaves	$\frac{3}{16}$
Camber	1.85 (flat at 500–520 lb)

TD, TF (coil springs):

Free length	$9.59 \pm\frac{1}{16}$
Mean coil diameter	3.238
No. of effective coils	7.5
Diameter of wire (ground)	.498
Maximum deflection	4.24

REAR SUSPENSION

Type:

TA, TB	Half-elliptic leaf springs, sliding trunnions. Axle above chassis members
TC	Half-elliptic leaf springs, swing shackles. Axle above chassis members
TD, TF	Half-elliptic leaf springs, swing shackles. Axle below upswept chassis members

Rear spring dimensions:

TA, TB:

Length (spring eye centre to rear end of main leaf)	37
Rear end of main leaf to trunnion centre	1
No. of leaves	9
Thickness of leaves	$1...\frac{3}{16}$
	$1...\frac{1}{4}$
	$7...\frac{7}{32}$
Camber	$1\frac{1}{16}$ (flat at 385 lb)

TC:

Length	$36\frac{1}{2}$
Width	$1\frac{1}{4}$
No. of leaves	9 (7+2 rebound)
Thickness of leaves	Main $\frac{1}{4}$
	1st rebound $\frac{3}{16}$
	Others $\frac{7}{32}$
Camber	1.687 (flat at 385 lb)

TD:

Length	42
Width	$1\frac{1}{2}$
No. of leaves	7
Thickness of leaves	$\frac{7}{32}$
Free camber	4.1
Working load	500 lb at $\frac{1}{2}$ inch positive camber

TF:

Length	$42\frac{1}{2}$
Width	$1\frac{1}{2}$
No. of leaves	7
Thickness of leaves	$\frac{7}{32}$
Camber (free)	2.85
Working load	397 lb at nil camber

DAMPERS (front and rear)

	Type	Fluid
TA, TB	Luvax vane type	Vane type shock-absorber fluid
TC	Luvax-Girling piston type	Castrol Girling piston-type damper fluid (thin)
TD, TF	Girling piston type	Castrol Girling piston-type damper fluid (thin)
TD,TF	Armstrong piston type	Armstrong piston-type damper fluid
TD Mark II	Andrex TE 1/N friction	Esso Cantona LK 190 (oil)

STEERING

Type:

TA, TB, TC	Bishop cam (beam axle)
TD, TF	Rack and pinion (ifs)

Steering and suspension geometry:

	Castor angle deg.	Swivel pin inclination deg	Camber angle deg	Toe-in inch
TA, TB	6 (3 on beam, 3 on chassis)	$7\frac{1}{2}$		$\frac{1}{2}$
TC	8 (3 on beam 5 on chassis Reduced to $5\frac{1}{2}$ if $2\frac{1}{2}$ deg. taper plate is fitted	$7\frac{1}{2}$	3	$\frac{1}{4}$
TD	$2 \pm \frac{1}{2}$ (side members parallel to ground)	9 to $10\frac{1}{2}$ (full bump)	Nil ± 1 (static position)	Nil
TF	As TD	As TD	1 deg positive ± 1 (static position)	Nil

BRAKING SYSTEM

All models	Lockheed hydraulic, 9 inch diameter drums
TA, TB, TC	Leading & trailing shoe, front & rear
TD, TF	2-leading shoe front; leading & trailing shoe rear
Handbrake	'Fly-off' lever. Operates on rear wheels only

Brake fluid:

UK	Lockheed Brake Fluid
Overseas	Lockheed No. 5 (normal conditions) Wagner 21 Fluid (extreme cold conditions)

Capacity of system	Approximately 1 pint (1.2 US pints)
Brake lining material	Ferodo MR

ELECTRICAL EQUIPMENT

Lucas equipment originally fitted to model TA 1937/8:

	Model	Service No.
Dynamo (Generator) 3-brush type	C45-NV-DA21	228194
Starter	M418A-A-84	255667
Switch	PLC2-L14	344130
Cut-out and fuse unit	CJR3-L35	336181
Battery	2 units SLTW-11E	
Distributor	DK4A-DA27	405556
Coil	Q12-L	401650

Bulbs:

	Lucas No.
Headlamps	54
Side, stop and tail	207
Ignition warning light	C252A
Panel lamps	1224M
Foglamp	2
30 mile/hr warning lamp, map-reading and dash lamps	207

Fuses:

Dynamo field	No FA 4.5	4.5 amperes
Headlamps	No. FA 25	25 amperes
Sidelamps	No. FA 25	25 amperes
Accessories	No. FA 25	25 amperes
Dipping reflector	No. FA 6	6 amperes

Electrical equipment, other models:

Generator type:

TB	3-brush
TC, TD, TF	2-brush

Generator speed:

TB, TC, TD, TF	1.16 engine speed

Output control:

TB	3rd brush and PLC switch Cut-out and fuse CJR3
TC, early TD	CVC, RF95 regulator and fuse box
Late TD, TF	CVC regulator, separate fuse box

Battery:

TB	Two 6-volt 50 ah
TC	12-volt SLXW9A 51 ah
TD	12-volt GTW9A 51 ah
TF	12-volt GTW9A2 51 ah

Starter pinion:

TB, TC	10 tooth
TD, TF	9 tooth

GENERAL DIMENSIONS

	TA, TB, TC	TD	TF Disc wheels	TF Wire wheels
Wheelbase	94	94	94	
Track, front	45	$47\frac{3}{8}$	$47\frac{3}{8}$	$48\frac{3}{16}$
rear	45	50	50	$50\frac{1}{16}$
Turning circle	37 feet	31 ft 3	31 ft 3	
Steering, lock to lock ...	$1\frac{1}{2}$ turns	$2\frac{3}{4}$ turns	$2\frac{3}{4}$ turns	
Overall length...	$139\frac{1}{2}$	145	147	
width	56	$58\frac{5}{8}$	$59\frac{3}{4}$	
Ground clearance	6	6	6	
Wheels	Wire	Vent disc (Conversion to wire possible)	Vent disc or wire (optional)	
Tyre size	4.50—19	5.50—15	5.50—15	
Normal tyre pressure	Front 24 lb/sq in Rear 26 lb/sq in	18 lb/sq in	18 lb/sq in	

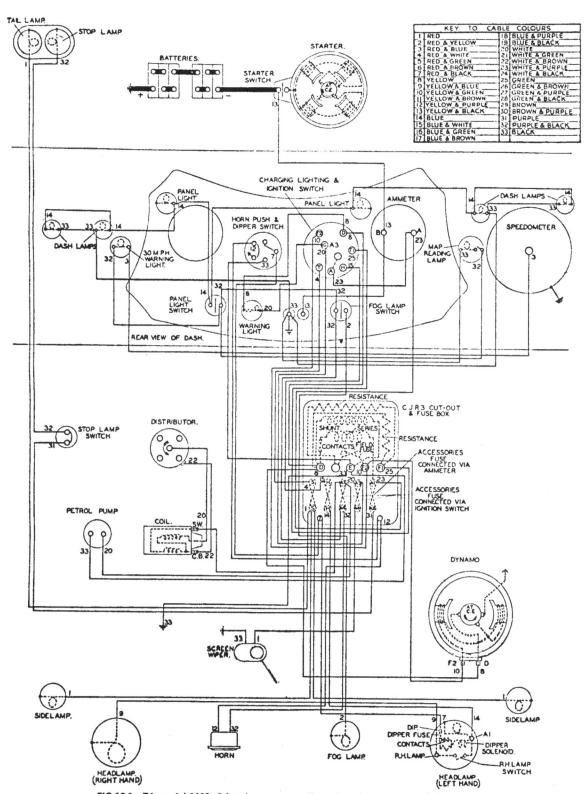

FIG 13:1   TA model 1938: 3-brush generator, dip-and-switch headlamp (solenoid)

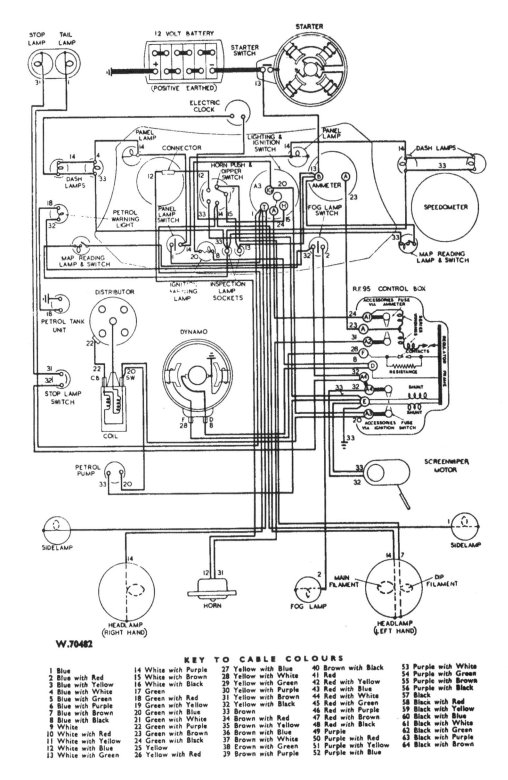

W.70482

KEY TO CABLE COLOURS

1 Blue	14 White *with* Purple	27 Yellow *with* Blue	40 Brown *with* Black	53 Purple *with* White
2 Blue *with* Red	15 White *with* Brown	28 Yellow *with* White	41 Red	54 Purple *with* Green
3 Blue *with* Yellow	16 White *with* Black	29 Yellow *with* Green	42 Red *with* Yellow	55 Purple *with* Brown
4 Blue *with* White	17 Green	30 Yellow *with* Purple	43 Red *with* Blue	56 Purple *with* Black
5 Blue *with* Green	18 Green *with* Red	31 Yellow *with* Brown	44 Red *with* White	57 Black
6 Blue *with* Purple	19 Green *with* Yellow	32 Yellow *with* Black	45 Red *with* Green	58 Black *with* Red
7 Blue *with* Brown	20 Green *with* Blue	33 Brown	46 Red *with* Purple	59 Black *with* Yellow
8 Blue *with* Black	21 Green *with* White	34 Brown *with* Red	47 Red *with* Brown	60 Black *with* Blue
9 White	22 Green *with* Purple	35 Brown *with* Yellow	48 Red *with* Black	61 Black *with* White
10 White *with* Red	23 Green *with* Brown	36 Brown *with* Blue	49 Purple	62 Black *with* Green
11 White *with* Yellow	24 Green *with* Black	37 Brown *with* White	50 Purple *with* Red	63 Black *with* Purple
12 White *with* Blue	25 Yellow	38 Brown *with* Green	51 Purple *with* Yellow	64 Black *with* Brown
13 White *with* Green	26 Yellow *with* Red	39 Brown *with* Purple	52 Purple *with* Blue	

FIG 13:2   TC 1945/8 Home model: CVC, dip-and-switch (double filament lefthand headlamp)

142

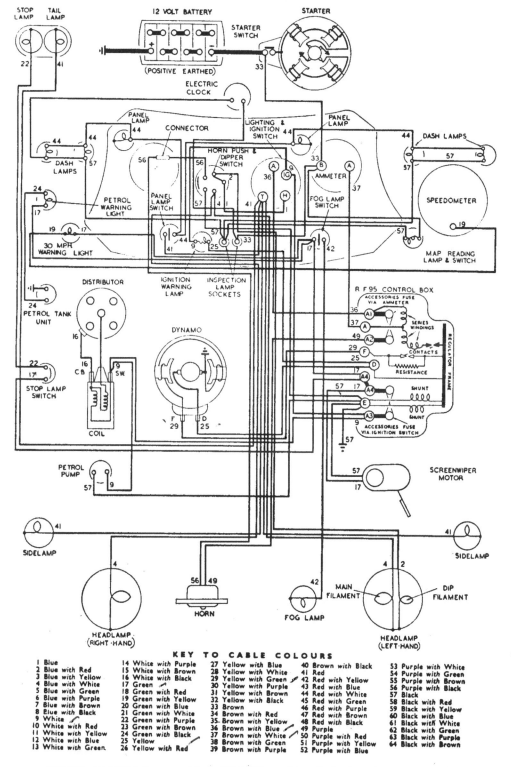

KEY TO CABLE COLOURS

1 Blue	14 White with Purple	27 Yellow with Blue	40 Brown with Black	53 Purple with White
2 Blue with Red	15 White with Brown	28 Yellow with White	41 Red	54 Purple with Green
3 Blue with Yellow	16 White with Black	29 Yellow with Green	42 Red with Yellow	55 Purple with Brown
4 Blue with White	17 Green	30 Yellow with Purple	43 Red with Blue	56 Purple with Black
5 Blue with Green	18 Green with Red	31 Yellow with Brown	44 Red with White	57 Black
6 Blue with Purple	19 Green with Yellow	32 Yellow with Black	45 Red with Green	58 Black with Red
7 Blue with Brown	20 Green with Blue	33 Brown	46 Red with Purple	59 Black with Yellow
8 Blue with Black	21 Green with White	34 Brown with Red	47 Red with Brown	60 Black with Blue
9 White	22 Green with Purple	35 Brown with Yellow	48 Red with Black	61 Black with White
10 White with Red	23 Green with Brown	36 Brown with Blue	49 Purple	62 Black with Green
11 White with Yellow	24 Green with Black	37 Brown with White	50 Purple with Red	63 Black with Purple
12 White with Blue	25 Yellow	38 Brown with Green	51 Purple with Yellow	64 Black with Brown
13 White with Green	26 Yellow with Red	39 Brown with Purple	52 Purple with Blue	

FIG 13:3   TC 1948/9 Home model: As FIG 13:2 but with revised cable colours (standardized)

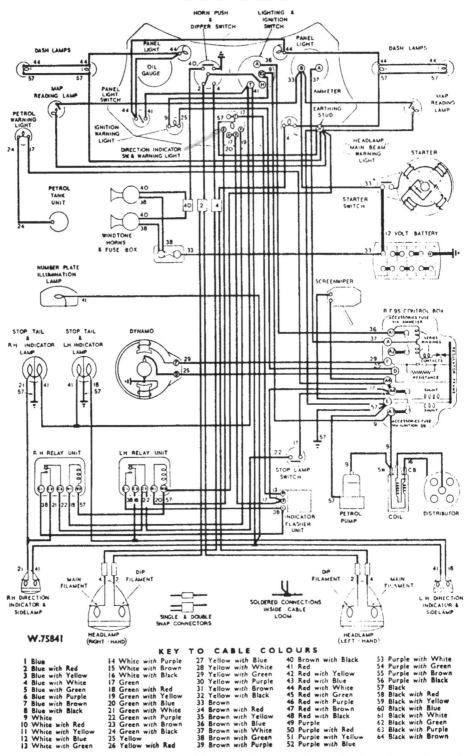

FIG 13:4 TC 1948/9 Export model USA: CVC, double-dipping headlamps, flashing indicators (two relays)

KEY TO CABLE COLOURS

1 Blue	14 White with Purple	27 Yellow with Blue	40 Brown with Black	53 Purple with White
2 Blue with Red	15 White with Brown	28 Yellow with White	41 Red	54 Purple with Green
3 Blue with Yellow	16 White with Black	29 Yellow with Green	42 Red with Yellow	55 Purple with Brown
4 Blue with White	17 Green	30 Yellow with Purple	43 Red with Blue	56 Purple with Black
5 Blue with Green	18 Green with Red	31 Yellow with Brown	44 Red with White	57 Black
6 Blue with Purple	19 Green with Yellow	32 Yellow with Black	45 Red with Green	58 Black with Red
7 Blue with Brown	20 Green with Blue	33 Brown	46 Red with Purple	59 Black with Yellow
8 Blue with Black	21 Green with White	34 Brown with Red	47 Red with Brown	60 Black with Blue
9 White	22 Green with Purple	35 Brown with Yellow	48 Red with Black	61 Black with White
10 White with Red	23 Green with Brown	36 Brown with Blue	49 Purple	62 Black with Green
11 White with Yellow	24 Green with Black	37 Brown with White	50 Purple with Red	63 Black with Purple
12 White with Blue	25 Yellow	38 Brown with Green	51 Purple with Yellow	64 Black with Brown
13 White with Green	26 Yellow with Red	39 Brown with Purple	52 Purple with Blue	

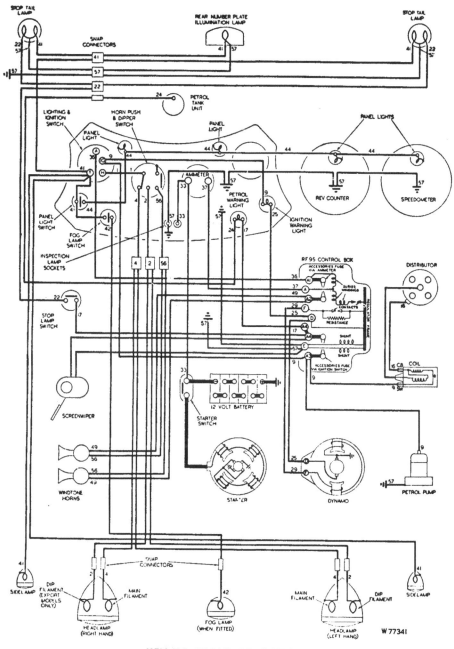

KEY TO CABLE COLOURS

1 Blue	15 White with Brown	28 Yellow with White	41 Red	54 Purple with Green
2 Blue with Red	16 White with Black	29 Yellow with Green	42 Red with Yellow	55 Purple with Brown
3 Blue with Yellow	17 Green	30 Yellow with Purple	43 Red with Blue	56 Purple with Black
4 Blue with White	18 Green with Red	31 Yellow with Brown	44 Red with White	57 Black
5 Blue with Green	19 Green with Yellow	32 Yellow with Black	45 Red with Green	58 Black with Red
6 Blue with Purple	20 Green with Blue	33 Brown	46 Red with Purple	59 Black with Yellow
7 Blue with Brown	21 Green with White	34 Brown with Red	47 Red with Brown	60 Black with Blue
8 Blue with Black	22 Green with Purple	35 Brown with Yellow	48 Red with Black	61 Black with White
9 White	23 Green with Brown	36 Brown with Blue	49 Purple	62 Black with Green
10 White with Red	24 Green with Black	37 Brown with White	50 Purple with Red	63 Black with Purple
11 White with Yellow	25 Yellow	38 Brown with Green	51 Purple with Yellow	64 Black with Brown
12 White with Blue	26 Yellow with Red	39 Brown with Purple	52 Purple with Blue	65 Dark Green
13 White with Green	27 Yellow with Blue	40 Brown with Black	53 Purple with White	66 Light Green
14 White with Purple				

FIG 13:5   TD model: CVC (RF95 regulator and fuse box), double-dipping headlamps

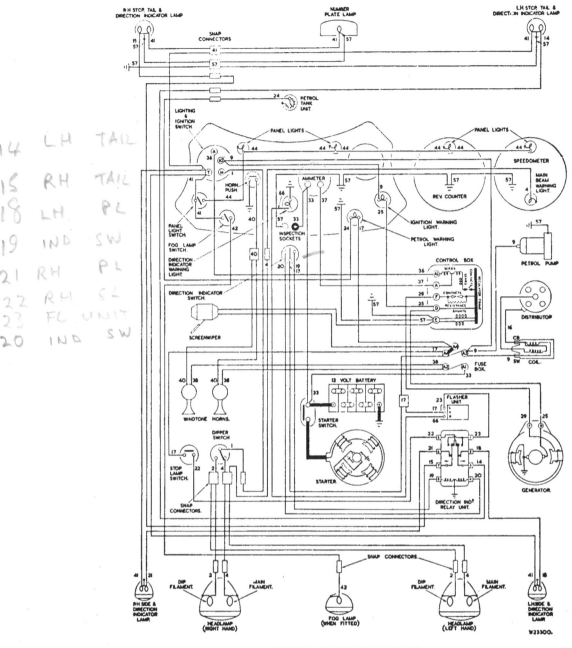

Handwritten notes (left margin):

14 LH TAIL
15 RH TAIL
18 LH PL
19 IND SW
21 RH PL
22 RH SL
23 FL UNIT
20 IND SW

KEY TO CABLE COLOURS

1 Blue	15 White with Brown	28 Yellow with White	41 Red	54 Purple with Green
2 Blue with Red	16 White with Black	29 Yellow with Green	42 Red with Yellow	55 Purple with Brown
3 Blue with Yellow	17 Green	30 Yellow with Purple	43 Red with Blue	56 Purple with Black
4 Blue with White	18 Green with Red	31 Yellow with Brown	44 Red with White	57 Black
5 Blue with Green	19 Green with Yellow	32 Yellow with Black	45 Red with Green	58 Black with Red
6 Blue with Purple	20 Green with Blue	33 Brown	46 Red with Purple	59 Black with Yellow
7 Blue with Brown	21 Green with White	34 Brown with Red	47 Red with Brown	60 Black with Blue
8 Blue with Black	22 Green with Purple	35 Brown with Yellow	48 Red with Black	61 Black with White
9 White	23 Green with Brown	36 Brown with Blue	49 Purple	62 Black with Green
10 White with Red	24 Green with Black	37 Brown with White	50 Purple with Red	63 Black with Purple
11 White with Yellow	25 Yellow	38 Brown with Green	51 Purple with Yellow	64 Black with Brown
12 White with Blue	26 Yellow with Red	39 Brown with Purple	52 Purple with Blue	65 Dark Green
13 White with Green	27 Yellow with Blue	40 Brown with Black	53 Purple with White	66 Light Green
14 White with Purple				

FIG 13:6 TD model: CVC (regulator and separate fuse box), foot-operated dipswitch, main-beam warning lamp, flashing indicators (8-terminal relay)

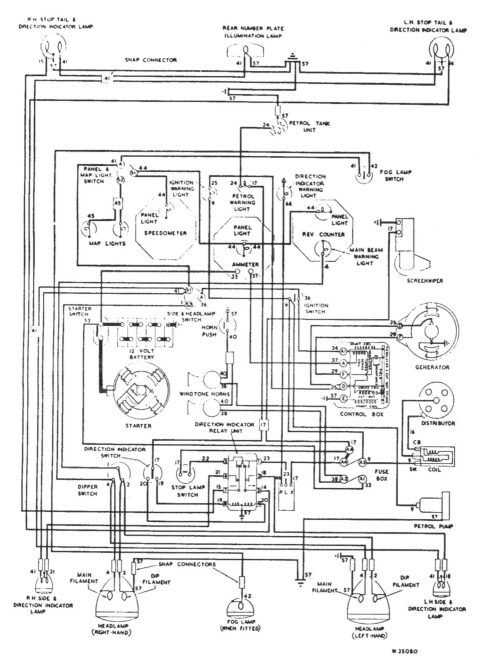

KEY TO CABLE COLOURS

1 Blue	15 White with Brown	28 Yellow with White	41 Red	54 Purple with Gree
2 Blue with Red	16 White with Black	29 Yellow with Green	42 Red with Yellow	55 Purple with Brow
3 Blue with Yellow	17 Green	30 Yellow with Purple	43 Red with Blue	56 Purple with Black
4 Blue with White	18 Green with Red	31 Yellow with Brown	44 Red with White	57 Black
5 Blue with Green	19 Green with Yellow	32 Yellow with Black	45 Red with Green	58 Black with Red
6 Blue with Purple	20 Green with Blue	33 Brown	46 Red with Purple	59 Black with Yellow
7 Blue with Brown	21 Green with White	34 Brown with Red	47 Red with Brown	60 Black with Blue
8 Blue with Black	22 Green with Purple	35 Brown with Yellow	48 Red with Black	61 Black with White
9 White	23 Green with Brown	36 Brown with Blue	49 Purple	62 Black with Green
10 White with Red	24 Green with Black	37 Brown with White	50 Purple with Red	63 Black with Purple
11 White with Yellow	25 Yellow	38 Brown with Green	51 Purple with Yellow	64 Black with Brown
12 White with Blue	26 Yellow with Red	39 Brown with Purple	52 Purple with Blue	65 Dark Green
13 White with Green	27 Yellow with Blue	40 Brown with Black	53 Purple with White	66 Light Green
14 White with Purple				

FIG 13:7 TF model: Revised panel layout

HINTS ON MAINTENANCE AND OVERHAUL

There are few things more rewarding than the restoration of a vehicle's original peak of efficiency and smooth performance.

The following notes are intended to help the owner to reach that state of perfection. Providing that he possesses the basic manual skills he should have no difficulty in performing most of the operations detailed in this manual. It must be stressed, however, that where recommended in the manual, highly-skilled operations ought to be entrusted to experts, who have the necessary equipment, to carry out the work satisfactorily.

Quality of workmanship:

The hazardous driving conditions on the roads to-day demand that vehicles should be as nearly perfect, mechanically, as possible. It is therefore most important that amateur work be carried out with care, bearing in mind the often inadequate working conditions, and also the inferior tools which may have to be used. It is easy to counsel perfection in all things, and we recognize that it may be setting an impossibly high standard. We do, however, suggest that every care should be taken to ensure that a vehicle is as safe to take on the road as it is humanly possible to make it.

Safe working conditions:

Even though a vehicle may be stationary, it is still potentially dangerous if certain sensible precautions are not taken when working on it while it is supported on jacks or blocks. It is indeed preferable not to use jacks alone, but to supplement them with carefully placed blocks, so that there will be plenty of support if the car rolls off the jacks during a strenuous manoeuvre. Axle stands are an excellent way of providing a rigid base which is not readily disturbed. Piles of bricks are a dangerous substitute. Be careful not to get under heavy loads on lifting tackle, the load could fall. It is preferable not to work alone when lifting an engine, or when working underneath a vehicle which is supported well off the ground. To be trapped, particularly under the vehicle, may have unpleasant results if help is not quickly forthcoming. Make some provision, however humble, to deal with fires. Always disconnect a battery if there is a likelihood of electrical shorts. These may start a fire if there is leaking fuel about. This applies particularly to leads which can carry a heavy current, like those in the starter circuit. While on the subject of electricity, we must also stress the danger of using equipment which is run off the mains and which has no earth or has faulty wiring or connections. So many workshops have damp floors, and electrical shocks are of such a nature that it is sometimes impossible to let go of a live lead or piece of equipment due to the muscular spasms which take place.

Work demanding special care:

This involves the servicing of braking, steering and suspension systems. On the road, failure of the braking system may be disastrous. Make quite sure that there can be no possibility of failure through the bursting of rusty brake pipes or rotten hoses, nor to a sudden loss of pressure due to defective seals or valves.

Problems:

The chief problems which may face an operator are:
1 External dirt.
2 Difficulty in undoing tight fixings.
3 Dismantling unfamiliar mechanisms.
4 Deciding in what respect parts are defective.
5 Confusion about the correct order for reassembly.
6 Adjusting running clearance.
7 Road testing.
8 Final tuning.

Practical suggestions to solve the problems:

1 Preliminary cleaning of large parts—engines, transmissions, steering, suspensions, etc.,—should be carried out before removal from the car. Where road dirt and mud alone are present, wash clean with a high-pressure water jet, brushing to remove stubborn adhesions, and allow to drain and dry. Where oil or grease is also present, wash down with a proprietary compound (Gunk, Tepol etc.,) applying with a stiff brush—an old paint brush is suitable—into all crevices. Cover the distributor and ignition coils with a polythene bag and then apply a strong water jet to clear the loosened deposits. Allow to drain and dry. The assemblies will then be sufficiently clean to remove and transfer to the bench for the next stage.

On the bench, further cleaning can be carried out, first wiping the parts as free as possible from grease with old newspaper. Avoid using rag or cotton waste which can leave clogging fibres behind. Any remaining grease can be removed with a brush dipped in paraffin. If necessary, traces of paraffin can be removed by carbon tetrachloride. Avoid using paraffin or petrol in large quantities for cleaning in enclosed areas, such as garages, on account of the high fire risk.

When all exteriors have been cleaned, and not before, dismantling can be commenced. This ensures that dirt will not enter into interiors and orifices revealed by dismantling. In the next phases, where components have to be cleaned, use carbon tetrachloride in preference to petrol and keep the containers covered except when in use. After the components have been cleaned, plug small holes with tapered hard wood plugs cut to size and blank off larger orifices with grease-proof paper and masking tape. Do not use soft wood plugs or matchsticks as they may break.

2 It is not advisable to hammer on the end of a screw thread, but if it must be done, first screw on a nut to protect the thread, and use a lead hammer. This applies particularly to the removal of tapered cotters. Nuts and bolts seem to 'grow' together, especially in exhaust systems. If penetrating oil does not work, try the judicious application of heat, but be careful of starting a fire. Asbestos sheet or cloth is useful to isolate heat.

Tight bushes or pieces of tail-pipe rusted into a silencer can be removed by splitting them with an open-ended hacksaw. Tight screws can sometimes be started by a tap from a hammer on the end of a suitable screwdriver. Many tight fittings will yield to the judicious use of a hammer, but it must be a soft-faced hammer if damage is to be avoided, use a heavy block on the opposite side to absorb shock. Any parts of the steering system which have been damaged should be renewed, as attempts to repair them may lead to cracking and subsequent failure, and steering ball joints should be disconnected using a recommended tool to prevent damage.

3 It often happens that an owner is baffled when trying to dismantle an unfamiliar piece of equipment. So many modern devices are pressed together or assembled by spinning-over flanges, that they must be sawn apart. The intention is that the whole assembly must be renewed. However, parts which appear to be in one piece to the naked eye, may reveal close-fitting joint lines when inspected with a magnifying glass, and, this may provide the necessary clue to dismantling. Left-handed screw threads are used where rotational forces would tend to unscrew a right-handed screw thread.

Be very careful when dismantling mechanisms which may come apart suddenly. Work in an enclosed space where the parts will be contained, and drape a piece of cloth over the device if springs are likely to fly in all directions. Mark everything which might be reassembled in the wrong position, scratched symbols may be used on unstressed parts, or a sequence of tiny dots from a centre punch can be useful. Stressed parts should never be scratched or centre-popped as this may lead to cracking under working conditions. Store parts which look alike in the correct order for reassembly. Never rely upon memory to assist in the assembly of complicated mechanisms, especially when they will be dismantled for a long time, but make notes, and drawings to supplement the diagrams in the manual, and put labels on detached wires. Rust stains may indicate unlubricated wear. This can sometimes be seen round the outside edge of a bearing cup in a universal joint. Look for bright rubbing marks on parts which normally should not make heavy contact. These might prove that something is bent or running out of truth. For example, there might be bright marks on one side of a piston, at the top near the ring grooves, and others at the bottom of the skirt on the other side. This could well be the clue to a bent connecting rod. Suspected cracks can be proved by heating the component in a light oil to approximately 100°C, removing, drying off, and dusting with french chalk, if a crack is present the oil retained in the crack will stain the french chalk.

4 In determining wear, and the degree, against the permissible limits set in the manual, accurate measurement can only be achieved by the use of a micrometer. In many cases, the wear is given to the fourth place of decimals; that is in ten-thousandths of an inch. This can be read by the vernier scale on the barrel of a good micrometer. Bore diameters are more difficult to determine. If, however, the matching shaft is accurately measured, the degree of play in the bore can be felt as a guide to its suitability. In other cases, the shank of a twist drill of known diameter is a handy check.

Many methods have been devised for determining the clearance between bearing surfaces. To-day the best and simplest is by the use of Plastigage, obtainable from most garages. A thin plastic thread is laid between the two surfaces and the bearing is tightened, flattening the thread. On removal, the width of the thread is compared with a scale supplied with the thread and the clearance is read off directly. Sometimes joint faces leak persistently, even after gasket renewal. The fault will then be traceable to distortion, dirt or burrs. Studs which are screwed into soft metal frequently raise burrs at the point of entry. A quick cure for this is to chamfer the edge of the hole in the part which fits over the stud.

5 **Always check a replacement part with the original one before it is fitted.**

If parts are not marked, and the order for reassembly is not known, a little detective work will help. Look for marks which are due to wear to see if they can be mated. Joint faces may not be identical due to manufacturing errors, and parts which overlap may be stained, giving a clue to the correct position. Most fixings leave identifying marks especially if they were painted over on assembly. It is then easier to decide whether a nut, for instance, has a plain, a spring, or a shakeproof washer under it. All running surfaces become 'bedded' together after long spells of work and tiny imperfections on one part will be found to have left corresponding marks on the other. This is particularly true of shafts and bearings and even a score on a cylinder wall will show on the piston.

6 Checking end float or rocker clearances by feeler gauge may not always give accurate results because of wear. For instance, the rocker tip which bears on a valve stem may be deeply pitted, in which case the feeler will simply be bridging a depression. Thrust washers may also wear depressions in opposing faces to make accurate measurement difficult. End float is then easier to check by using a dial gauge. It is common practice to adjust end play in bearing assemblies, like front hubs with taper rollers, by doing up the axle nut until the hub becomes stiff to turn and then backing it off a little. Do not use this method with ballbearing hubs as the assembly is often preloaded by tightening the axle nut to its fullest extent. If the splitpin hole will not line up, file the base of the nut a little.

Steering assemblies often wear in the straight-ahead position. If any part is adjusted, make sure that it remains free when moved from lock to lock. Do not be surprised if an assembly like a steering gearbox, which is known to be carefully adjusted outside the car, becomes stiff when it is bolted in place. This will be due to distortion of the case by the pull of the mounting bolts, particularly if the mounting points are not all touching together. This problem may be met in other equipment and is cured by careful attention to the alignment of mounting points.

When a spanner is stamped with a size and A/F it means that the dimension is the width between the jaws and has no connection with ANF, which is the designation for the American National Fine thread. Coarse threads like Whitworth are rarely used on cars to-day except for studs which screw into soft aluminium or cast iron. For this reason it might be found that the top end of a cylinder head stud has a fine thread and the lower end a coarse thread to screw into the cylinder block. If the car has mainly UNF threads then it is likely that any coarse threads will be UNC, which are not the same as Whitworth. Small sizes have the same number of threads in Whitworth and UNC, but in the $\frac{1}{2}$ inch size for example, there are twelve threads to the inch in the former and thirteen in the latter.

7 After a major overhaul, particularly if a great deal of work has been done on the braking, steering and suspension systems, it is advisable to approach the problem of testing with care. If the braking system has been overhauled, apply heavy pressure to the brake pedal and get a second operator to check every possible source of leakage. The brakes may work extremely well, but a leak could cause complete failure after a few miles.

Do not fit the hub caps until every wheel nut has been checked for tightness, and make sure the tyre pressures are correct. Check the levels of coolant, lubricants and hydraulic fluids. Being satisfied that all is well, take the car on the road and test the brakes at once. Check the steering and the action of the handbrake. Do all this at moderate speeds on quiet roads, and make sure there is no other vehicle behind you when you try a rapid stop.

Finally, remember that many parts settle down after a time, so check for tightness of all fixings after the car has been on the road for a hundred miles or so.

8 It is useless to tune an engine which has not reached its normal running temperature. In the same way, the tune of an engine which is stiff after a rebore will be different when the engine is again running free. Remember too, that rocker clearances on pushrod operated valve gear will change when the cylinder head nuts are tightened after an initial period of running with a new head gasket.

Trouble may not always be due to what seems the obvious cause. Ignition, carburation and mechanical condition are interdependent and spitting back through the carburetter, which might be attributed to a weak mixture, can be caused by a sticking inlet valve.

For one final hint on tuning, never adjust more than one thing at a time or it will be impossible to tell which adjustment produced the desired result.

GLOSSARY OF TERMS

AF   Across Flats. Width across the flats of nut or bolt heads, or between jaws of associated spanners.

Allen key   Cranked wrench of hexagonal section for use with socket-head screws.

Alternator   Electrical generator producing alternating current. Rectified to direct current for battery charging.

Ambient temperature   Surrounding atmospheric temperature.

ANF   American National Fine screw thread.

Annulus   Used in engineering to indicate the outer ring gear of an epicyclic gear train.

Armature   The shaft carrying the windings, which rotates in the magnetic field of a generator or starter motor. That part of a solenoid which is activated by the magnetic field.

Asymmetrical   Not symmetrical.

Axial   In line with, or pertaining to, an axis.

BA   British Association screw thread.

Backlash   Play in meshing gears.

Balance lever   A bar where force applied at the centre is equally divided between connections at the ends.

Banjo axle   Axle casing with large diameter housing for the crownwheel and differential.

Bendix pinion   A self-engaging and self-disengaging drive on a starter motor shaft.

Bevel pinion   A conical shaped gearwheel, designed to mesh with a similar gear with an axis at 90 deg. to its own.

bhp   Brake horse power, measured on a dynamometer.

bmep   Brake mean effective pressure. Average pressure on a piston during the working stroke.

Brake cylinder   Cylinder with hydraulically operated piston(s) acting on brake shoes or pad(s).

Brake regulator   Control valve fitted in hydraulic braking system which limits brake pressure to rear brakes during heavy braking to prevent rear wheel locking.

BSF   British Standard Fine screw thread.

BSW   British Standard Whitworth screw thread.

Bypass filter   Oil filter—one which cleans a small volume of oil from the pump and returns it to the sump.

Camber   Angle at which a wheel is tilted from the vertical.

Capacitor   Modern term for an electrical condenser. Part of distributor assembly, connected across contact breaker points, acts as an interference suppressor.

Castellated   Top face of a nut, slotted across the flats, to take a locking splitpin.

Castor   Angle at which the kingpin or swivel pin is tilted when viewed from the side.

cc   Cubic centimetres. Engine capacity is arrived at by multiplying the area of the bore in sq cm by the stroke in cm by the number of cylinders.

Clevis   U-shaped forked connector used with a clevis pin, usually at handbrake connections.

Clockwise   In the direction of rotation of the hands of a clock, movement in the opposite direction is normally referred to as anti-clockwise.

Collet   A type of collar, usually split and located in a groove in a shaft, and held in place by a retainer. The arrangement used to retain the spring(s) on a valve stem in most cases.

Commutator   Rotating segmented current distributor between armature windings and brushes in generator or motor.

Compression ratio   The ratio, or quantitative relation, of the total volume (piston at bottom of stroke) to the unswept volume (piston at top of stroke) in an engine cylinder.

Condensor   See capacitor.

Core plug   Plug for blanking off a manufacturing hole in a casting.

Crownwheel   Large bevel gear in rear axle, driven by a bevel pinion attached to the propeller shaft. Sometimes called a 'ring wheel'.

'C' Spanner   Like a 'C' with a handle. For use on screwed collars without flats, but with slots or holes.

Damper   Modern term for shock-absorber used in vehicle suspension systems to damp out spring oscillations.

Depression   The lowering of atmospheric pressure as in the inlet manifold and carburetter.

Dowel   Close tolerance pin, peg, tube, or bolt, which accurately locates mating parts.

Drag link   Rod connecting steering box drop arm (pitman arm) to nearest front wheel steering arm in certain types of steering systems.

Dry liner   Thinwall tube pressed into cylinder bore.

Dry sump	Lubrication system where all oil is scavenged from the sump, and returned to a separate tank.
Dynamo	See Generator.
Electrode	Terminal part of an electrical component, such as the points or 'electrodes' of a sparking plug.
Electrolyte	In lead-acid car batteries a solution of sulphuric acid and distilled water.
End float	Or end play. The endwise movement between associated parts.
EP	Extreme pressure. In lubricants, special grades for heavily loaded bearing surfaces, such as gear teeth in a gearbox, or crownwheel and pinion in a rear axle.
Fade	Of brakes. Reduced efficiency due to overheating.
Field coils	Windings on the polepieces of motors and generators.
Fillets	Narrow finishing strips usually applied to interior bodywork.
First motion shaft	Input shaft from clutch to gearbox.
Fullflow	Oil filters. Filters all the oil pumped to the engine. If the element becomes clogged, a bypass valve operates to pass unfiltered oil to the engine.
FWD	Front wheel drive.
Gear pump	Two meshing gears in a close fitting casing. Oil is carried from the inlet round the outside of both gears in the spaces between the gear teeth and the casing to the outlet, the meshing gear teeth prevent oil passing back to the inlet, and the oil is forced through the outlet port.
Generator	Modern term for 'dynamo'. When rotated produces electrical current.
Grommet	A ring of protective or sealing material. Can be used to protect pipes or leads passing through bulkheads.
Gudgeon pin	Shaft which connects a piston to its connecting rod. Sometimes called 'wrist pin', or 'piston pin'.
Halfshaft	One of a pair transmitting drive from the differential gearing to the wheel hubs.
HC	High-compression. See Compression ratio.
Helical	In spiral form. The teeth of helical gears are cut at a spiral angle to the side faces of the gear wheel.
Hot spot	Hot area that assists vapourisation of fuel on its way to cylinders. Often provided by close contact between inlet and exhaust manifolds.

HT	High Tension. Applied to electrical current produced by the ignition coil for the sparking plugs.
Hydrometer	A device for checking specific gravity of liquids. Used to check specific gravity of electrolyte.
Hypoid bevel gears	A form of bevel gear used in the rear axle drive gears. The bevel pinion meshes below the centre line of the crownwheel, giving a lower propeller shaft line.
Idler	A device for passing on movement. A free running gear between driving and driven gears. A lever transmitting track rod movement to a side rod in steering gear
IFS	Idenpendent Front Suspension.
Impeller	A centrifugal pumping element. Used in water pumps to stimulate flow.
Journals	Those parts of a shaft that are in contact with the bearings.
Kerosene	Paraffin.
Kingpin	The main vertical pin which carries the front wheel spindle, and permits steering movement. May be called 'steering pin' or 'swivel pin'.
Layshaft	The shaft which carries the laygear in the gearbox. The laygear is driven by the first motion shaft and drives the third motion shaft according to the gear selected. Sometimes called the 'Countershaft' or 'Second motion shaft'.
lb ft	A measure of twist or torque. A pull of 10 lb at a radius of 1 ft is a torque of 10 lb ft.
lb/sq in	Pounds per square inch.
LC	Low Compression. See 'Compression ratio'.
Little end	The small, or piston end of a connecting rod. Sometimes called the 'Small end'.
ls	Leading shoe in brake drum. Tends to wedge into drum, when applied, so increasing the braking effect.
LT	Low Tension. The current output from battery.
Mandrel	Accurately manufactured bar or rod used for test or centring purposes.
Manifold	A pipe, duct, or chamber, with several branches.
Needle rollers	Bearing rollers with a length many times their diameter.
Oil bath	Reservoir which lubricates parts by immersion. In air filters, a separate oil supply for wetting a wiremesh element and holding the dust.
Oil wetted	In air filters, a wiremesh element lightly oiled to trap and hold airborne dust.

Overlap	Period during which inlet and exhaust valves are open together.
Panhard rod	Bar connected between fixed point on chassis and another on axle to control sideways movement.
Pawl	Pivoted catch which engages in the teeth of a ratchet to permit movement in one direction only.
Peg spanner	Tool with pegs, or pins, to engage in holes in the part to be turned.
Pendant pedals	Pedals with levers that are pivoted at the top end.
Phillips screwdriver	A cross-point screwdriver for use with the cross-slotted heads of Phillips screws.
Pinion	A small gear, usually in relation to another gear.
Piston-type damper	Shock absorber in which damping is controlled by a piston working in a closed oil filled cylinder.
Preloading	Preset static pressure on ball or roller bearings not due to working loads.
Radial	Radiating from a centre, like the spokes of a wheel.
Radius rod	Pivoted arm confining movement of a part to an arc of fixed radius.
Ratchet	Toothed wheel or rack which can move in one direction only, movement in the other being prevented by a pawl.
Ring gear	A gear toothed ring attached to outer periphery of flywheel. Starter pinion engages with it during starting.
Runout	Amount by which a rotating part is out of truth.
SAE	Society of Automotive Engineers.
Semi-floating axle	Outer end of rear axle halfshaft is carried on bearing inside axle casing. Wheel hub is secured to end of shaft.
Servo	A hydraulic or pneumatic system for assisting, or augmenting a physical effort. See 'Vacuum Servo'.
Setscrew	One which is threaded for the full length of the shank.
Shackle	A coupling link, used in the form of two parallel pins connected by side plates to secure the end of the master suspension spring, and absorb the effects of deflection.
Shell bearing	Thin walled, steel shell lined with anti-friction metal. Usually semi-circular and used in pairs for main and big-end bearings.
Shock absorber	See 'damper'.
Silentbloc	Rubber bush bonded to inner and outer metal sleeves.
Socket-head screw	Screw with hexagonal socket for an Allen key.
Solenoid	A coil of wire creating a magnetic field when electric current passes through it. Used with a soft iron core to operate contacts or a mechanical device.
Spur gear	A gear with teeth cut axially across the periphery.
Stator tube	A stationary tube inside the steering column, carrying wiring to steering wheel controls.
Stub axle	Short axle fitted at one end only.
Tachometer	An instrument for accurate measurement of rotating speed. Usually indicates in revolutions per minute.
TDC	Top Dead Centre. The highest point reached by a piston in a cylinder, with the crank and connecting rod in line.
Thermostat	Automatic device for regulating temperature. Used in vehicle coolant systems to open a valve which restricts circulation at low temperatures.
Third motion shaft	Output shaft of gearbox.
Three-quarter floating axle	Outer end of rear axle halfshaft flanged and bolted to wheel hub, which runs on bearing mounted on outside of axle casing. Vehicle weight is not carried by the axle shaft.
Thrust bearing or washer	Used to reduce friction in rotating parts subject to axial loads.
Torque	Turning or twisting effort. See lb ft.
Track rod	The bar(s) across the vehicle which connect the steering arms and maintain the front wheels in their correct alignment.
ts	Trailing shoe, in a drum brake assembly. Tends to be pushed away from drum.
UJ	Universal joint. A coupling between shafts which permits angular movement.
UNF	Unified National Fine screw thread.
Vacuum Servo	Device used in brake system, using difference between atmospheric pressure and inlet manifold depression to operate a piston which acts to augment pressure as required. See 'Servo'.
Venturi	A restriction or 'choke' in a tube, as in a carburetter, used to increase velocity to obtain a reduction in pressure.
Vernier	A sliding scale for obtaining fractional readings of the graduations of an adjacent scale.
Welch plug	A domed thin metal disc which is partially flattened to lock in a recess. Used to plug core holes in castings.
Wet liner	Removable cylinder barrel, sealed against coolant leakage, where the coolant is in direct contact with the outer surface.
Wet sump	A reservoir attached to the crankcase to hold the lubricating oil.

INDEX

A

Air cleaner.. 39
Antifreeze 49
Armature, generator 113
Armature, starter motor 116
Automatic ignition control.. 41
Axleshafts (Halfshafts) 74

B

Balancing wheels 109
Ball joints, steering 93, 97
Battery maintenance 112
Belt tension 49
Big-end removal 23
Big-end refitting 26
Bleeding, brake system 107
Bodywork 121
Breather pipe modification, TD 29
Brake adjustment 101, 108
Brake cables 108
Brake hoses 103
Brake linings 107
Brake pedal clearance 107
Brushes, generator 112, 114
Brushes, starter motor 116
Bulbs, headlamp 118, 120

C

Cables, handbrake 108
Cables, torque TA 83
Camber angle 88
Camshaft removal and refitting 19
Camshaft types 29
Capacitor (Condenser) 44
Carburetters 35
Carburetter jet centring 38
Carburetter synchronisation 38
Castor angle 88
Choke, carburetter.. 36
Clutch adjustment 55
Clutch, competition 57
Clutch, dry plate 55
Clutch, wet plate, TA 53
Clutch, 8-inch 57
Clutch overhaul 56
Clutch plate alignment 57
Clutch spigot bearing 66
Coil, ignition 45
Commutator 114
Condenser (Capacitor) 44
Connecting rod removal 23
Connecting rod refitting 26
Contact breaker 41
Control box—see Regulator
Control link, engine 28
Cooling system 47
Cooling system draining 48
Crankshaft regrinding 25
Crankshaft removal and refitting 25

Cut-out

Cut-out 117
Cylinder head removal 13
Cylinder head refitting 18
Cylinder head bolt tightening sequence .. 19
Cylinder reboring 25

D

Dampers, Andrex friction 88
Dampers, front 78, 87
Dampers, rear 78
Decarbonizing 15
Differential 71
Direction indicators 119
Distributor cam types 43
Distributor maintenance 42
Distributor overhaul 43
Doors 126
Draining cooling system 48

E

Electrical system 111
Electrolyte, battery.. 112
Engine control link 28
Engine dismantling 13
Engine mountings 27
Engine reassembly.. 25
Engine removal 11
Engine refitting 27
Engine types 9

F

Fan belt 49
Field coils 114
Flasher unit 119
Flywheel removal 23
Flywheel refitting 27
Flywheel ring gear.. 23
Front axle TA, TB, TC 81
Front hubs.. 86
Front springs 83
Front suspension TD, TF 81
Fuel warning lamp 118
Fuel pump.. 31
Fuel pump, later TF 34
Fulcrum pins TD, TF 81, 84
Fuses 117

G

Gaskets, cylinder head 18, 29
Gaskets, engine 25
Gasket, sump 21
Gearbox description 59
Gearbox modification, TD 67
Gearbox overhaul 63
Gearbox removal 61
Gearbox refitting 66
Generator, three brush 112

Generator, two brush 113
Gudgeon pins 24

H

Handbrake adjustment 108
Headlamp beam setting 118
Headlamp dipping systems .. 118, 120
Horn adjustment 119
Hoses, hydraulic brakes 103
HT cables 45
Hubs, front 86
Hubs, Knock-on wheels 74, 108
Hubs, rear 74
Hub modification 88
Hydraulic brake operation 99
Hydraulic components, servicing .. 104
Hydraulic system, bleeding 107
Hydrometer test of electrolyte 112

I

Idling adjustment, carburetters 38
Ignition automatic advance 41
Ignition timing 44

K

King-pins and bushes TA, TB, TC 87
Knock-on wire wheels 108

L

Lighting and charging switch TA, TB .. 112
Lighting system 118
Lubrication system, engine 11

M

Main bearings 11, 25
Master cylinder 101
Micrometer timing adjustment, distributor .. 41

O

Oil filter 25
Oil filter bypass valve 23
Oil pump 22
Oil pressure relief valve 23
Oil seal, crankshaft 21
Oil seals, front hub 86, 88
Oil seals, rear axle 74
Oilways, clearing 25

P

Pedal clearance, brake 107
Pedal clearance, clutch 55
Petrol pump—see Fuel pump
Petrol warning lamp 118
Pinion, starter 115
Pistons 11, 26
Piston rings 24

PLC lighting and charging switch 112
Propeller shaft 69
Pushrod removal 15
Pushrod refitting 18

R

Rack and pinion steering TD, TF 91, 93
Radiator 47
Rear axle construction 71
Rear axle removal 72
Rear axle refitting 74
Rear springs 75
Rear spring trunnions TA, TB 75, 78
Regrinding crankshaft 25
Regulator (CVC) 116
Revolution counter—see Tachometer
Rocker gear 15, 18

S

Selector mechanism, gearbox 59
Shackles, front springs 83
Shackles, rear springs 75
Sleeve, propeller shaft 69
Sliding trunnions TA, TB 75, 78
Slow running adjustment 38
Solenoid-operated headlamp reflector 118, 120
Sparking plugs 45
Specific gravity, battery electrolyte .. 112
Splines, propeller shaft 69
Springs, front 83
Springs, rear 75
Starter drive 115
Starter motor 115
Starter pinion 115
Steering 91
Steering column TA, TB, TC 92
Steering column TD, TF 96
Steering geometry 88, 97
Sump removal and refitting 21
Suspension, front 81
Suspension geometry 88
Suspension, rear 71
Switch, PLC lighting and charging .. 112
Swivel pins TD, TF 83
Swivel pin inclination 88
Synchronising twin carburetters 38

T

Tachometer (Rev. counter) drive 112
Tappets 20
Thermostat 51
Tie rods 92, 97
Timing chain tensioner 20
Timing, ignition 45
Timing gear 19
Timing, valve 20
Toe-in 97
Torque cables, TA 83
Track rod TA, TB, TC 97
Trunnions, rear spring TA, TB 75, 78

U

Unified thread modifications   79
Universal joints   69

V

Valves   15
Valve clearances   18
Valve guides   17
Valve springs   18
Valve timing   20

W

Warning light, petrol   118
Warning light, 30 mile/hr   118
Water circulation   47
Water pump   47
Wheel balancing   109
Wheels, disc   109
Wheels, wire   108
Wheels, Dunlop centre lock (knock-on's)..   108
Windscreen wiper   119
Wiring   111
Wiring, headlamps..   120
Wishbone, independent front suspension .. 81, 83

GREEN	GREEN	BLACK	WHITE	YELLOW	BROWN BLUE	BROWN WHITE	YELLOW GREEN	PURPLE
A 4	A 4	E	A 3	D	A 1	A	F	A 2
WIPER MOTOR STOPLAMP SW FOG LAMP SW	AMMETER	IG SW COIL PETROL PUMP	DYNAMO IG WARN LAMP	AMMETER TO LIGHT SW	AMMETER	DYNAMO FIELD	AMMETER	

RF 91
REGULATOR.

R H

GREEN WITH WHITE   RD

L H

GREEN WITH RED   RED

Lightning Source UK Ltd.
Milton Keynes UK
UKOW07f1059150116

266406UK00002B/151/P